I0828352

Pearl

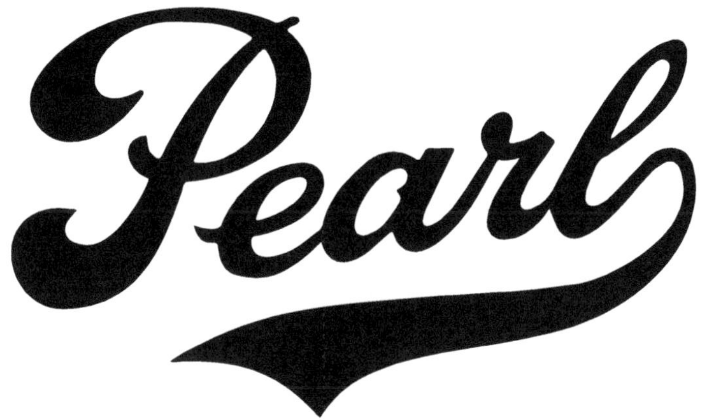

A History of SAN ANTONIO'S ICONIC BEER

JEREMY BANAS

Foreword by Kit Goldsbury
Preface by Bill Jones

Published by American Palate
A Division of The History Press
Charleston, SC
www.historypress.net

Front cover image of can by Steve Fernandes. Pearl logo courtesy Pabst Brewing. Back cover top image courtesy Pearl LLC Archives. Smokestack image courtesy of author.

First published 2018

ISBN 9781540227942

Library of Congress Control Number: 2017955993

To my boys, Quinn, Jack and Max: My love for you knows no bounds. You inspire me to be the best father I can be. To my parents, Milton and Cathy Banas: Your unconditional love and support are what keep me going. To my baby sister, Cari Gordonne: I grow more in awe of you each and every year that passes by. I love you all.

CONTENTS

Foreword, by Christopher "Kit" Goldsbury 9
Preface, by Bill Jones 11
Acknowledgements 13
Introduction 17

Period I. City Brewery and the San Antonio Brewing Association, 1883–1887 21
Period II. The Rise of the San Antonio Brewing Association, 1887–1918 30
Period III. Prohibition, 1918–1933 53
Period IV. Otto A. Koehler and Pearl's Golden Age, 1933–1969 65
Period V. The Decline of the Pearl, 1969–2001 88
Period VI. The New Pearl, 2002–2017 101

Appendix I. The Koehler House 127
Appendix II. The Texas Transportation Company 139
Bibliography 145
Index 149
About the Author 155

FOREWORD

Over the last fifteen years, we have had the honor of working in the footprint of the historic Pearl Brewery as we've tried to reimagine and rebuild this stately neighborhood that is home to so many stories, traditions and histories that we as San Antonians hold dear.

What drew us to this property and this project were the beautiful buildings, evidence of an era when pride in quality meant everything, and the opportunity to bring a place back to life that had faded in relevance and energy.

Our aim at Pearl over these fifteen years has been to use the principles that made the brewery great—commitment to people, pride in quality and, most importantly, a sense of place and community indelible and rooted in South Texas culture—to build a next chapter filled with people making things that make us proud, public space, beautiful architecture and an invitation to all of San Antonio to make it their own.

As we complete our final project, the Bottling Department Food Hall, we take stock in the dense, diverse, well-loved and well-used neighborhood that has grown up around and in the beautiful bones of the brewery.

Beer is brewed here again, students are educated at the Culinary Institute of America, homegrown and far-flung chefs are honing their craft in our nineteen restaurants and San Antonians and visitors alike bask in the special and inimitable beauty of the Hotel Emma, located in the original San Antonio Brewing Association brewhouse.

Foreword

As you read this book, we invite you to absorb the history so that you may look for clues of this place's illustrious past in this contemporary iteration—chandeliers made of bottle cappers, cabanas and fountains made of tank ends and a conveyor belt as a boardroom table. But more than the things, it's truly the spirit of the people who built, worked in and led this place that we hope you feel here today. Their spirit, ingenuity, boldness and creativity live in the community that is here now, writing the next chapter of Pearl.

—Christopher "Kit" Goldsbury

PREFACE

At Pearl Brewing, everyone was family. Everyone watched out for one another, from Bubba at the grain rail sidings to Leo Kitchen, the keeper of the yeast. Cowboy Wallace took care of the fermentation, all the while making sure that everyone had peanut butter to snack on. Manuel Rodriguez and Howell Parker headed up the filtration crew, which kept Pearl and Pearl Light flowing, and James Burns handled the packaging department by way of the government cellar. The department lunches included great barbecue and homemade tamales and were always good times. One of the better memories was when a certain supervisor from Rhode Island ate a tamale for the first time and didn't know to remove the cornhusk.

I am very proud to follow in the steps of past brewmasters G.J. Billmeier, Howard Nagle and Richard Kromar, not to mention working with past brewmaster Kenneth Schmidt, who came to Pearl in the 1980s (via the Lone Star Brewing Company) as a packaging manager; another big shout-out goes to our plant manager, Eddie Mueller, who kept the boat afloat.

Pearl finally has a future, but I always remember the past, as it's quite literally carved into the walls of my office. The hidden office was part of the original brewery and full of dark oak paneling, as well as the handmade Triple X chairs and historic beer steins lining the walls. I would always take my two kids to the brewery on the weekends when I had to work. They loved sitting on the big leather sofa in my office, running around, riding the big elevators and checking fermentation in the cellars.

Preface

With the sweaty aroma of the beer being brewed coming from the huge copper kettles, it was an industrial playground that reminded me of how beer making runs in my blood and now runs in the blood of future brewers and Pearl drinkers.

I started my brewing career working at my family's brewery in Smithtown, Pennsylvania, at the age of sixteen. I later attended the Siebel Institute Master Brewer Program, graduating in 1979. I was the master brewer at the Jones Brewing Company, the makers of Stoney's Beer, until 1984, when I joined the Pearl Brewing Company in San Antonio, Texas. After the Pearl plant was closed, I moved on to the Miller Brewery Company, working at its Fort Worth plant.

To all the Pearl enthusiasts and future generations of Pearl beer drinkers:

Let's drink the liquid of amber so bright;
Let's drink the liquid with foam so bright;
Let's drink the liquid that brings all good cheer;
Prost to the past, present and the future Pearl beer drinkers.

—Bill Jones

Bill Jones is now retired and living with his wife, Christy, in Fort Worth, Texas. He has two children: a son, Benjamin Jones, living in Arlington, Virginia, and working for Keller Williams Realty, and a daughter, Isa Jones, living in Jackson, Wyoming, and working as a journalist for the Jackson Hole News & Guide. *Bill won numerous brewing awards while working at Pearl: Gold Medal for Pearl Larger at the 1991 Great America Beer Festival, Gold Medal for Old Milwaukee NA in 1999 and Best Amber for Salado Creek Beer at the World Expo of Beer in 1997.*

ACKNOWLEDGEMENTS

The best part of writing a book on a subject you have a passion about and maybe a fair amount of knowledge is the research—exploring and discovering things that not only you did not know, but tidbits of information that also previously had been lost to time. All this cumulative knowledge tells the story of your subject, as well as the stories of the people involved.

This comprehensive history of the Pearl Brewery tells such a story of people. I would be remiss, however, if I did not acknowledge the many people who helped with this wonderful book. My sincerest apologies if anyone was left out.

To my Heidi, thank you for your love, support and putting up with all my late nights and weekends of researching and writing. I love you, sweetie.

Mike Hood, thank you for being an inspiration with writing, as well as a mentor and friend. It means more than you know.

Charlie Staats, your knowledge and passion for the history of Texas breweries know no bounds. Thank you for keeping me historically on track. Your guidance and friendship were invaluable.

Travis Poling, thank you for all your friendship and advice in guiding me to be a better writer.

To my friends at Silver Ventures/Pearl LLC, specifically Christopher "Kit" Goldsbury, Elizabeth Fauerso and Anne Marie Nikolich, your openness and generosity helped to make this project more robust. Thank you for helping me to preserve this piece of San Antonio history.

Tim Craig, thank you for sharing the fruits of your archival labors. The archives you've built for the Pearl will stand the test of time.

Dr. Paul Pace, thank you for opening up your family to me and sharing your history (as well as healing my broken hand!). It has been an honor and a pleasure to be a part of it.

Bill Jones and Grant Ward, thank you for sharing your work experiences at the Pearl and for the grand tradition you added to.

Pabst Brewing Company and Alya Wilhelm, thank you for use of the Pearl Lager Beer logo.

To the staff at the Trinity University Coates Library in San Antonio, thank you for guiding me in the early stages of my research. It proved to be invaluable.

To the impeccable folks at Southerleigh Fine Food and Brewery, the current occupants of the Pearl Brewhouse, thank you for continuing such a grand tradition of brewing—in particular, chef Jeff Balfour, head brewer Les Locke and my favorite Frenchman, manager Philippe Place.

To all my friends and family who have supported me throughout this: my oldest friend, Clinton "Buck" Davis; Eric Cruzan; Brian Orosco; Marco and Tiana Ortega; Brooke Barker; my grandparents Richard and Marie Mauro; RJ Mauro; Rich Mauro; Mary Kay Mauro; Ron Mauro; Claire Marie TeBockhorst; Randy Mauro; Mary and Keith Beuchel; Chris and Julia Scott; John TeBockhorst; Leah TeBockhorst; Paul TeBockhorst; Joe TeBockhorst; Laura Johnson; Kristin Turner; Devin Mauro; Janice Bates; Nicholas Bates; Jane Mauro; Tricia Gallegos; Stephanie and Greg Vetter; and Scott Graham.

To my brewing industry family who always inspire me: Brad Farbstein, Megan Parisi, Jason Armstrong, Mark McDavid, TJ Miller, Dennis Rylander, James Hudec, Eugene Simor, Greg Spickler, Vera Deckard, Keith and Anna Kilker, Jason Barrier, Kelly Meyer, Ray Mittledorf, Jason Ard, Paul Ford, Matt "Chaca" Menchaca, Blake Murrah, Zach Harris, Jeremy Karney, Seth Weatherly, Aaron Mendiola, Jason Davis, Alicia Spence-Schlesinger, Scott Metzger, Chris Mobley, Boyan Kalusevic, Jody and Steve Newman, Rob Martindale, Scotty Kretchman, Forrest Clay Hyde, Mike Holt, Seth Parker, Marcus Baskerville, Mike DiCiccio, Rob Garza, Roland Tamez, Randy Ward, Tim Schwartz, Jaime Jurado, Paul and Kim Kavulak, Joey and Maggie Villareal, Jeff Stuffings, Averie Swanson, Mitch Steele, Greg Koch, Steve Wagner, Chris Spradley, Pedro Longoria, Aaron Mendiola, Tony Drewery, Drew and Leah Watson, Tim Myers, Jon Airheart, Denise Aguirre, Kerrie Crosby, Kevin and Chrissy Hobbins, Holland Lawrence and Garrett Marrero.

Acknowledgements

Arcadia Publishing and The History Press, specifically acquisitions editor Ben Gibson and senior editor Ryan Finn, thank you for your encouragement and guidance.

Debra Martin, executive director of the Alamo Colleges Foundation, thank you for the use of your photos of the Koehler House, as well as the college's continued preservation of such a historic home.

INTRODUCTION

The idea for this book arose out of research that was done on my first book, *San Antonio Beer: Alamo City History by the Pint*, co-written with my good friend Travis Poling. A plethora of information was found on the Pearl that was confined into two chapters of that book. It would take much more to properly tell the story of the Pearl, and so here we are: a comprehensive account of one of the largest regional breweries in the country, a brewery that would last 115 years and have a long-lasting effect on San Antonio and all of Texas.

The history of the Pearl Brewing Company is the history of beer itself in San Antonio, for Pearl—or the San Antonio Brewing Association, as it was known as for its first seven decades—was there in the beginning and would be there almost to our present. Subsequently, the history of beer in San Antonio is the history of German and European settlements in Texas. It is all connected to a larger aspect of our culture here in South Texas.

Fermented beverages were alive and well in Texas in the city's earliest days. In the eighteenth century, Spanish missionaries in many ways kicked off what would be the start of San Antonio's culture and reputation as a fairly boozy city. Records in the Bexar County Clerk's Office show inventories of Spanish missionaries that include wine in their possession. Tax certificates at the time show that wine was transported around what is now Texas, specifically from Laredo to the Spanish for Presidio De Bexar.

The Bexar County clerk's resident Spanish archivist, Alfred Rodriguez, suggested that grapes could have been grown within a short distance of the irrigated San Antonio River and that these local grapes may have even made their way into locally made wines. It is also quite possible that alcoholic beverages from Mexico and Central America, such as chicha—a corn-based beer in which enzymes from the corn are released by chewing the corn itself—may have made their way to San Antonio. That's not hard to imagine when there were well-established trade routes from Central America into the United States.

The Spanish brought wine, but the English and Germans would bring beer. In most English settlements throughout what would become the United States, ales prevailed, whether it be porters or pale ales. Where Germans landed, it was primarily lager beer, and it was lager beer that would come to define brewing in San Antonio, although it didn't start off that way. Charles Degen and the Western Brewery popped up in 1855, though some records indicated 1853, right next to the famous "Shrine of Texas Liberty," the Alamo. William Menger, who would later build the famed Menger Hotel, hired Degen, and together they started the state's first commercially licensed brewery in San Antonio. The beer they brewed was not the popular lager of their native Germany, but rather ale.

It would not be until the late 1870s when breweries would begin making lager beer. Once they did, however, the floodgates were opened. The Lone Star Brewing Association, started by Adolphus Busch, really kicked things off, but it would be J.B. Belohradsky and his City Brewery in 1883 that would have the biggest influence.

By 1886, San Antonio residents Otto Koehler, Otto Wahrmund, Oscar Bergstrom and Frederick Hartz had assumed control of City Brewery and sought to modernize it further, not only with new equipment but also with a secret recipe and a new name. The brewery was re-chartered in 1887 as the San Antonio Brewing Association. Less than a decade later, the soon-to-be-iconic brewhouse was built in 1894, along with the Pearl Stables.

By the early twentieth century, the San Antonio Brewing Association was one of half a dozen breweries in the Alamo City that were a driving force in its evolution. It was not just beer. No, the San Antonio Brewing Association was a major employer in San Antonio and along with other breweries accounted for one-fourth of San Antonio's total income. From 1914 to 1933, Pearl would see many challenges to its business. Founder Otto Koehler was shot and killed in 1914, leaving a void in leadership. Prohibition hit in 1918, forcing Pearl to modify its model in order to stay in business and keep food on the table for its employees. Emma Koehler, wife of Otto Koehler, would see the brewery through Prohibition and its growth beyond.

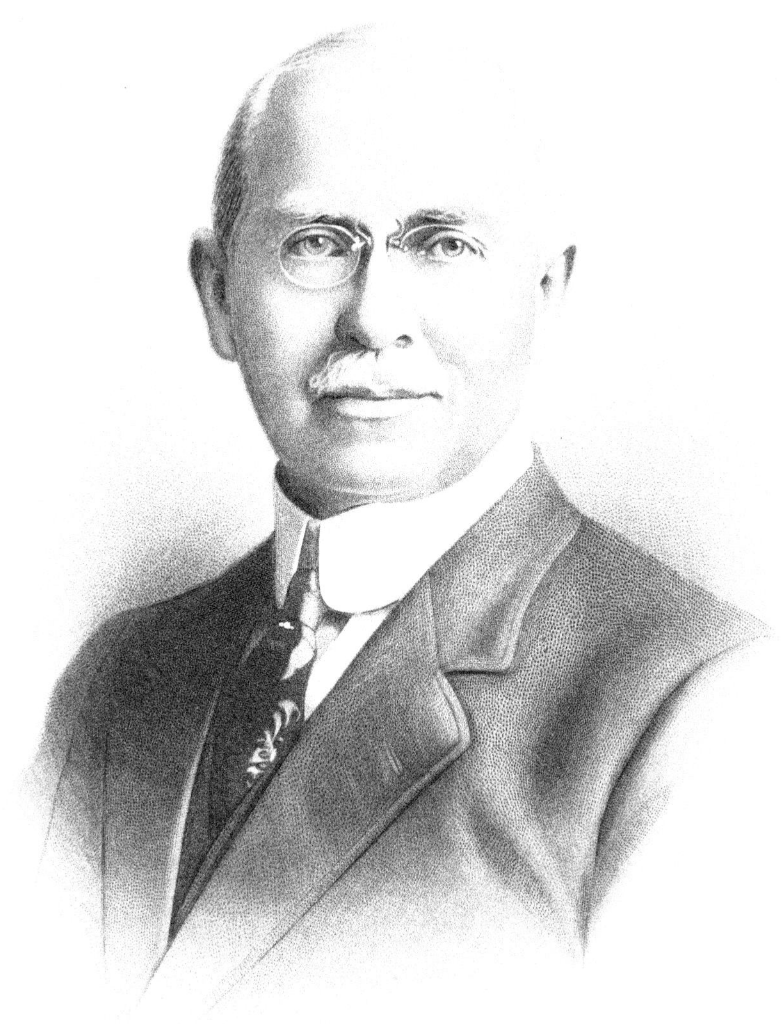

Portrait of Otto Koehler in his later years. *UTSA Libraries Special Collections.*

After Prohibition ended, a reorganized San Antonio Brewing Association emerged with Otto A. Koehler, nephew of Emma and Otto Koehler, at the helm of the brewery, leading it to what would be its golden age. Unparalleled growth occurred along with a name change in the 1950s, making Pearl the largest brewery in Texas. This growth would continue into the '60s, making these two decades the best in Pearl's history.

Soon after the death of the second Otto Koehler, the brewery was sold to Houston-based Southdown Corporation, ending Koehler ownership for the first time in eighty years and signaling what would become a fast decline for Pearl. The '70s saw extravagant spending and a disregard for brewery maintenance. As the '70s were coming to a close, Pearl was sold to Paul Kalmanovitz's General Brewing, whose holdings would later become the Pabst Brewing Company. Pabst ran Pearl much as it did the other regional breweries in its portfolios, with very little concern for the brand and its employees, focusing instead on maximizing exposure and the fortune and glory aspect of ownership. These led Pearl into a decline that it would not survive, closing for good in 2001.

Pearl's story did not end in 2001, however. By 2002, local billionaire Christopher "Kit" Goldsbury had purchased the Pearl facility, including its buildings. Goldsbury would renovate the grounds and all of the brewery buildings, including the iconic brewhouse, into a mixed-use facility for the community that includes shopping, dining and brewing.

The story of the Pearl Brewing Company is a story not only of a historic regional brewery but also of its people, who poured their hearts and souls into a family business and into San Antonio itself.

PERIOD I

CITY BREWERY AND THE SAN ANTONIO BREWING ASSOCIATION, 1883–1887

CITY BREWERY ARRIVES

The early 1880s were an interesting time for San Antonio. The population was 225,000 by 1880; the city's second railroad, the International–Great Northern, had arrived; and an industrial revolution had gripped the city. Modernization was in full swing, paralleling that of the country's growth at the time. Having dropped slightly from being the largest city in Texas, San Antonio's infrastructure boomed as well, with hospitals, paved roads, telephones and the like bringing San Antonio into the modern era and helping it once again claim the title of the state's largest city.

San Antonio's fledgling beer industry was not spared this growth, as the influx of immigrants into the Alamo City comprised mainly Germans, and the one thing Germans wanted most was beer. It was this thirst for beer that drove German immigrants William A. Menger and Charles Degen to open the Western Brewery in San Antonio in about 1855. The Western Brewery, however, produced ale, unusual for a German immigrant at the time, as lagers required very cold temperatures for fermentation and a longer aging time. What the growing German population wanted, however, was the lager beer that was so popular in their native Germany and much of Europe at the time. Lager beer, produced in other parts of the state, including the nearby town of New Braunfels, was often brewed in the winter to take advantage of the lower temperatures. However, lager beer was lacking in San Antonio.

It would take another immigrant to San Antonio to quench this thirst. Fast-forward to 1883 San Antonio. Local resident (and Bohemian immigrant) Jaroslav B. Belohradsky was looking to open a brewery in San Antonio. Not just any brewery, though. Belohradsky wanted to open one that would produce lager beer. Belohradsky came to San Antonio in 1880 along with others of the St. Louis brewing industry, including brewing magnate Adolphus Busch, who would help open the Lone Star Brewing Association the following year. With the recent advent of refrigeration technology, it was now possible to get and maintain the lower temperatures needed for lager beer, and Belohradsky planned to take advantage of this.

When Belohradsky came to San Antonio, he left behind his wife, Marie A. Nemeck, whom he had married in St. Louis on February 20, 1868, and their children, who would remain in St. Louis most of the time. When he met Marie, Belohradsky was already a father and had a son, Joseph W. Belohradsky, who was born in 1860. It has been speculated that Marie Nemeck could have been the younger Joseph's mother, as she arrived in the United States in 1859. Speculation is all we have, as records from this period are scant to say the least.

Feeling that he could fill the need for lager beer in San Antonio, Belohradsky made plans for his brewery, naming it City Brewery and pushing it to be the most modern site in Texas, with a focus on brewing a specific style of lager known as pilsner. The pilsner style was a relatively new type of lager that was gaining in popularity and hailed from the Pilsen region of Bohemia, now located in the Czech Republic. Belohradsky planned to sell his pilsner for about $3.50 per keg, about a dollar lower than the more popular national brands that had recently come to San Antonio with the railroad.

With a plan in place, he set out to get the financing needed for his brewing venture, one that was not going to be cheap if he was going to do this his way. Belohradsky came upon a bit of luck when he met fellow San Antonio resident Stephen Baker. Baker helped him get his fundraising started. It would take quite a lot more to complete his venture, so Belohradsky used the contacts he had in San Antonio and was introduced to Joseph S. Lockwood and John Hermann Kapmann. Lockwood was the president of Lockwood National Bank, and Kapmann was a venture capitalist from Westphalia. Together they composed the financial firm of Lockwood and Kapmann.

Lockwood and Kapmann seemed keen on the idea of another brewery in San Antonio and offered to loan Belohradsky the sum of $100,000. Although not all of what he was looking for, Belohradsky accepted the funds. Evidence points to Lockwood and Kapmann having more to invest, although it is unclear as to why it loaned only $100,000 to Belohradsky. Although underfinanced, Belohradsky pressed on, not realizing that one reason why he had not received as much financing from Kapmann might have been due to the fact that Kapmann was vested in the Lone Star Brewing Association and even held a seat on its board of directors, providing quite the conflict of interest.

In the late summer of 1883, construction started and was completed the following summer in 1884. One month later, the first barrel of Belohradsky's new brew left the brewery doors. The beer was immensely popular and sold well almost immediately, but soon it became difficult to keep up with the debts he incurred in starting City Brewery.

After only two years in business, Belohradsky encountered trouble he may have thought he left behind from his time in Chicago many years before. In March 1886, a local newspaper, most likely the *San Antonio Light*, led with the headline "Prominent Brewer: Arrest of J.B. Belohradsky for Alleged Embezzlement in Chicago." The accusation came from a former employer back in Chicago, a local Polish benevolent society. It accused him of taking approximately $1,750.

No real support existed for this accusation, and many at the time thought that Belohradsky was being framed. Regardless of the validity of the accusations, it was enough to spook his investors, who abandoned Belohradsky soon after the accusation came to light, resulting in the value of City Brewery dropping faster than hops in a brew kettle. Soon after, Lockwood Bank assigned a receiver by the name of Robert Tendick, who took control of City Brewery, signaling that the end was very likely near. It is possible that Belohradsky could have proven the accusations false, reassured his investors and gotten City Brewery moving again, but another roadblock lay in his path from an unlikely source: his own attorney, Oscar Bernard Bergstrom.

At some point after the accusation came to light, Belohradsky retained the services of Oscar Bergstrom. How he found Bergstrom is not known, but Bergstrom appeared to be Belohradsky's saving grace. Bergstrom quickly defended the brewer, eventually keeping Belohradsky out of jail. Of course, a little help from then Texas governor John Ireland didn't hurt either. It seemed this young attorney from San Antonio had a few connections in high places. Eventually, Belohradsky squared his affairs in San Antonio, although he would never return.

It was during this defense of Belohradsky that Bergstrom appeared to show his true intentions. While Belohradsky struggled for freedom and his business, Bergstrom saw a great opportunity with very little startup cost involved. At some point in 1886, a sheriff's sale took place in San Antonio, and one of the items up for grabs was City Brewery. Bergstrom wasted no time in purchasing the City Brewery stock from its spooked investors, thus saving the drowning brewery and effectively dooming his own client.

BELOHRADSKY DEPARTS CITY BREWERY

At age twenty-seven, Oscar Bernard Bergstrom was suddenly in control of a business that he really knew little about. He had neither brewed beer before nor worked at a brewery. For this, Bergstrom would call in an acquaintance—though possibly a friend, too—from his time in St. Louis: Otto Koehler. It is not clear who approached whom first, Koehler or Bergstrom; however, the pair wasted no time in reorganizing and modernizing City Brewery. Brought in as an initial partner was local businessman Frederick H. Hartz, although Hartz was primarily an investor and had no real role in the day-to-day operations of City Brewery.

In addition to the San Antonio Brewing Association, Bergstrom dabbled in other ventures as well. He had his hand in railroads, mining, a dye and clothing factory and politics. Much of his time with these ventures was spent in New York City, where Bergstrom seemingly fled to get away from what was becoming a volatile environment at City Brewery.

Bergstrom was an interesting character. He was charismatic, industrious and perhaps a little vain. He seems to have become very rich very fast. How much of this may have been due to questionable business practices is hard to say. After all, he had pulled City Brewery right from under Belohradsky. Perhaps it was also this aggressive and controlling nature that caused him to leave San Antonio and the City Brewery for the city of New York around 1896. What prompted the move? Very likely he saw New York as a more lucrative business environment than the Alamo City.

When Bergstrom arrived in New York, he was absent his wife, Phillipa. What became of her is not well known, although the 1920 Bexar County census listed a Philomena Bergstrom who was head of a household, so it is possible that they simply divorced. What is known is that in 1901 Bergstrom was remarried to one Eleanor Elliott, also a Texas native and also previously married. The 1910 census in Manhattan, New York, supports they had been married nine years and that each was in a second marriage. Although he had left the San Antonio Brewing Association behind him, Bergstrom was still a member of the board of directors, a point that he would later take legal action on.

While in New York, Bergstrom established a banking company in the Wall Street district, as well as mining and railroad investments, a citrus grove in Florida and a clothing and dye factory in New York. It seems that our man Bergstrom had quite the variety of job interests in which he wanted to invest his time and money. In his master's thesis at Trinity University, "Business History of the San Antonio Brewing Association," published in 1976, James Nelson states that according to Bergstrom's family, "he was always ready to part with his money for the wildest schemes if they appealed to his fancy."

Despite all his other undertakings, when Bergstrom left San Antonio around 1896, he appears not to have abandoned the life of an attorney altogether. The same 1910 Manhattan census that discussed his marriage also listed him as "a lawyer in general practice." Self-styled as O. Bergstrom and Company, he maintained several offices over his time in New York, all of which were in the Wall Street area. In fact, Bergstrom and his new wife appear to have lived in Kings County, New York, in the high society area of Brooklyn Heights, known to be an area where many a Wall Street financier took up residence.

Bergstrom and his family seem to have taken quite well to New York upper-crust society and were often mentioned in the society columns of local papers when they took vacations abroad as well as in Atlanta, Georgia.

Bergstrom did not have it easy in New York, with his business practices also being called into question. In 1906, Wall Street brokers were beginning to question one of his mining investments, the La Chiva Mining Company, wondering if anything was even being mined at all. It was not uncommon at the time for stock certificates to be forged, and many certificates were almost impossible to cash. It seems that Bergstrom disavowed all knowledge of, or investment in, the La Chiva Mining Company, despite the fact that many of the mining company's investors had offices next to Bergstrom's banking offices.

Outside an active social life in New York, which included his daughter, Eleanor, marrying a gubernatorial candidate and high-profile trips to Atlanta, Bergstrom himself felt the need to get back to San Antonio. By 1921, perhaps sooner, Bergstrom was back living in San Antonio and staying primarily at the Menger Hotel. His reasons for returning to San Antonio on a more permanent basis became clear when, in 1921, the San Antonio Brewing Association, now known as Alamo Industries but known by other

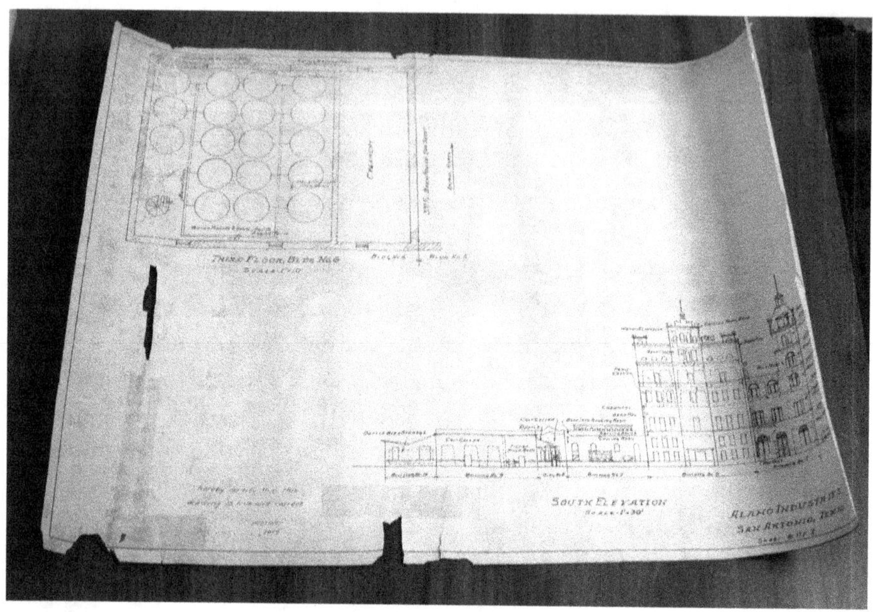

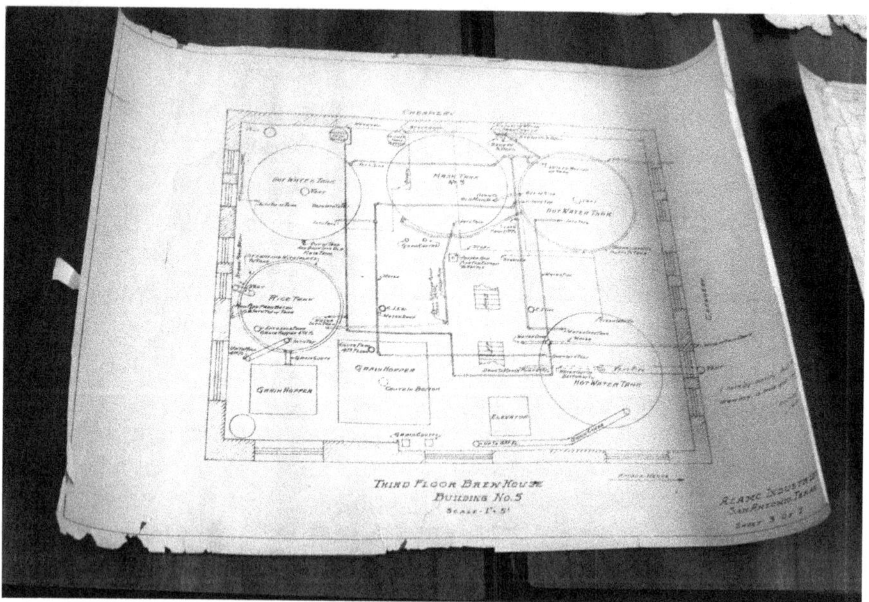

This page: Blueprints of Pearl Brewhouse when it was known as Alamo Industries. *Jeremy Banas*.

names during Prohibition, barred Bergstrom from taking part in company decisions and even excluded him from the brewery grounds.

With San Antonio Brewing Association's profit margins close to bankruptcy and his own personal debts weighing on him, Bergstrom filed suit against San Antonio Brewing Association in the Thirty-Seventh Judicial Court in the spring of 1921. He demanded access to the brewery grounds and asked for the court to appoint different receivers. With Otto Koehler having passed seven years earlier, the suit focused primarily on Koehler's widow, Emma, and Bergstrom's partners. The San Antonio Brewing Association answered the suit stating that Bergstrom had been consulted prior to every business decision, even when he was living outside Texas, and that when he was in San Antonio, he spent the majority of his time at the San Antonio Brewing Association offices.

The judge eventually ruled against Bergstrom but did force San Antonio Brewing Association executives to allow Bergstrom to the brewery grounds and its records, although it would be another six years before the case was closed. When Bergstrom exited San Antonio in 1896, little did he know that he would create a vacuum that his co-president and co-founder, Otto Koehler, was more than happy to fill.

CITY BREWERY TRANSITIONS FOR THE FUTURE

When Otto Koehler took over San Antonio Brewing Association upon Bergstrom's departure, he ushered in the second period in the brewery's history. There was to be no more opposition to his and the board's wishes. They were now firmly in control, or so they thought at the time.

To understand Otto Koehler and his approach to the business of the San Antonio Brewing Association, we must understand the man himself. Otto Koehler was born in the village of Aldfeld in the kingdom of Hanover, and although Hanover is in Germany now, when Koehler was born in 1855, Hanover was a separate kingdom under English rule. Koehler was born to August W. and Johanne Koehler and was one of ten children growing up, making their home a crowded one; however, his parents made sure that all were taken care of. Koehler's twin brother, Karl, would precede him in a move to the United States.

Despite the many opportunities available to him in his hometown, the allure of the United States and the promise of greater success won him over.

In 1873, Koehler left for the United States and the bustling city of St. Louis at the tender age of seventeen, using his sister Johanna's wedding in St. Louis as the excuse he needed to leave Hanover and claim his opportunities in the United States.

Once in St. Louis, Koehler was determined to become a naturalized citizen and acclimate to his new country. He was granted U.S. citizenship the same year of arrival. His first job as an American citizen was that of a clerk in his brother's general store, where he would begin to learn the ins and outs of the business world and hone his ability to relate and interact with his fellow man. This first job didn't last long for Koehler, for soon he would run into St. Louis beer baron Adolphus Busch and was introduced to Anton Griesedieck, another German immigrant who owned a malting house, as well as what would later become the A. Griesedieck and Company Brewery, among others. It was one of Anton's sons, Joseph—or "Papa Joe," as he was affectionately called—who would later open the Griesedieck Brothers Brewing Company, one of the few breweries to later survive Prohibition and remain open until 1977.

The young Otto Koehler took a job as a bookkeeper and quickly proved himself, bringing him once again to the attention of Adolphus Busch, who himself had been busy with Anheuser-Busch's first expansion outside of its St. Louis headquarters, to San Antonio, Texas—it would later become the first brewery to bear the name Lone Star. Koehler quickly jumped into the Anheuser-Busch Lone Star Brewing Association and was soon on his way to what would become his passion: brewing.

When Koehler arrived in San Antonio to help head up Lone Star, he would meet two individuals who would later become key to his brewing career: John J. Stevens and A.B. Frank, both involved financially with Lone Star. Koehler quickly established long-lasting personal and business relationships with these men, quick enough that within a few years he would be involved in a different business venture that would last 115 years.

Koehler's time at Lone Star was short-lived, however. Having whet his appetite with the first Lone Star, he had his sights on his own brewing operation and took steps toward this goal while still with Lone Star. In 1886, Koehler took a trip to Germany, where he acquired the rights to the recipe and the name Pearl beer. At the same time, he also took a loan of about $10,000 from his brother-in-law, John Bentsen, with the intention of investing in Lone Star's primary rival in San Antonio. To plan and take steps to open your own rival brewery, while still working at one and using its resources, is ballsy, to say the least. This, however, was who Otto

Koehler was, and it would later both work to his benefit and serve to be the end of him.

Returning now to City Brewery, we see J.B. Belohradsky and his ever-popular brewery struggling. Belohradsky was knee deep in his legal and financial scandal, leaving him exposed enough for Koehler and his partners to swoop in and take control. With an initial partnership consisting of Koehler, Oscar Bergstrom and local businessman Frederick Hartz, the three pooled their collective personal resources and took financial control of City Brewery from Belohradsky in early 1887. The new partners continued to operate as City Brewery until August 1887, when they re-chartered it as the San Antonio Brewing Association. With the help of John J. Stevens, they obtained a loan of $300,000 from Trader's National Bank, which they used to upgrade City's equipment and brewing processes and introduce a new recipe that would come to be known as XXX Pearl Beer.

Now somewhat established, City Brewery's new managing directors included Koehler, Bergstrom, Hartz, Otto Wahrmund and Robert Tendick. Tendick had been running City Brewery as a receivership since 1886, when Belohradsky was forced out. With Koehler's brewing experience, the new directors were poised to create what would become the San Antonio Brewing Association, a force to be reckoned with. Although not involved with breweries himself, Wahrmund's father-in-law was Charles Nimitz of Fredericksburg, Texas, who not only operated a small brewery out of his saloon but grew his own hops as well—no small feat in Texas, where the soil is not suited to large-scale hop growing. This being the case, Nimitz likely was able to grow enough for his own purposes. Not too many years later, another famous Nimitz would come out of Fredericksburg: Charles's grandson, Admiral Chester Nimitz.

PERIOD II

THE RISE OF THE SAN ANTONIO BREWING ASSOCIATION, 1887–1918

BUBBLES, BUBBLES, BOILERS AND STABLES

Although the San Antonio Brewing Association's beginning is set in 1886, Koehler did not actually leave the Lone Star Brewing Association until 1887. It was during that year that Koehler is reputed to have made his now well-known trip from San Antonio to Bremen, Germany, and to the Kaiser-Beck Brewery to acquire what would become the recipe and trademark for San Antonio Brewing Association's XXX Pearl Beer.

Another thought as to how Otto Koehler came upon the name Pearl, and possibly the recipe, lies with a recently discovered match safe bearing the name "Compliments of A. Griesedieck Brewing Co., Pearl Lager Beer, St. Louis, Mo.," with dates stamped on it ranging from 1879 to 1886, the very year the San Antonio Brewing Association debuted its XXX Pearl beer. Coincidence? Perhaps, but consider again that Otto Koehler worked for Anton Griesedieck. "Kaiser-Beck did not have a Pearl beer and Anton, as well as his future sons, did not continue to call their beer Pearl," noted Charlie Staats, a local historian and collector of Texas brewing memorabilia and who also discovered the match safe. "It is possible that Otto struck a deal with Anton to purchase the recipe and the Pearl name from him, making one wonder what Otto Koehler was actually doing in Germany if he was not at Kaiser-Beck."

Although many know the famous brew as Pearl, it was known as XXX Pearl for quite a long time. "Pearl" referred to the pearl-like bubbles that resulted from

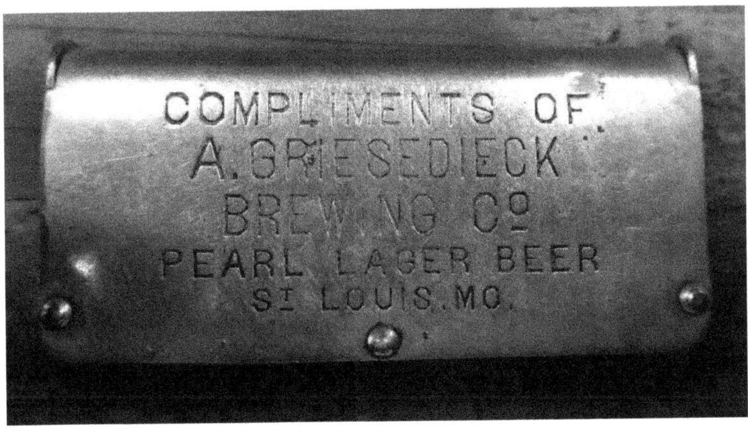

Match safe from the A. Griesedieck Brewing Company, suggesting that Otto Koehler may have obtained the name and recipe for Pearl lager beer from someone other than Kaiser-Beck Brewery in Germany, as is commonly accepted. Dates on the back range from 1879 to 1886, with 1886 being the year Pearl launched XXX Pearl Beer. *Charlie Staats.*

the carbonation. The XXX designation had, since medieval times, been used to designate the quality of the beer produced by European monasteries, with XXX being the highest quality. In fact, a brewery representative in 1887 promoted the beer in print, paying homage to the brewery name that folks had become accustomed to, as well as the brewery's new name: "The new City Beer, just out, and very fine, try it. Have you tried the new brand of City Pearl Beer? The finest flavored beer in the market. Be sure and try, and you will be convinced. Warranted to be the same at all times. Ask for it, drink no other."

As the San Antonio Brewing Association gained steam, Oscar Bergstrom, staying true to his opportunistic nature, assumed the presidency of the fledgling brewery. Despite this, it was really Koehler's brewery management experience that steered the ship. It was this very business acumen that had impressed Adolphus Busch in St. Louis, prompting him to bring Koehler to San Antonio for Lone Star. Would it be enough for Koehler?

While leading San Antonio Brewing Association forward in a new sea of breweries in San Antonio, Koehler began to invest in other businesses as well. At one point, Koehler had his hands in the Monarch Mining Company in Idaho; the Continental Mining Company and the Panuco Mountain and Monclova Railroad in Mexico; the American Lignite and Briquette Company of Texas; and the Texas Transportation Company, which served as the railroad used by San Antonio Brewing Association to transport its beer from the brewery to the main railroad line at Sunset Station in San Antonio. "His name as president or director of fifteen large corporations spoke of his versatility and business acumen," stated James Nelson in his 1976 master's thesis. "He had the ability to handle large business interests and groups of men."

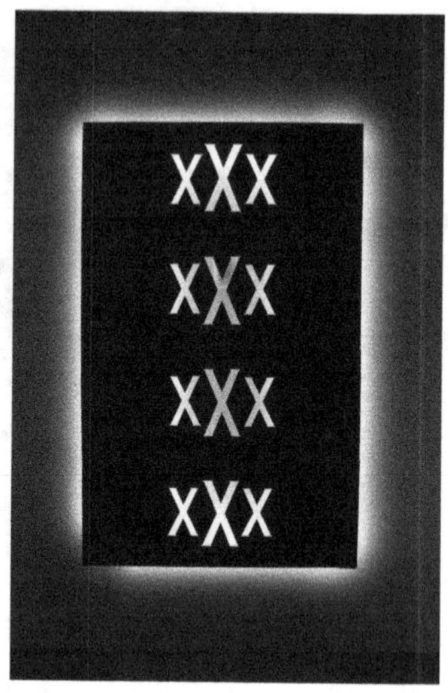

The XXX logo harkens back to medieval days, when XXX meant the best-quality beer. *Nan Palmero.*

As with many things, necessity is the mother of invention, and with demand for its beer reaching greater heights each year, distribution around the city and beyond was becoming a challenge for the company. The creation of the Texas Transportation Company was the result of this need, with the board of the San Antonio Brewing Association determining that its horse-drawn carriages would not be enough on their own. This short rail would allow XXX Pearl to be transported from the brewery to the nearby tracks of the Southern Pacific Railroad, as well as bringing much-needed brewing supplies from the arriving trains.

In addition to his business investments, Koehler invested heavily in real estate, further increasing what would become one of the largest fortunes in San Antonio at the time. One of the biggest of these investments was the now long-abandoned Hot Wells Resort and Sanitarium, started by McClellan Shackleton. Koehler was one of many investors in the grand four-story Victorian building that included numerous pools and eighty guestrooms. Not surprisingly, Otto Koehler sat at the top as president.

Koehler was a shrewd businessman indeed, leveraging not only his money but also that of the San Antonio Brewing Association, all with the approval of the San Antonio Brewing Association's board and stockholders. Often this money would be charged back to Koehler either individually or as Koehler and Company. Koehler was not alone. His partner at the San Antonio Brewing Association, Otto Wahrmund, dabbled in investments in just this same manner.

Perhaps one of the most interesting of his many investments was that of his partnership and friendship with his former employer Adolphus Busch. Together they were silent partners in the buyout of the first brewery to bear the name of the "Shrine of Texas Liberty," the Alamo Brewing Company, in 1895. Alamo Brewing would later be absorbed into the Lone Star Brewing Association.

Busch continued to keep an eye on Koehler throughout the decades, even expressing concern for the San Antonio beer magnate in a letter to Koehler

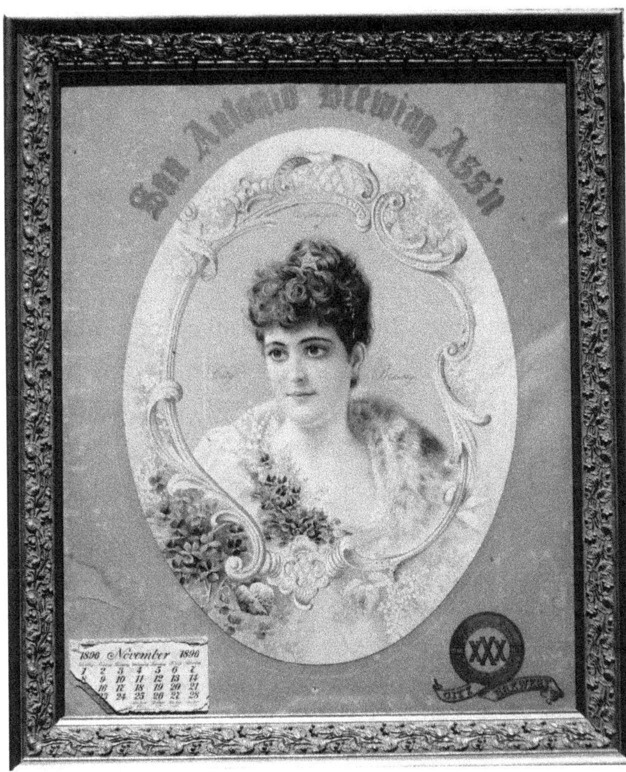

Page from San Antonio Brewing Association's 1896 calendar. *Jeremy Banas.*

on June 2, 1904: "You take good care of the brewery and promote its interest to the fullest extent; this is a far better investment than dabbling in mines and all kinds of outside affairs which give one nothing but worry and bring losses. Now you have no children and there is no earthly reason why you should burden yourself with all these responsibilities and cares; you ought to live like a king and enjoy life." Ironic, as later in the next century Busch's own brewery, Anheuser-Busch, was opening regional breweries and buying out others, a practice that would continue into the next two centuries.

By the late 1880s and early 1890s, the popularity of XXX Pearl Beer and the San Antonio Brewing Association had caused production to increase at a rapid rate, with XXX Pearl being delivered all over the Alamo City, much to the pleasure of its thirsty residents. "The brewery also purchased several saloons in San Antonio paying between $100 to $5,000 including all furniture and fixtures," said Charlie Staats, "thus becoming an official XXX Pearl Saloon." One of the more well-known and frequented of these saloons was the Scholz Palm Garden in downtown San Antonio, a three-story building that stands today. Between 1887 and 1894, the brewery would see many upgrades, including new offices, refrigeration equipment, a cooperage, a bottling building, a washing house and a storage room. The cooperage for San Antonio Brewing Association would be run by another German immigrant, Ernest Charles Mueller, whose home near San Antonio Brewing Association would later be repurposed as the Granary 'Cue and Brew in 2012 after being purchased from the Mueller family in 2004 by the Pearl's current ownership.

Mueller was enticed to come to the United States and later San Antonio by his friend and former coworker at Anheuser-Busch, Ignatz Hrovat, who was San Antonio Brewing Association's brewmaster at the time. Although Koehler brought the now famous recipe from Germany to San Antonio, it was Hrovat who weaved magic into it.

By 1892, production at the San Antonio Brewing Association had grown to near sixty thousand barrels per year, with more than sixty employees needed to keep that wonderful elixir rolling out the brewery doors. Clearly Koehler, Bergstrom and the gang had outgrown their wooden brewery. A more modern brewery with extra space was needed and fast. In 1893, the *San Antonio Daily Light* reported, "The City Brewing Company now in contemplation of extensive enlargements as they feel justified by their success and increasing demand for their product in doubling their capacity. The plans for a new brewing house of latest design, additional storage vault for 10,000 bottles, new stables for horses, are now in the hands of architects, the building to be built of brick and iron and fireproof."

The new brewhouse, stables and offices would be under the design of Chicago architect August Maritzen, already very well known nationally for his brewery designs. The new brewery would be done in two phases, with the now iconic brewhouse finished in 1894, while the washhouse, bottling building and stock house were completed in 1897. Also completed in 1894, and designed by local architect Otto Kramer, were the equally famous Pearl Stables. The year 1897 also saw the San Antonio Brewing Association leverage its holdings to borrow about $150,000 from the St. Louis Trust company to shore up its capital, as well as update and expand the brewery. In 1899, the troubled Oscar Bergstrom left for New York, allowing Otto Koehler to assume the presidency of the San Antonio Brewing Association. In 1901, Koehler, Wahrmund and J.J. Stevens bought out their other partners during the brewery's re-chartering that same year.

In addition to the new brewery, upgraded equipment and icehouse, Koehler focused a little of his attention on the exterior aesthetics of the new brewery. One such addition was a garden on the grounds. The *San Antonio Express* reported in its November 14, 1914 edition that "Otto Koehler took the greatest pride and pleasure in the plants and trees of his home and brewery. Whenever he left San Antonio, he charged the gardener to give special care to the flowers and trees. Recently he completed a fence around his house grounds that is unique and in keeping with the beautiful surroundings."

The home and grounds referred to are that of Koehler's residence in Laurel Heights off West Ashby Place, just north of what is now the campus of the San Antonio Community College. As legend has it, Otto Koehler picked that particular location for his $133,000 mansion so that he could keep an eye on the brewery and his employees by observing the color of the smoke coming from the brewery's smokestacks. If true, this is quite interesting, considering Koehler's devotion to his employees and the trust he gained from them as a result.

Not that Otto Koehler had much to worry about. His brewery was in the hands of brewmaster Oscar Oswald Schreiber, who kept the formula written down in a secret book and made sure that the brewhouse ran smoothly and without incident. Such was the responsibility of a brewmaster, and that tradition has carried into present times. However, thirteen short years after the brewery opened, Schreiber passed away. Schreiber was going to be hard to replace, but the San Antonio Brewing Association board took a stab at it and hired Gottfried Schober, who left in 1904, opening his own brewery and ice factory in 1905 a mere two blocks from the San Antonio Brewing Association. Schober was replaced by the venerable Gustav Etter, who would see the San Antonio Brewing Association through the best and worst of times, until his retirement in 1945.

Gustav Etter was known at the time as one of the most respected brewmasters in the country, as well as being the treasurer for the United States Brewmasters Association. Etter had been born in 1865 in Rotweil, Germany, and arrived in the United States in the late 1880s. Prior to his arrival at the San Antonio Brewing Association, Etter had worked as brewmaster at Tosetti Brewing Company in Chicago, Illinois. Though known primarily for XXX Pearl, the San Antonio Brewing Association brewed other brands as well, such as Muenchener and Texas Pride, which were introduced by Etter. Texas Pride itself would see multiple incarnations over the next seven decades. Little is known about these styles, but Nelson stated that "Etter established a continued record of brewing perfection. Under his firm guidance, brewing facilities were considered a marvel of excellence. In 1907, Texas Pride was acclaimed as their most popular bottled beer."

In the early 1900s, in response to increased competition from new and expanding breweries, the San Antonio Brewing Association joined other

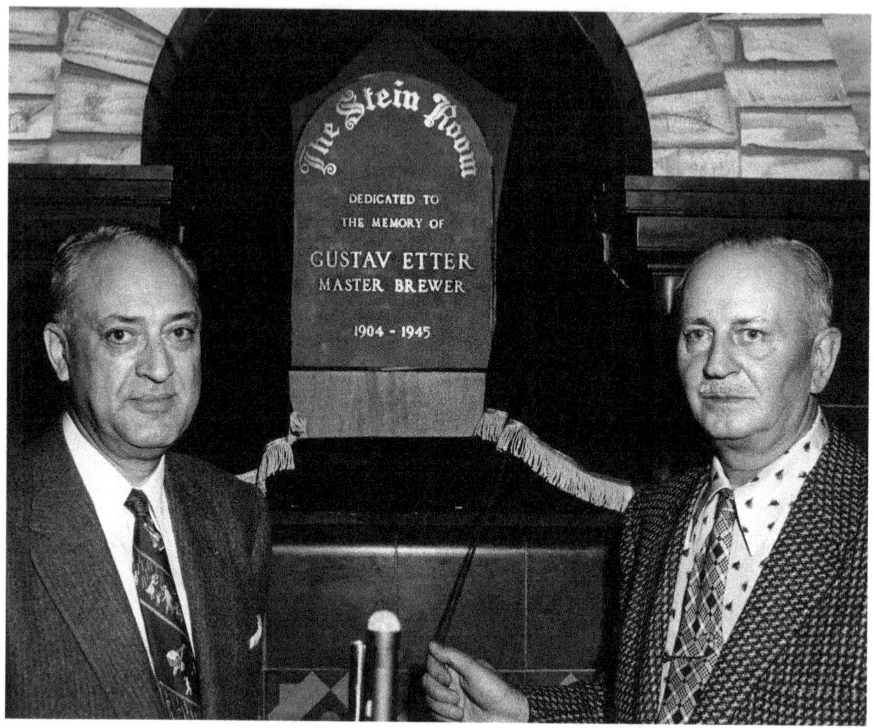

Otto A. Koehler and the Stein Room dedication. *Pearl LLC Archives.*

Texas breweries like the Lone Star Brewing Company, the Texas Brewing Company of Fort Worth, the American Brewing Association of Houston and several others to form the Texas Consolidated Brewing Association. Joint stock ownership was given to each member; with this new partnership, the breweries hoped to stabilize beer prices in the Lone Star State, which were fixed by the association at about $2.50 per barrel, although eventually these beer giants of Texas would face an antitrust case that would hurt the member breweries dearly and accelerate prohibition in Texas.

Along with a stabilization of the common brewing process for lager beer, purchase of grain from the same malting companies in the United States, the use of similar equipment and stringent federal guidelines on ingredients, mainly the Pure Food Law of 1906, lager beer continued to rise in popularity not only in Texas but also throughout the United States, largely due to these changes.

In a letter to his father in 1903, Otto Koehler exulted in his excitement for the future:

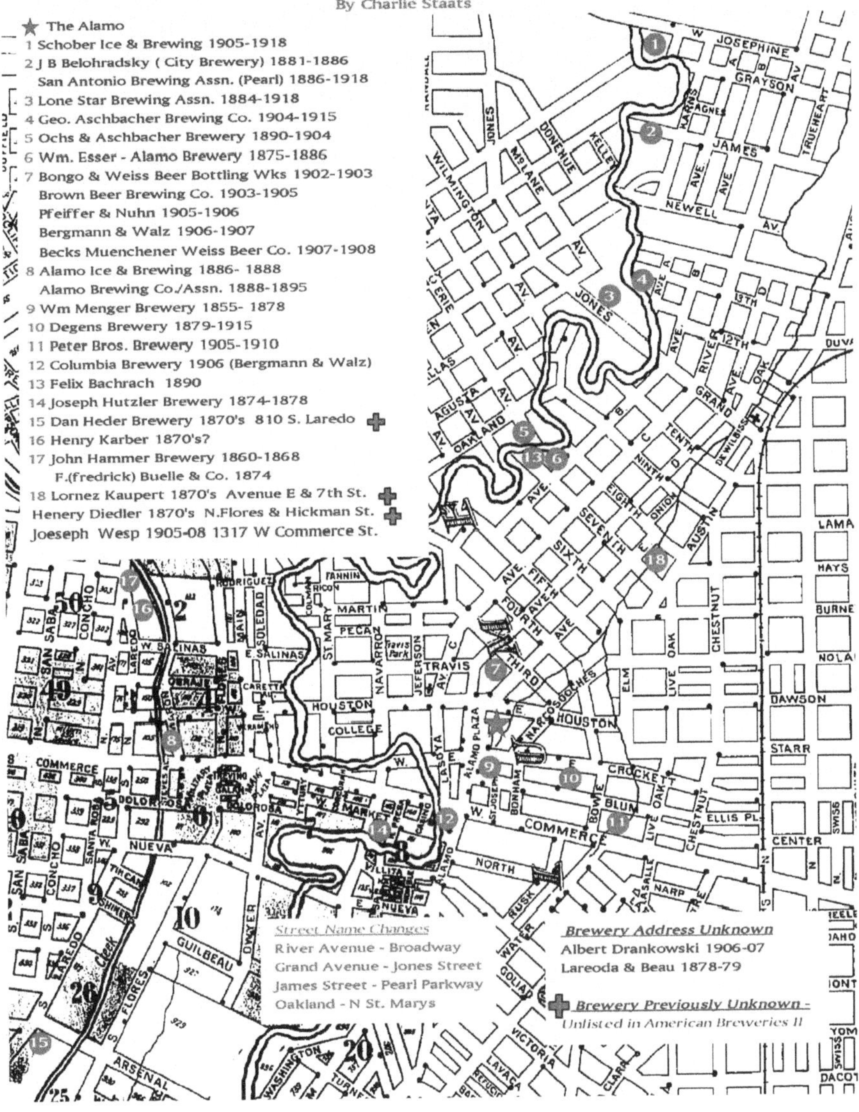

Pre-Prohibition San Antonio brewery locations. *Charlie Staats.*

> *Everything with us here is in excellent shape, business and otherwise and I hope that in the coming years everything will fall into place so that I and the members of our entire family will have nothing to worry about anymore. I recently got involved in a number of big deals all of which promise to turn out tremendously great; and furthermore is our brewing business so organized that our profits are greatly increased and I am manager of seven breweries.*

What's interesting is Otto Koehler's mention of being manager for seven breweries. Considering that he worked only for the San Antonio Brewing Association, it is possible that he was taking credit for the other breweries that were a part of the Texas Consolidated Brewing Association. Although no records are found to support this, he may have been elected to head the overall association. In addition, he still had shares in the Lone Star Brewing Association.

EARLY RUMBLINGS OF PROHIBITION

Despite the popularity of XXX Pearl and Texas Pride, rumblings from the so-called dry camp were heating up around the same time. Anti-drinking rhetoric from the Anti-Saloon League was weighing heavily on the booming beer business in Texas. In an attempt to slow this momentum and a possible future prohibition on alcohol, the Texas Consolidated Brewing Association added the Dallas Brewing Company and the Galveston Brewing Association to its ranks, re-forming the group into the Texas Brewers' Association.

This new group's sole purpose was to pour money into a campaign to stop the possible ban on all alcohol. Each member brewing pledged twenty cents per barrel to the endeavor in an attempt to persuade lawmakers and judges that the "wet side" was the right one. These efforts did bring an ally to the wet side in Oscar Branch, who occupied the Governor's Mansion, gaining him the nickname "Budweiser Branch" to his pro-dry opponents.

Not all of its efforts could be dedicated to staving off what would be the inevitable, and thus the San Antonio Brewing Association brewed on. By 1910, the association appears to have switched to metal barrels, although photos of that time suggest that it was still using a fair number of wooden barrels. The brewery also began adding an enzyme to its beer that

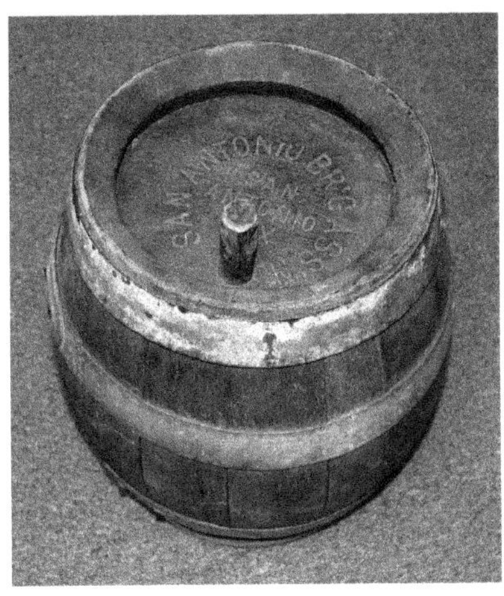

A barrel that once held XXX Pearl Beer, unknown year. *Jeremy Banas.*

helped with clarification of its natural haziness, and it even moved past a labor strike that lasted just one day.

By 1911, though, dry legislation support was increasing, with much of the support coming from rural counties and from within the Texas legislature. Governor Branch went so far as to cut funding for the enforcement of dry laws in those counties where they already existed. Coupled with behind-the-scenes shenanigans by the wet crowd, the proposed legislation was defeated. In 1913, the Anti-Saloon League went national and petitioned Congress for a federal amendment banning alcohol. By 1915, the pro-dry sentiment had morphed into a bill and was voted on, with 197 in favor and 190 against.

Despite the success and growth of the San Antonio Brewing Association, 1914 would prove a vital year in its history. War broke out in Europe that July. Koehler was overseas visiting his German family when war broke out, stranding him and his wife, Emma, in Germany. The Koehlers of Germany were nervous about their fate, as well as that of the visiting Otto and Emma. While in Germany, Otto Koehler drew up a new will, thereby giving each of his brothers and sister the equivalent of $25,000 1914 dollars if he were to leave this earth—it would turn out to be rather prophetic.

Otto and Emma Koehler were able to return to the United States in the fall of 1914. On the way to their ship, the SS *New Amsterdam*, lightning struck the limousine they were traveling in, and the German police detained them. After a series of interrogations, the Koehlers were released, and they were finally able to return home. What was to come in the ensuing months would make Otto Koehler wish he had still been stranded in Germany.

Upon his return, Otto Koehler tackled issues at the brewery with the energy of someone half his age. Despite the threat to his interests in Mexico from Pancho Villa, Koehler seemed completely at ease. However, that would not last long, as a secret he had been hiding from everyone would prove to be his end and alter the San Antonio Brewing Association for the foreseeable future; a scandal would soon take center stage over all else that would rock San Antonio and the United States.

TROUBLE IN PARADISE?

In the early 1900s, Emma Koehler is reported to have been involved in a terrible car accident that left her virtually an invalid and perpetually bedridden. No evidence is actually found to support this, leading one to ponder the actual cause of the injury. "It could even be that she was injured during her summer 1909 visit to Germany, which would explain hiring a German nurse, rather than starting out from San Antonio with help," mused San Antonio researcher Martha Rand Hix. It is also possible for this to be the truth, as there is mention in the memoirs of Emma Koehler's great-niece, Margaret Pace Willson, that her Aunt Emma had been injured in an auto accident. To ease his burden yet make sure his wife was attended to, Koehler hired a nurse in 1909 by the name of Emma Dumpke.

The Koehlers had hired Dumpke while on one of their many trips back to Germany. Dumpke was described in a later account as a "pretty, petite brunette." Dumpke appears to have taken a shine to Mrs. Koehler, even as she and Otto Koehler became closer. Not long after Dumpke's hiring, Koehler and Dumpke's affair began in earnest. Not much is known about Otto and Emma Koehler's relationship at the time, but it most certainly looks to have taken a turn after her accident.

At some point after Dumpke was hired, she brought around a nurse friend of hers to the Koehler mansion. Dumpke had already spoken to her friend about her affair with Otto Koehler. When this friend, Emma Hedda Burgermeister, arrived with Emma Dumpke to the Koehler mansion, she could not escape the wandering eye of the San Antonio Brewing Association president. She soon joined the love triangle. Each was given a stipend, with Dumpke receiving $125 and Burgermeister receiving only $50 per month. It's hard to say if this caused any friction between the two friends, although it most certainly could not have helped matters any.

It is not known at what point Koehler bought the two mistresses their own residence, but he would often take unaccompanied trips to their Hunstock cottage not far from South Presa Street. Odd, considering that Burgermeister would later testify that Dumpke had been let go by Mrs. Koehler later in 1909 and before Otto Koehler purchased the Hunstock cottage for the two Emmas. Always known as a good neighborhood, it remains so today. The house itself was modest, about 1,500 square feet, give or take. It included a living room, a kitchen and bedrooms in the back, with a roof high enough for a good-sized attic. Oddly enough, the cottage was also a small walk of a few blocks from Otto Koehler's Hot Wells investment.

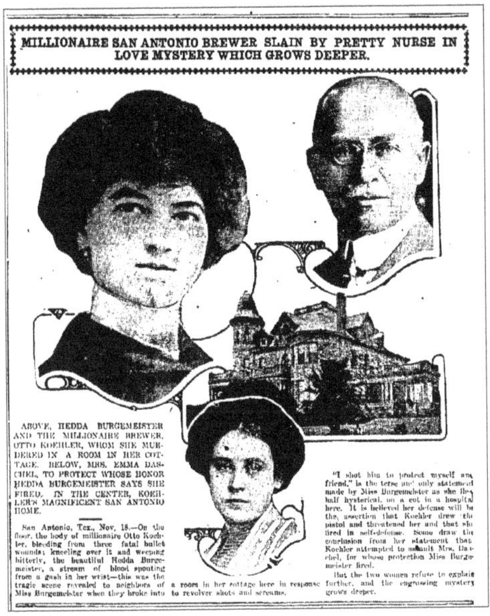

MILLIONAIRE SAN ANTONIO BREWER SLAIN BY PRETTY NURSE IN LOVE MYSTERY WHICH GROWS DEEPER.

ABOVE, HEDDA BURGEMEISTER AND THE MILLIONAIRE BREWER, OTTO KOEHLER, WHOM SHE MURDERED IN A ROOM IN HER COTTAGE. BELOW, MRS. EMMA DASCHEL, TO PROTECT WHOSE HONOR HEDDA BURGEMEISTER SAYS SHE FIRED. IN THE CENTER, KOEHLER'S MAGNIFICENT SAN ANTONIO HOME.

San Antonio, Tex., Nov. 18.—On the floor, the body of millionaire Otto Koehler, bleeding from three fatal bullet wounds; kneeling over it and weeping bitterly, the beautiful Hedda Burgemeister, a stream of blood spouting from a gash in her wrist—this was the tragic scene revealed to neighbors of Miss Burgemeister when they broke into a room in her cottage here in response to revolver shots and screams.

"I shot him to protect myself and friend," is the terse and only statement made by Miss Burgemeister as she lies half hysterical, on a cot in a hospital here. It is believed her defense will be the assertion that Koehler drew the pistol and threatened her and that she fired in self-defense. Some draw the conclusion from her statement that Koehler attempted to assault Mrs. Daschel, for whose protection Miss Burgemeister fired.

But the two women refuse to explain further, and the engrossing mystery grows deeper.

Copy of article describing the trial of Emma Burgermeister. *Charlie Staats.*

Around the time of Otto and Emma Koehler's return from Europe, Emma Dumpke laid a bomb on poor Otto: she was going to be married. One can only imagine what was going through Otto Koehler's head. Clearly, he had hinged his happiness on his relationship with the two nurses, for Otto Koehler took a drastic measure soon after. Dumpke married Dr. Martin Dachsel and left San Antonio. When a neighbor of the Emmas sent a telegram to Dumpke in the fall of 1914 advising that Burgermeister was sick, Dumpke returned to San Antonio immediately to see her friend. After Dumpke's return, Otto Koehler had a dilemma. Realizing that he was going to lose Dumpke and could do nothing about it, Otto Koehler made a proposal of marriage to Emma Burgermeister, stating that he would seek a divorce from his wife.

Burgermeister turned Koehler down. She could not in good conscience marry Koehler and have him leave his wife, a helpless and injured woman, by herself with no way to support herself. At some point after this encounter, Otto Koehler seems to have changed his mind about his divorce and marriage proposal, as suggested by details gathered from the later trial of Emma Burgermeister. One can only speculate as to why Otto Koehler changed his mind. Had someone intervened and convinced him to stop, or had he come to the realization that perhaps he had made some very bad decisions? Burgermeister herself later alluded that someone had gotten to Otto Koehler and helped him see reason.

Regardless, events were already set in motion. On a very fateful Friday, November 13, 1914, Otto Koehler left his mansion in Laurel Heights and got into his buggy, tearing off to the Hunstock cottage, a trip that would take him almost an hour.

By all accounts, Koehler appears to have gone to the cottage that night to officially end the affairs with the two nurses. Some speculate that he went to the cottage to beg Burgermeister to change her mind. Regardless of the reason, Otto Koehler arrived at the cottage in the early evening and entered with great fanfare. At the door was Dumpke, whom he swiftly passed right by without saying a word. Koehler headed straight to the bedroom, where he assumed Burgermeister would be. As Koehler entered the bedroom, he saw her in bed with a cold rag on her forehead. Koehler eventually sat at the edge of the bed.

Not fifteen minutes later, Koehler was lying on the floor dead with bullet wounds in his chest, face and neck. It took three bullets—ironic considering he had three women in his life. If we were to believe in conspiracies, one might think Burgermeister planned this all along, down to the three shots getting revenge for her, Dumpke and Otto Koehler's wife, Emma Bentsen Koehler. A lot transpired in those fifteen minutes. The trial revealed that Otto Koehler leaned in to kiss Burgermeister, who spurned his advances. An argument ensued, with Burgermeister suddenly pulling out a gun, aiming it at Koehler and then firing.

When police arrived at some point after, Burgermeister was in a fit. She had to be carried out from the cottage and taken to Baylor Hospital. Burgermeister was treated for a wound she had sustained in her left forearm from a knife. It would not be unreasonable to surmise that Koehler had the knife and tried to defend himself at some point, but no mention of a knife being present was found. The Koehler family's official statement was somewhat typical, for they noted that Otto Koehler had gone to the cottage that night to settle a bill with the two nurses when the argument occurred. This alternative fact would not stand up for long once the grand jury trial began.

Koehler himself was also taken from the scene. Although San Antonio Undertaking and Embalming took the larger-than-life brewer away in a body bag, it was not the end of the drama surrounding Otto Koehler and his three Emmas.

Letters poured in from all over to Emma Koehler, expressing their sorrow to the newly widowed brewer's wife. Otto Koehler, despite his faults, was beloved around the world. Koehler's own obituary was even carefully crafted to ensure that everyone remembered that Koehler "was widely known and

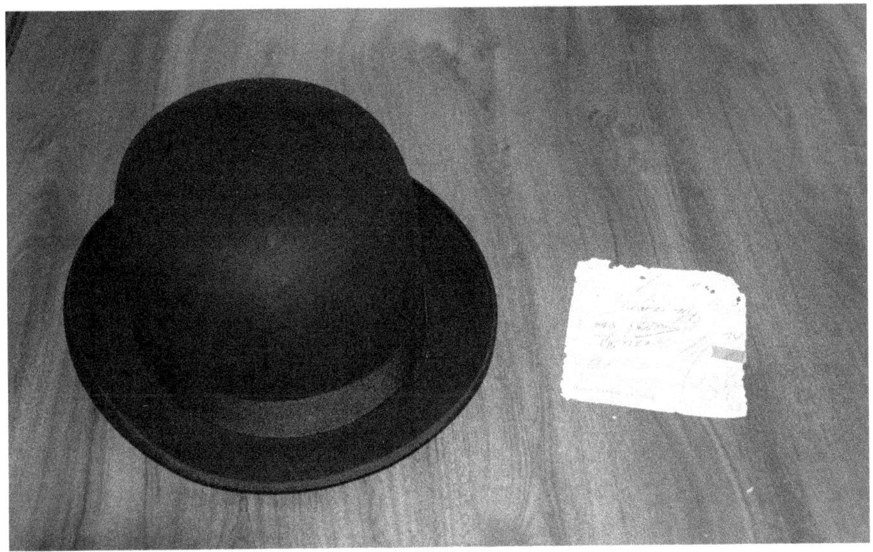

Otto Koehler's original bowler hat. Purchased at Saks Fifth Avenue on April 5—unknown year but likely in the late 1890s. *Jeremy Banas.*

he had many friends." Although he was gone, Koehler had lived his life exactly how he wanted and made no apologies for it. He had given much back to his beloved San Antonio community, for which he was honored in death. Koehler had been a member of the long-standing German heritage society Beethoven Mänerchor (still open today) along with fellow German (and San Antonio's first commercial brewer) Charles Degen. In fact, the Beethoven Choir, with whom Koehler also sang, opened its pipes during his funeral in honor of a fallen friend.

At a San Antonio Brewing Association board meeting a few days after Otto Koehler's death, his partner and close friend Otto Wahrmund addressed the brewery's board regarding his friend's death:

> *Whereas, Otto Koehler, our president with whom we have been intimately associated both personally and in the business since the organization of this association, met with an untimely death on the twelfth day of this month.... Words cannot convey the sorrow we feel at his death in the prime of manhood. Possessed of all his facilities and energy would have made him in the future, as he was in the past, one of the most useful citizens of his adopted home. We deeply deplore the fact that he has left us, and extend to those left behind our heartfelt sympathies and bow to the inevitable.*

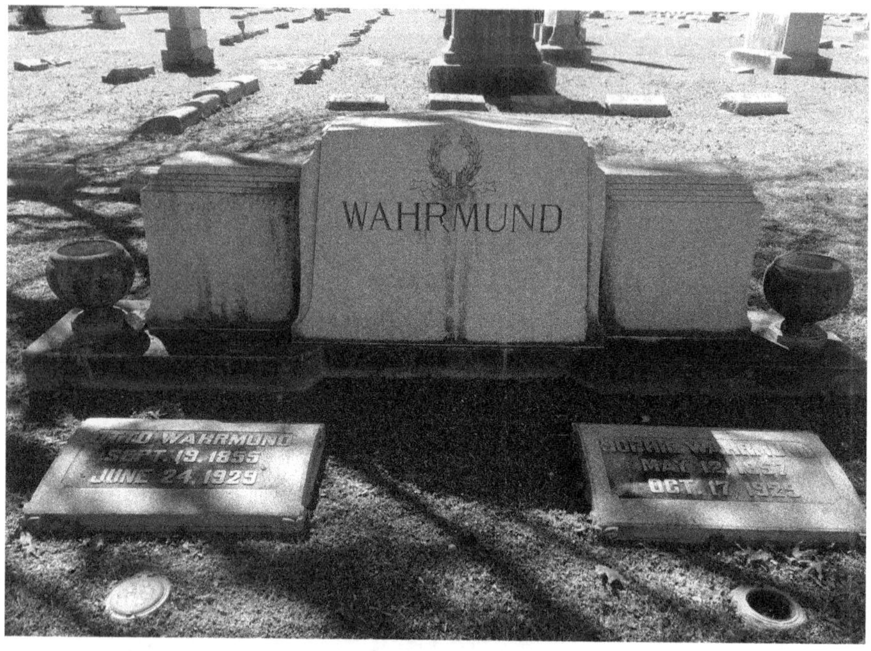

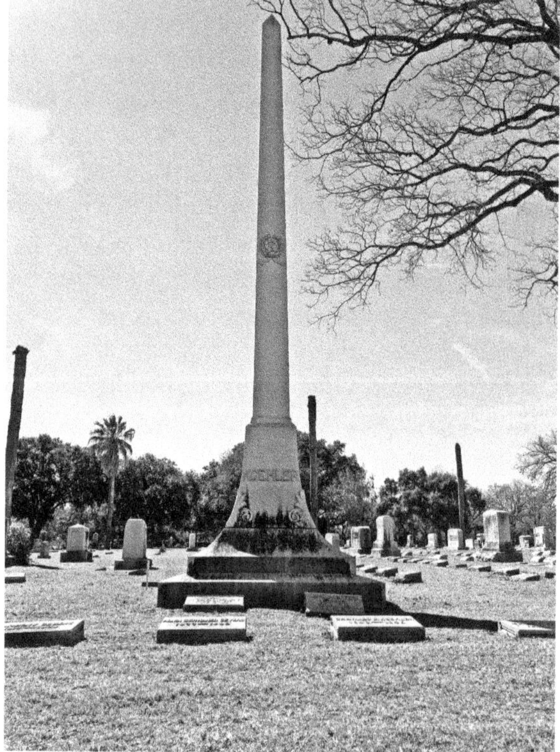

Above: Gravestone of Otto Wahrmund at Mission Park South Cemetery. *Jeremy Banas*.

Left: Otto Koehler's epitaph at Mission Park South Cemetery. *Jeremy Banas*.

> *Resolved further, that in recognition of the fact that the best energies of his life have been devoted to the success of this enterprise, and in respect of his memory, that there be no change in the presidency of this Association at this time.*

Koehler's funeral saw about one thousand attendees, and his pallbearers were some of the San Antonio Brewing Association's and San Antonio's elite. They included Andrew Stevens (brother of co-founder J.J. Stevens), Harry Wahrmund (Otto Wahrmund's nephew), Otto Wahrmund, Oscar Bergstrom (who was still living in New York City), J.J. Stevens, William Wurzbach (brother of the well-known Harry Wurzbach) and almost fifty other pallbearers, with the services being held at the Koehler mansion in Laurel Heights.

A *San Antonio Light* article in 1914 estimated Otto Koehler's net worth as somewhere around $3 million, a sum that would now equal $73,710,436. Not too bad for someone (especially an immigrant) who started at the

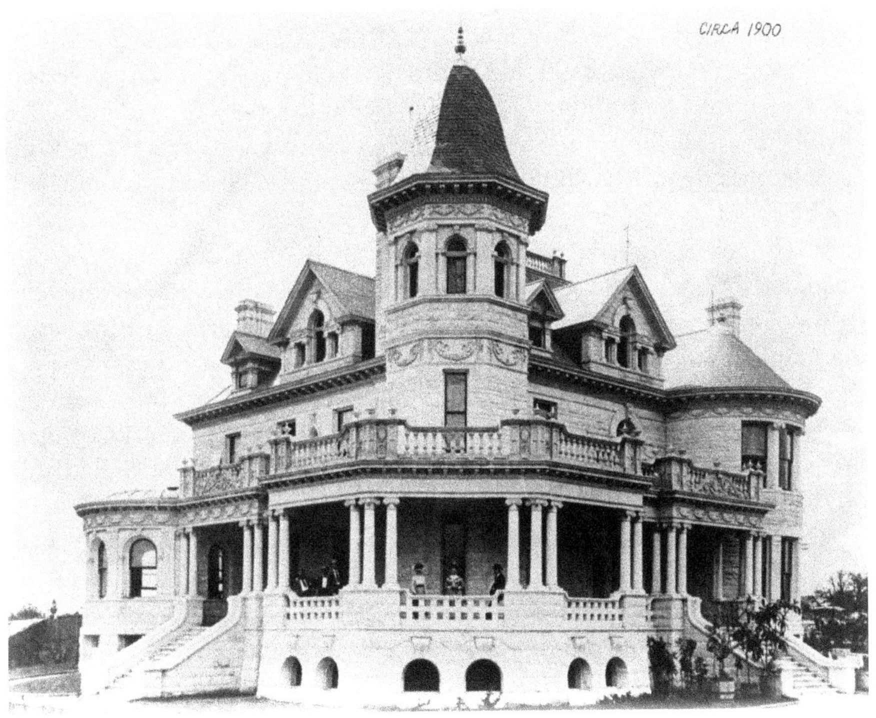

Exterior of the Koehler House, 1900s. *San Antonio College and the Alamo Colleges District Foundation.*

bottom of the industry and worked his way up. The article also mentioned that his wife, Emma Koehler, as well as two nephews, Charles E. and Otto A. Koehler, both of whom would figure prominently in the brewery's future, survived Koehler.

WHO SHOT OTTO?

What of the two Emmas who were present and involved in Otto Koehler's death? Conflicting reports exist regarding Emma Dumpke, known as Emma Dumpke Daschel after her marriage. One article noted that she was detained at the scene for murder or conspiracy to commit murder of Otto Koehler, although the district attorney, merely holding her as a "witness" to the murder, did not formally arrest her.

With no evidence to support that Dumpke was involved in any type of conspiracy to murder Koehler, San Antonio district attorney W.C. Linden released her on November 19, 1914, after her husband paid her bail in the amount of $500. Yet another article stated that Dumpke was arrested at the scene and then later released due to lack of evidence. The grand jury also found no evidence of Dumpke's involvement in Otto Koehler's death and essentially let her go; Dumpke left San Antonio with her husband soon after.

Burgermeister remained at Baylor Hospital for four days, receiving treatment for her wound. One could speculate that she was exaggerating her injuries in order to avoid facing the music. When it was time for her to leave the hospital, she was taken to the Bexar County Jail by then Bexar County sheriff Tobin. Mrs. N.S. Brooks, a jail matron at the time, processed her. Burgermeister continued to plead that she only shot Otto Koehler to protect herself, as Koehler had threatened her with a gun—despite the fact that no other gun was found at the scene.

A grand jury chose not to indict Emma Dumpke but pushed forward with the indictment of Emma Burgermeister with as much force as one of the trains that carried San Antonio's beloved XXX Pearl Beer. In order to avoid the charges, Burgermeister did what any self-respecting innocent would do: she fled, claiming that her attorney told her to run, although not before she paid her $5,000 bail fee, leaving her $2,000. She didn't just hide out in some far-away state in the United States. No, she fled to Europe to put her nursing skills to use in the war effort as World War I raged on.

In early 1915, Burgermeister's attorney received a letter from her advising that she was "nursing wounded soldiers." By July 1915, and for an unknown reason, Burgermeister had returned to America on the SS *New Amsterdam* and settled in New York. Having missed a court date of February 1 that year, her bail was revoked. She had been hiding out in New York a mere two years when Duncan McAskill, the Bexar County district attorney, came to New York to get her. Burgermeister then hired an attorney, and *The State of Texas v. Emma Hedda Burgermeister* began on January 16, 1918.

The circus of a trial that ensued would not soon be eclipsed, becoming something we might today label as a "trial of the century." Burgermeister's attorney was none other than former Texas governor Thomas Mitchell Campbell. While governor, Campbell had created the position of Bexar County assistant district attorney to help with enforcement of laws against saloons. On the prosecuting side were Assistant District Attorney James F. Onion, who had been a pallbearer at Otto Koehler's funeral; S.G. Newton, a San Antonio Brewing Association attorney; and W.C. Linden, who was Bexar County district attorney when Burgermeister skipped bail in 1915. Coincidentally, Campbell was a dry supporter and Onion and his team were wets.

Everything appeared to be in the prosecution's favor, especially with an all-male jury of local residences. One person who could have helped immensely was missing: Emma Dumpke. Without her testimony that Koehler and Dumpke were not together anymore at the time of the incident, that Koehler was upset over money and that Burgermeister was planning for trouble, the defense would have its fair share of challenges.

TRIAL OF THE CENTURY

Many witnesses testified for and against Emma Burgermeister. One witness was Henry Cordt, who resided across from the "Emma" cottage with his wife. At the time Dumpke was living out of town with her husband, Cordt advised the court that Burgermeister had forged a telegram in his name, sending it to Dumpke in St. Louis and urging her to come back to San Antonio to her aid. Dumpke had earlier confirmed this, stating that she returned to find Burgermeister just fine.

Cordt would also testify that he heard Dumpke yell Burgermeister's name on the night of the murder, prompting him to run across the street to the cottage. Upon entering the cottage, Cordt heard three or four shots. Burgermeister's bedroom door was half open when he approached, and after he fully opened it, Burgermeister portrayed herself as a victim, hunched over Koehler's body, cradling his head and crying. Cordt confirmed this, adding that he asked Burgermeister what she had done, to which the young nurse replied, "He tried to murder me," saying nothing more as Koehler's body still twitched.

Burgermeister must have been quite the charmer. She made friends with the jail matron, Brooks, who admitted during the trial that she and Burgermeister had become friends and she had accepted gifts from her. This possible friendship may have prompted Matron Brooks to provide questionable testimony in favor of her friend, including that Burgermeister had bruises on her body, including the throat. Even one of the responding officers, Detective Crosby Marsden, advised that two knives were found at the scene, one of them bloody, in addition to a loaded revolver and Burgermeister's used .32-caliber revolver. Perhaps the bloody knife, later shown to have been dull, led to Burgermeister's proclamation that Otto Koehler had tried to kill her. The detective, who would later serve as a Texas Ranger, admitted to having done some detective work for Burgermeister in the past, as well as giving her defense attorney photos from the crime scene that would aid in her defense.

Perhaps the best support for Burgermeister was that of local attorney Florence Ramer. She testified that Burgermeister had come to her on the day of the murder asking for help, stating that her life was in danger from Koehler. She noted that Burgermeister had told her that Koehler tried to meet her for a liaison at a shady place, after which she became fearful of him. Ramer also stated that Burgermeister said she had not sent Dumpke to the brewery that day to fetch Otto Koehler and bring him to the cottage to discuss their falling out and to settle their business affairs, nor had she arranged for Ramer to be there in the evening. This testimony was in response to other testimony that perhaps the Emmas had planned this ahead of time.

When Burgermeister herself took the stand, she no longer appeared to be the victim. Hardened and full of resolve, Burgermeister painted a picture of Otto Koehler that left some with a distaste for the Texas beer magnate. Tall, blond and alluring, Burgermeister used this to her advantage with her jurors. She described Koehler as "a bull when mad" and noted that she had never worked for the Koehlers, as all had been led to believe. She went so far as to deny any liaisons with Koehler herself, advising that any extramarital affairs were between Koehler and Dumpke, whom he said he would marry once his wife had the decency to wake up on the wrong side of the grass.

Burgermeister continued her story, painting a very desperate Otto Koehler once Dumpke was married and moved from San Antonio. At that time, Burgermeister said, Koehler then professed his love for her. However, she turned him down, not wanting to leave a sick Emma Koehler out on her own. After Koehler seemingly broke things off with her, Burgermeister advised that Koehler came to her after returning from his fall 1914 trip to see family in Germany. He asked her if she really loved him. She replied that she did. She noted that Koehler became confused about his life, stating that he would go to Galveston and make it look like an accident.

Concerned, she hired an investigator to follow Koehler and protect him, as she loved him, she said. That is when she telegraphed Dumpke. Burgermeister said that when Koehler asked her and Dumpke to bring all the papers that had his name on them, his intentions to kill her were clear, so she took precautions. When Koehler later arrived at the house, she asked him why he wanted to do away with her, to which he replied that she was not in her right mind. Burgermeister claimed that Koehler came toward her, at which point she fired the gun until he fell to the ground. During the trial, she also confirmed that both guns in the home were hers, kept for protection. After shooting Koehler, she claimed to have then turned the gun on herself and pulled the trigger, but nothing happened. Finding this clearly ridiculous, the district attorney remarked that her "aim at Mr. Koehler was better than your aim at yourself."

Despite this, Koehler had many residents testifying on his behalf, including many of his pallbearers. They testified to his character and lack of temper. The Koehler family's version of the events, primarily that of Emma Koehler, was that Otto Koehler had driven out to the Hunstock cottage to settle a bill that Burgermeister had submitted for the care of Emma Koehler and that the two argued, with Burgermeister panicking and shooting Koehler.

Then the unexpected happened: the trial resulted in an acquittal for Burgermeister—a little shocking considering the all-male jury. As if to add insult to the widow Koehler's already substantial embarrassment, Burgermeister married the jury foreman and moved to New Orleans. At some undisclosed time later, though, she moved back with her husband into the very cottage home where she and Dumpke had lived, for the cottage had been deeded to her by Otto Koehler years before.

Adjusting after Otto Koehler's death in late 1914, the San Antonio Brewing Association was hit hard. With no clear leadership at the brewery, the board needed to take action quickly. To stay on track, the board members agreed to Otto Wahrmund's suggestion in the meeting after Koehler's death that they would not elect another president for now. Wahrmund became the brewery's president in all but name.

LIFE WITHOUT OTTO KOEHLER

One individual who was brought on in the middle of 1914 and would help keep the San Antonio Brewing Association going in years to come, especially after Otto Koehler's death, was engineer William Isaacs, known as Billy to his friends. Isaacs worked at the San Antonio Brewing Association for almost fifty years and retired as vice-president of plant operations.

Isaacs was a Texas born and raised engineer. Born on July 4, 1896, he came to San Antonio around ten years later. He was hired by the San Antonio Brewing Association on July 14, 1914, after having completed his studies at St. Mary's College (now St. Mary's University). When World War I broke out for the United States in 1917, Isaacs served as an automotive instructor in Austin at Camp Mabry. He came back a few years later when the United States' involvement in the war ended.

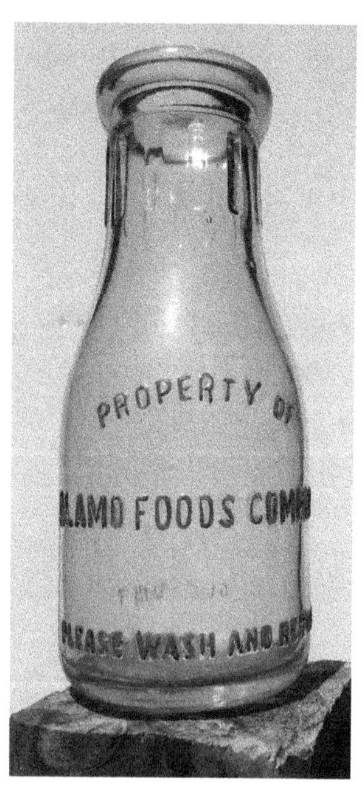

An empty bottle of milk from Alamo Foods. *Jeremy Banas.*

Things were a little different now compared to just two years earlier. Prohibition had begun, and the San Antonio Brewing Association was now Alamo Industries. By 1922, Isaacs had become chief engineer. In 1924, to further add more notches to his brewing belt, he attended the Siebel Institute of Technology in Chicago, a revered brewing school that exists today. While at Siebel, Isaacs took classes in baking, milling, engineering, refrigeration and other topics related to the food industry, as teaching people how to brew was not allowed. He later became a registered engineer and a member of the Texas Society of Professional Engineers. His wife, Dorothy, may have even worked as a stenographer for Alamo Industries. By 1943, Isaacs had been promoted to plant manager. In 1952, he was plant superintendent, and by the time of his departure in 1957, he was a member of the board of directors and vice-president of plant operations.

Isaacs would remain vice-president all the way until his retirement in 1969. The Pearl Brewing Company honored William Isaacs at the San Antonio Country Club with a lunch. Otto A. was present and gave Isaacs a bronze plaque praising his dedicated service, which saw the brewery through Prohibition, World War I and World War II.

Isaacs diversified himself a little and was a member of the board of the Exchange Club, the building committee for St. Luke's Church and the board for the Texas Diocese of the Episcopal Church. Isaacs passed away on October 19, 1991, at the age of ninety-five, having had one heck of a life and career.

However, it would not just be its beloved founder, president and manager's passing that would give the San Antonio Brewing Association its fair share of challenges. Conflicts with the dry camp, as well as the state government, would come into play after Koehler's death. Before 1903, the members of the Texas Consolidated Brewing Association worked toward an anti-prohibition agenda, with members agreeing to pay twenty cents per barrel of beer that was kegged and one cent per six-pack of bottled beer, raising more than $2 million. The State of Texas alleged that these funds were used to commit a multitude of campaign interferences between 1902 and 1911. Specifically, the organization was accused of messing with specific whole tax laws, contributing toward political campaigns that would support its wet agenda and the political acts of corporations aligned with its ideals. Although it was collectively fined a mere $281,000, its actions served only to fuel the growing sentiment against alcohol.

So worried were Otto Koehler and the San Antonio Brewing Association that Koehler himself expressed his concerns over the funds needed to support their anti-prohibition campaign in a letter to August A. Busch on February 1, 1911:

> *From the above general outline you can see that we are entering into a very costly campaign and I do not believe that the amount of money which can be raised outside the brewing interests will amount to very much. The Texas Brewers have assessed themselves 60 cents a barrel on 600,000 barrels, which will make a total of $360,000. Your contributions of $100,000 and the 30 cent assessment on Lemp, Pabst and Schlitz well at $45,000 more to this amount, which (if paid in) will make a total of*

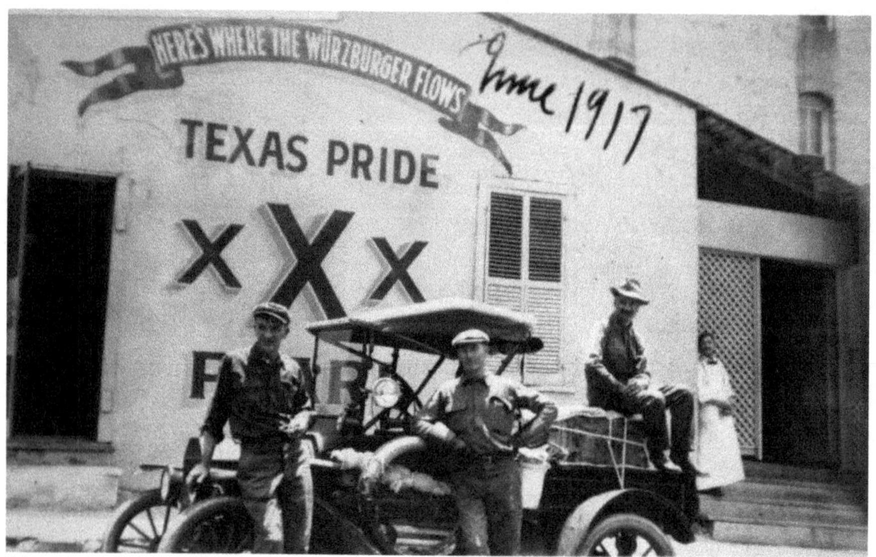

A San Antonio Brewing Association delivery truck parked in front of a building advertising Texas Pride, another of SABA's brands. *Pearl LLC Archives.*

> *$505,000, which ought to be enough, but I have requested Mr. Clauss take up immediately with the wholesale liquor people the question of a contribution from them, switch on their usual basis of one-third the number of shipping brewers, would amount to $50,000 more. If all this money is paid* IT OUGHT *to be sufficient for our campaign.*

PERIOD III

PROHIBITION, 1918–1933

TEMPERANCE WINS OUT

In the two years leading up to the start of Prohibition, San Antonio, and Texas in general, was in its prime. San Antonio boasted six breweries: the San Antonio Brewing Association, Peter Bros Brewery, Degen's Brewery, the Lone Star Brewing Association, Schober's and the Och's and Aschbacer's Brewery. The year 1916 saw these San Antonio breweries realize a combined annual income of $8 million, which was a ridiculously high sum that amounted to about one-fourth of the city's overall income. With 1,200 employees and a total payroll of $1 million, San Antonio's brewing industry was three times larger than any other industry in the Alamo City. In 1917, with Prohibition on the horizon, the San Antonio Brewing Association introduced "La Perla—A Near Beer" while still brewing XXX Pearl Beer.

As World War I heated up in 1917, a nationwide conservation of resources was well underway, and the brewing industry was not immune. In September 1917, President Woodrow Wilson ordered the distillation of spirits to stop. It was not long after that beer and wine were ordered halted as well. The Food and Drug Administration even forbade corn to be distilled for any reason, even medicinal. Brewers were limited in the amounts they could buy to 30 percent, and the alcohol by volume (ABV) was reduced to a maximum of 2.75 percent. Later the next year, the serving of alcohol within a ten-mile radius of a military base was prohibited.

Between the temperance movement and federal restrictions on grain, breweries around the country were hit hard. On June 15, 1918, Texas governor William P. Hobby declared that Texas would be dry statewide. Earlier than the federal government, Texas was now in a true state of prohibition. Later that year, the president declared a stoppage of grain use by breweries, although they were able to use what they had on hand until December 1, 1918.

The monetary effects of Prohibition would hit the San Antonio Brewing Association as hard as it hit all breweries around the country, dropping from net profits of $551,564.45 in 1916 to a mere $265,588.59 in 1918. Its main products at this point were kegged beer, bottled beer, ice and spent grain given to farmers as cattle feed. By mid-1918, when prohibition hit, the San Antonio Brewing Association faced a difficult decision: keep going or shut down. Considering that the federal government only allowed breweries to take a 20 percent loss if they liquidated, Emma Koehler and the San Antonio Brewing Association board chose to keep going instead. To do this, they would need a drastic modification to their business. Thus, Alamo Industries was born, and Emma and company entered the dairy business.

At this time, many in the beer, wine and spirits industry believed that Prohibition would not last—that it would be repealed along with the end of the war—and the San Antonio Brewing Association fit right into this camp. When the war did not end as quickly as expected, Alamo Industries had to think more long term. With co-founder Colonel Otto Wahrmund stepping into the role of brewery manager and de facto president, the brewery at least had some direction and the appearance of leadership to the public and investors.

Having attained his military education at the Texas Military Institute in Austin, Texas, Wahrmund also led a political career. Oddly enough, the San Antonio Brewing Association was not Wahrmund's first foray into the brewing industry. A San Antonio city directory at the time listed Wahrmund as the general manager of J.B. Belohradsky's City Brewery, just prior to its purchase by Koehler and company that same year. It appears that Wahrmund had loaned Belohradsky about $4,000 when the latter was trying to keep City Brewery under his control. After the takeover of City Brewery was finalized, Wahrmund joined the San Antonio Brewing Association.

By 1908, Wahrmund had been elected to the Texas state legislature and would later be reelected to three more terms, always keeping his mind on the legislature that would be favorable to his beloved San Antonio Brewing Association. By early 1919, Wahrmund's four terms as a state representative would come to an end when he was asked to resign by the Texas Democratic Party for what appeared to be no good reason. With Wahrmund clearly on the wet side of the prohibition issue, it's possible that his party felt pressure from Texas's Governor Hobby (a dry) to do something about the beloved colonel.

Wahrmund himself insisted that poor health had factored into his departure. Later in 1919, months after his departure from politics, Wahrmund again claimed poor health as the reason he was not able to testify at the tax evasion trial of Emma Koehler's nephew, Corwin Priest. Priest had joined the San Antonio Brewing Association as vice-president in January 1915 two months after Koehler's death.

Priest was quite an interesting fellow. His prior employment included as a cashier for the German savings bank in St. Louis, showing that numbers were clearly his forte. This may not have helped Otto Wahrmund, as what he needed was somebody like Otto Koehler and not someone like himself. At this time, the Alamo Industries Board of Directors realized that it would need to modify its business plan. This led various board members, including Wahrmund, to kick in money out of their own coffers.

Although he lacked the Koehler zeal for dealing with the public, as well as a personality for dealing with employees, Wahrmund was more than up for the task of running the San Antonio Brewing Association. However, after opposing Emma Koehler's plans for turning the brewery into a dairy, he gave notice on December 2, 1918. On January 1, 1919, he officially resigned from Alamo Industries.

In 1922, with Priest resigning, it appeared that Wahrmund might be able to return to the brewery he helped found by repurchasing stock. However, this was not something that was in the cards for the old colonel. Wahrmund was not without means, though. He sold his interest in the Mexican mines and was still head of City National Bank and Sommers Drugstore, showing that his diversification would allow him to thrive outside of the brewery that he had helped found—the company that he would miss most dearly.

Wahrmund did return to the San Antonio Brewing Association/Alamo Industries for a brief time in the early 1920s. This, however, was short-lived, as Wahrmund's failing health again prevented his staying with Alamo Industries. Oscar Bergstrom's return was also key in this. With Emma Koehler not being firmly in control of the management of Alamo Industries, this paved the way for Bergstrom to bring in an outside company to manage the brewery, all the while Emma Koehler was working her tail off to keep things going. This harsh management of the outsiders caused trouble with the unions. Faith would not be restored until the arrival of Benjamin Brooks "B.B." McGimsey, whose leadership style was similar to Otto Koehler's and who was able to restore relations with the workers. It was this partnership between McGimsey and Emma Koehler that kept things going near the end of Prohibition and would see the brewery through Otto A.'s later transition as brewery president.

Wahrmund kept himself busy after his brewery days and was appointed as water director in 1925 by then mayor John Calvin. Showing that his organizational skill was just what the city needed, he soon placed the city's water system on solid financial ground.

Much like his fellow co-founder and friend Otto Koehler, Warhmund was not born with a silver spoon. He was born the son of Judge William Wahrmund and his wife, Amelia, in the Texas Hill Country town of Fredericksburg, a town that had its own modest brewing history. Fredericksburg was one of a number of towns along with New Braunfels that was settled by Germans in the mid-1800s. Many immigrants at that time applied to a well-known German organization known as the Society of Melbourne, headed by Prince Carl of Solms-Braunfels. Those who applied in Germany often listed their equipment skills and talents. Hoping to form their own version of the East India Company, Carl and his fellow barons purchased land in the area that would be known later as New Braunfels and Fredericksburg, not realizing, though, that it landed smack dab in the middle of Comanche Indian territory.

The second head of this organization, John O. Meusebach, also a German baron, was able to make peace with the Indians, and the settlement of Fredericksburg, Texas, officially began. About one year later, the colony was prospering, with peace between the new settlers and the Comanches.

Warhmund's parents were married in Germany and came to Texas in the 1840s, and the colonel's brother was born in 1849. His parents were supporters of Southern rights in the Civil War, and when they first arrived in the mid-1840s, they joined General Zachary Taylor's army as volunteers during the Mexican-American War. Upon their return, they were granted land.

Despite not having seen any military service like that of his father and uncle, Otto Wahrmund eventually gained his honorary title of "Colonel" from Texas governor Oscar Colquitt. On January 23, 1879, Wahrmund married Mary Sophie Nimitz, whose father operated a hotel in Fredericksburg. The hotel is now the site of the Museum of the Pacific War and the Nimitz Museum. His new family would later see the birth of

Chester W. Nimitz, later commander-in-chief of the Pacific navy fleet and who was present when Japan's Admiral Hirohito surrendered aboard the USS *Missouri*. In fact, Nimitz was our dear colonel's nephew.

Beginning his business career in Fredericksburg, he moved his family to San Antonio in the early 1880s and was the father of seven daughters and one son. Although reports are mixed, Otto Wahrmund and his wife, Sophie, settled by either River Avenue or Broadway, both rural areas at that time in San Antonio. Wahrmund passed away in neither San Antonio nor his hometown of Fredericksburg. On June 25, 1929, he passed away in Kerrville, Texas. He had recently sought refuge in the Texas Hill Country hoping to heal his ailing body. His funeral was held at his home in San Antonio, with many wealthy and well-known San Antonians in attendance. San Antonio Brewing Association brewmaster Gustav Etter, Judge S.G. Newton and C.T. Priest were among those in attendance.

When Wahrmund passed, he was survived by his wife and four of his seven daughters—all of whom would later be buried in south San Antonio at the Mission Park Cemetery. However, the colonel is not alone. To his right are buried Gustav Etter and his wife, Carey. To his left are his dear friend Otto Koehler and the venerable Emma Koehler. Hardly a coincidence, I would think.

HAIL TO THE CHIEF?

The brewery faced another challenge when Wahrmund resigned in 1919, leaving it again without leadership. Despite being the majority owner, Otto Koehler's widow, Emma, would not be elected president of the San Antonio Brewing Association for a while. For the time being, Corwin Priest would be elected the association's president in 1919——this, of course, despite charges of tax evasion. Emma was, however, elected vice-president.

Proving that it was easily adaptable and would not give up, the San Antonio Brewing Association did what even fellow brewing giant Lone Star could not do: it kept people working and did it in a way that maintained its facilities in case it ever was able to brew beer again. The now re-formed Alamo Industries, later known as the Alamo Foods Company in 1922, altered its production complex to make various sodas and created an ice plant to manufacture ice for the local San Antonio community and even a mechanics shop to help the city's residents repair their vehicles. When

Prohibition arrived in 1918, La Perla was dropped as a brand, and XXX Pearl Beer became XXX Pearl Near Beer.

Other buildings on the grounds were used as dry cleaners, cold storage, a dye plant, an ice cream shop and more. The spent grain left over from making near beer was sold to the nearby farmers as feed for their animals, a practice long used by breweries and one that continues to this day.

Many creative promotions came out of the brewery during its Alamo Foods Company days. On May 16, 1919, the dairy products department of Alamo Industries produced a popular Alamo ice cream. Multiple flavors were available, such as cherry nut salad, tutti-frutti, caramel nut, French orange and almond bisque. Around Christmas 1919, special flavors were introduced, like New York ice cream, caramel ice cream, frozen pudding, maple mousse, cranberry sherbet, marshmallow date brick (which was a three-layer brick of marshmallow date, pineapple sherbet and cherry nut) and angel cream brick (a three-layer brick of caramel, angel cream and tutti-frutti). Other items produced by the dairy department included Alamo cream, Sunnyvale milk and cream, Alamo butter, Sunbeam butter, Alamo cottage cheese and Alamo buttermilk.

In about 1921, a few short years after national Prohibition began, Alamo Industries changed its name to Alamo Foods Company, and the company's focus shifted from various businesses such as dry cleaning, auto repair, a

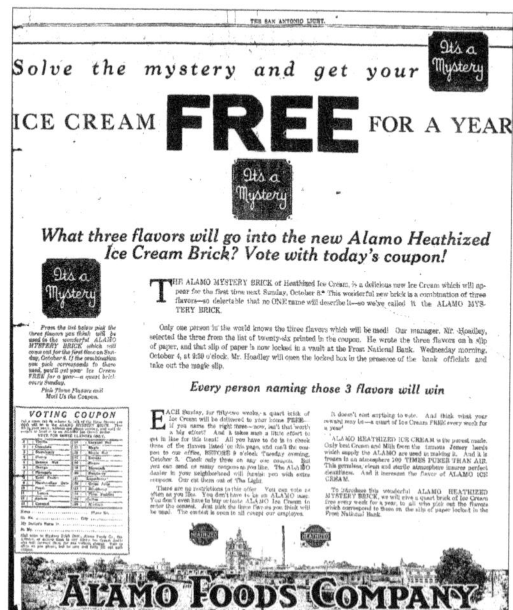

Alamo Foods' ice cream contest. The contest would put the ice cream division out of business. *Charlie Staats.*

billboard company (known as Sunset), soda making and the like to solely food-related businesses. Many of the other ventures were sold off to companies in the San Antonio area.

On October 8, 1922, the ice cream division of Alamo Foods Company decided to have a mystery ice cream contest, with winners getting a free quart of ice cream each week for one year. In all, there were 177 winners, which, when multiplied by fifty-two weeks, amounts to 9,204 free quarts of ice cream. The flavors were banana nut, cherry and orange. This was so much ice cream given away for free that it effectively put the ice cream division out of business. In 1923, the company sold the division to another local creamery, which, ironically enough, rented space out from the San Antonio Brewing Association for the creamery. In 1930, Blue Bell and Bluebonnet Creameries rented space on the top floor from Alamo Foods Company—Blue Bell would become an icon of its own in coming decades.

By 1930, Alamo Foods Company had also begun to bottle its Orange Crush soda. This is the very division that Otto A. Koehler would take over upon his return from the war, although 1930 would not prove to be the best year for the brewery. It was on December 12, 1930, that Otto Koehler's brother, Charles, who was the treasurer of Alamo Foods Company, was killed in a Laredo, Texas hunting accident.

The San Antonio Brewing Association still had a reason to brew during this period, and that was malt syrup. Drugstores were in need of this for various ice cream–related delights, and thus Hop Flavored XXX Pearl Malt Syrup was born and was distributed to anyone who wanted it. This syrup made it easy for industrious fans of XXX Pearl to brew up a batch of Pearl at home themselves.

All of these enterprises not only kept the association in business but also kept employees working; it showed the Alamo City that it was committed to more than just beer. The San Antonio Brewing Association was committed to its community. Although these various enterprises kept things going, by the end of the Roaring Twenties, things began to get worse for the country, as well as for Alamo Foods Company. The Great Depression hit everyone hard, even the association's board members, several of whom, feeling the pinch of the Depression, sold their shares to Emma Koehler, who was already majority owner, thus solidifying her position. Although she remained vice-president, it was Emma who used her determination to create ever-evolving plans to keep the business going. Much like many women at the time, although she was not in the limelight, she became the driving force behind the San Antonio Brewing Association and was critical to its survival.

Without the passing of her husband, it is likely that Emma Koehler would not have been as critical as she was to the San Antonio Brewing Association's survival and growth. Without Emma Koehler, the San Antonio Brewing Association's demise would have been a distinct possibility. During the hard times of the Great Depression and Prohibition, it was the return of Otto Andrew Koehler, the son of Otto Koehler's brother Karl, that signaled the possibility of a recovery and rebirth for the brewery. Otto Andrew returned home from serving in the war overseas to see his family's company, which he had grown up with, stripped down to next to nothing. He did not jump in right away. He even opened several businesses in San Antonio but stood ready to help his aunt whenever she may need him.

PROHIBITION ARRIVES

Although the Eighteenth Amendment was ratified in January 1919, Prohibition began as a federal program on January 16, 1920. Many thought this was only achievable if there were distinct laws against the manufacture and sale of alcohol. Many saw the distilling, beer and wine industries as motivated by profit and happy to encourage people to drink more. As with many things, though, the more you tell someone they can't do something, the more they do it. Many found ways to make bathtub beer, gin and other alcoholic beverages during Prohibition. If alcohol were not legally available, then that would solve the troubling issues of crime, violence and inappropriate sexual behavior, right?

Early in the 1840s, wets sought to prevent those who were against alcohol from ruining a good thing. As far back as 1843, the Republic of Texas passed what may have been one of the first prohibitionist laws in the United States. In 1845, saloons were often busted on liquor violations, although state officials never enforced it. The law was repealed in 1856; however, that only served to fuel the fire. The Texas organization the United Friends of Temperance began in 1870 to fight for a more sober Texas in the United States.

A few years later, in 1883, the Woman's Christian Temperance Union, a national organization, branched out in Texas with known temperance advocate Frances Willard. In 1887, the dry camp tried to get a referendum for prohibition passed, but it lost by more than ninety thousand votes. Not ones to give up, the feisty three counties in Texas were dry, and another seventy-nine counties were a mix of dry and wet under the 1876 constitutional local option law. In the early 1900s, the prohibition movement gained support from voters in North Texas, converting the majority of Texas voters. Not surprisingly, the wets continued to oppose with a very wealthy and public opposition that included the primary leaders. United Friends merged with the Anti-Saloon League, which was a national organization that appeared in Texas in 1907, and the dry camp gained control of seats in Congress.

The Texas state legislature ratified the amendment in 1918, with Texas residents approving the measure in 1919. Despite its traditionally conservative leanings, many in Texas just could not get on board with the idea of banning alcohol. Even the Anti-Saloon League's Texas representative was not able to get a strict enforcement of Prohibition. Smack dab in the middle of Prohibition, the year 1925 saw the Texas state legislature firmly in control by the wet camp. As one can imagine, it opposed enforcing statewide prohibition, although the dry camp was still able to get many to support educational training for state officials regarding abstaining from alcohol. Only a few short years later, in 1933, President Franklin Delano Roosevelt signed the Twenty-First Amendment that effectively crumpled Prohibition up and tossed it away in a trashcan. It wasn't until 1935, though, that residents of Texas voted to repeal the state's dry laws. At that point, prohibition went back to the local level, giving temperance advocates the local option statutes to rely on.

In 1933, the federal repeal of Prohibition did not go into effect right away. During the months before, the federal government granted those existing breweries permits to begin brewing beer in anticipation of the Twenty-First Amendment taking effect. Thus, within minutes of taking effect, around one hundred trucks and twenty-five railroad cars loaded with XXX Pearl Beer rolled out of the brewery and headed into the hands of thirsty Texans.

At this point, Otto Andrew Koehler returned to the San Antonio Brewing Association and to Aunt Emma. Otto Andrew headed the company's Orange Crush division and returned the name of Otto Koehler to the brewery's management.

Emma was officially named the president of the organization in 1933, finally making official what she had been doing since 1918, with Otto Andrew voted in as vice-president. Aunt Emma stayed on as an adviser to her nephew until her death in 1943. At that time, Otto Andrew was elected by the board as president of the San Antonio Brewing Association, ushering in the San Antonio Brewing Association's fourth period, one that saw unprecedented growth for the brewery. He stayed in this position until his death in 1969.

SAN ANTONIO BREWING ASSOCIATION GROWS DESPITE PROHIBITION

The growth of the new San Antonio Brewing Association started with one man hired during Prohibition. Aunt Emma and Otto Andrew would not have been nearly as successful without the expert guidance they received from Benjamin Brooks McGimsey, perhaps one of the best hires the San Antonio Brewing Association ever made. McGimsey was born in Louisiana in 1888 to Robert Hunter McGimsey and Alice Edna (Mathews) McGimsey and was one of six children.

McGimsey's impact would not be felt immediately, as the outside firm of Gregg and Company was brought on in January 1921 at the behest of Emma Koehler to help with solidifying the company's rapidly dropping profits. Gregg and Company was composed of Tresham Gregg and his brother, Kenneth, both originally employed by Adolphus Busch's Lone Star to help with its own Prohibition survival attempts in converting to a cotton mill. It was the recommendation of Lone Star president Henning Bruin and the strength of the Gregg brothers' ability to convert Lone Star that led Emma Koehler to hire the firm.

When he arrived at Alamo Industries during Prohibition, McGimsey had no experience in the brewing industry. In 1920, at age thirty-two, McGimsey came to the San Antonio Brewing Association, then operating as Alamo Industries, to work as a temporary employee for the Gregg and Company business firm brought in by Bergstrom. Soon after Gregg and Company left in December 1921, McGimsey stayed and was hired as general manager of the association.

When Wahrmund returned in 1922, after Corwin Priest left, it was McGimsey whom he worked with. During his first year, McGimsey made quite a splash. After tightening the ship, profits increased about 50 percent. Not having to do this all alone was a relief for Emma Koehler, who had been using a great portion of her own money to keep the brewery going—in fact, close to $1 million by 1921.

McGimsey's presence was immediately felt, although what he inherited from Gregg and Company was a mess. It had made a mockery of everything Otto Koehler stood for regarding his employees and how they should be treated. One of McGimsey's first orders of business was the shift in business focus to that of food only, changing the name to the Alamo Foods Company.

In addition to further distancing the company from its own employees, in 1921 Gregg and Company effectively ousted the International Union of

United Brewery, Flour, Cereal and Soft Drink Workers, whose members went on strike in 1921. Around this time, a devastating flood hit the San Antonio Brewing Association hard—it would take months to recover. McGimsey looked to restore good relations with members of Local 112. During the three years it would take to repair things, there was a general boycott of anything Alamo Foods Company produced. This included ice cream, soft drinks and all other businesses. Not that Alamo Foods Company needed any help from the union for its dairy business to go under.

At one point during Prohibition, even the City of San Antonio recalled all Alamo Foods Company products from Koehler Pavilion area at Brackenridge Park, land that had been donated to the City of San Antonio in 1915 by Emma Koehler in honor of her late husband. The one stipulation Emma Koehler had regarding the land donation was that it remain legal to consume alcoholic beverages at the park, and so it remains to this day the only area within Brackenridge Park where alcohol can be legally consumed.

McGimsey was so gung-ho about his approach to turning the association around that in 1924 he even predicted that the company would return to profitability before the end of that era: "If all our plans can be realized, we should begin to make money this year. So far our future amounts to plans, but I firmly believe that they can be realized by careful operation and the cooperation of all persons concerned. We cannot hope to get out of the woods the first year, for it took five years to get in the condition we are in. I believe that in the course of three or four years, this concern should be a very successful one with most, if not all, of its obligations taken care of."

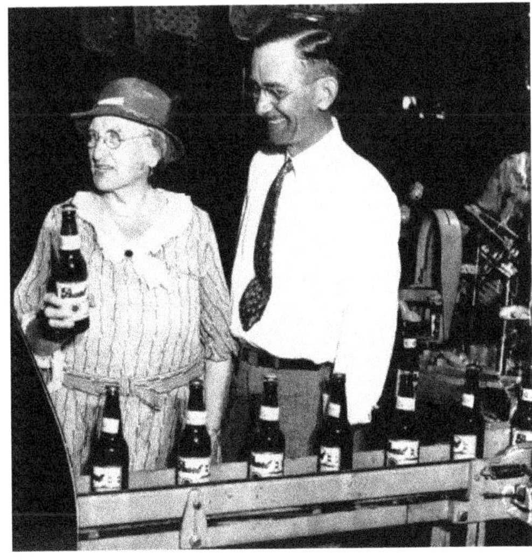

Emma Koehler (alongside B.B. McGimsey) holding the first bottle of XXX Pearl Beer off the line after Prohibition was repealed. *UTSA Libraries Special Collections, with permission of the* San Antonio Express-News.

Perhaps the flood was a bit of a mixed blessing. Upgrades had been deemed necessary recently, so in addition to restoring the damage to the property itself, new refrigeration units were installed and a whole lot of paint was applied. In fact, it took about the same amount of time to get San Antonio Brewing Association into tiptop shape as it did for B.B. McGimsey to restore relations with the union and work.

Although the return to profitability wasn't as immediate as promised, the Pearl also did not lose money during McGimsey's early years. Many breweries around Texas that attempted to survive Prohibition suffered greatly. One at a time, they all closed down. The only one left in 1933 was the San Antonio favorite that used to produce a gem of a fine beer, although true relief would not come until it could brew beer again.

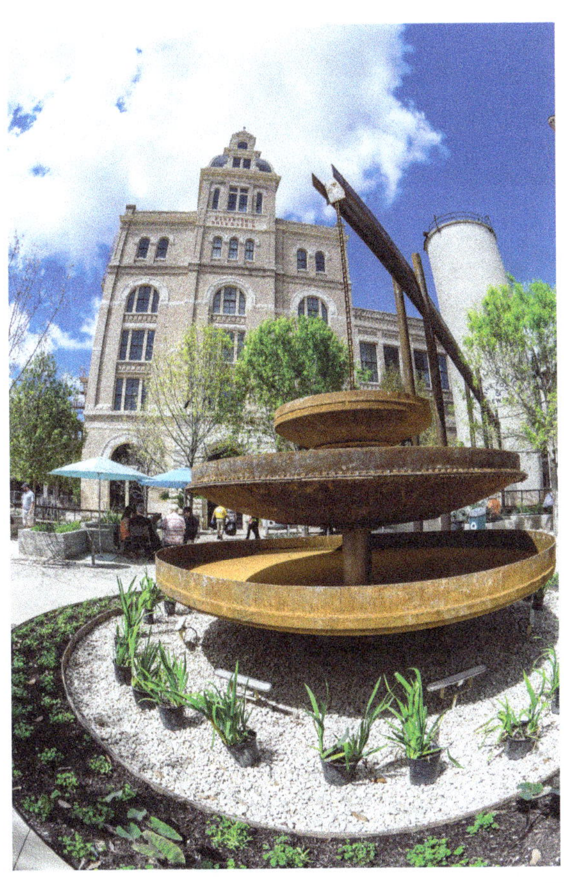

Left: View of Southerleigh Fine Food and Brewing from its courtyard. *Nan Palmero*.

Below: Another way that Silver Ventures honors the past.

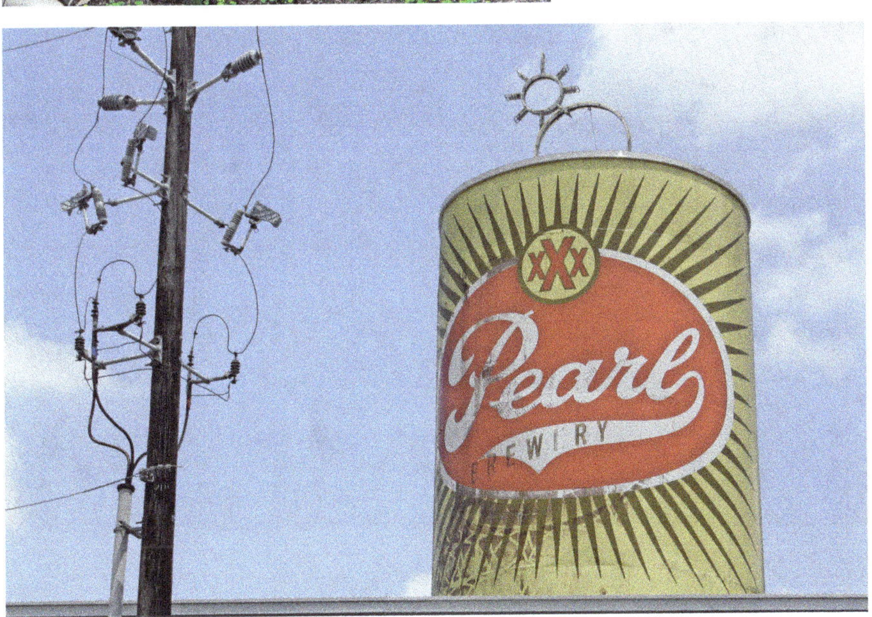

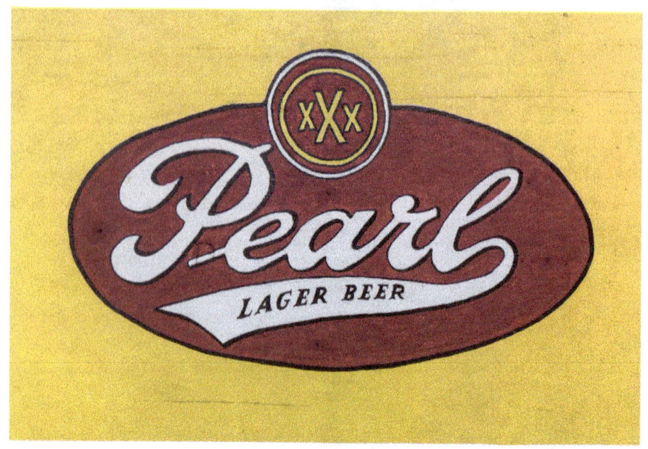

Pearl Lager Beer logo. *Jeremy Banas.*

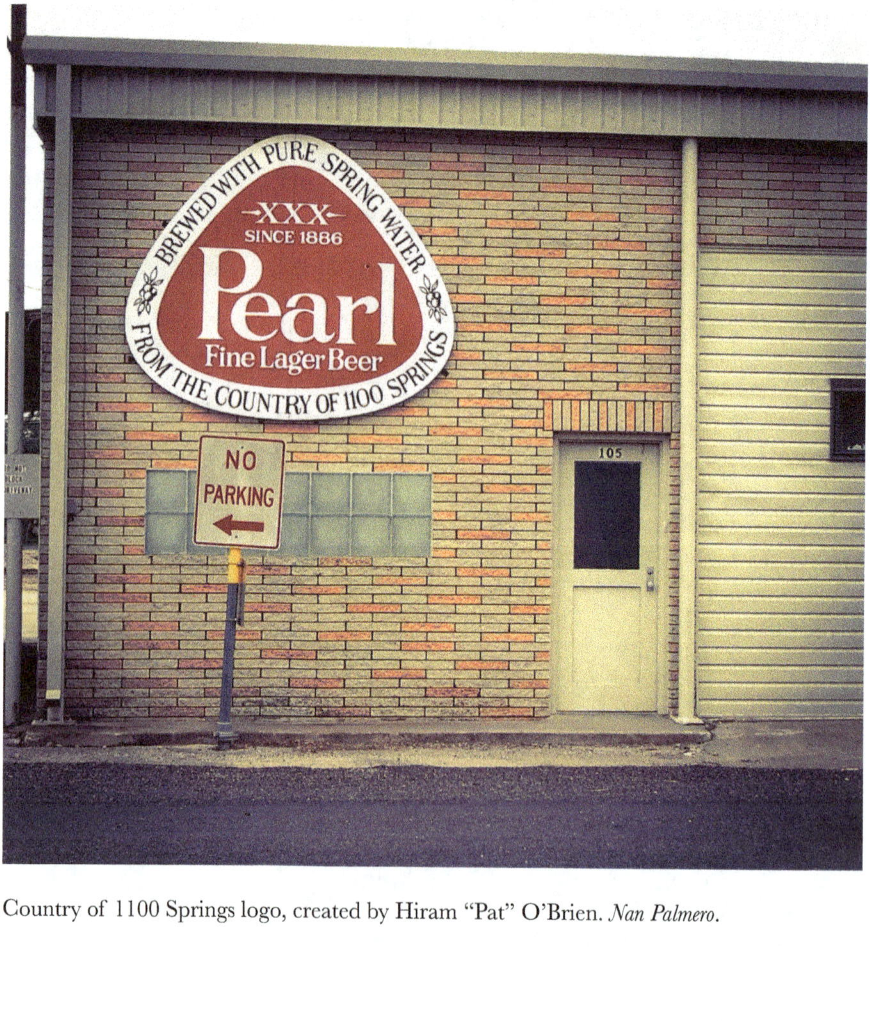

Country of 1100 Springs logo, created by Hiram "Pat" O'Brien. *Nan Palmero.*

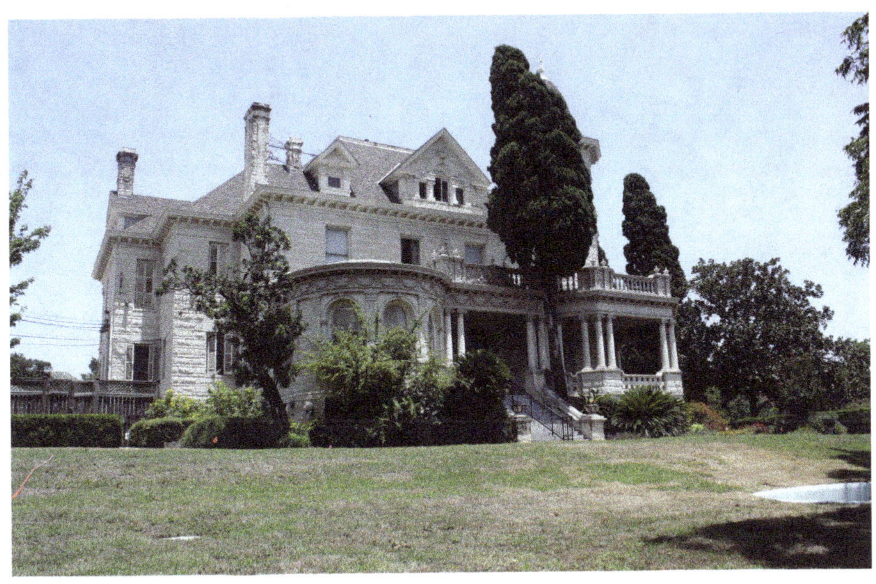

The Koehler House as it sits today. *Jeremy Banas.*

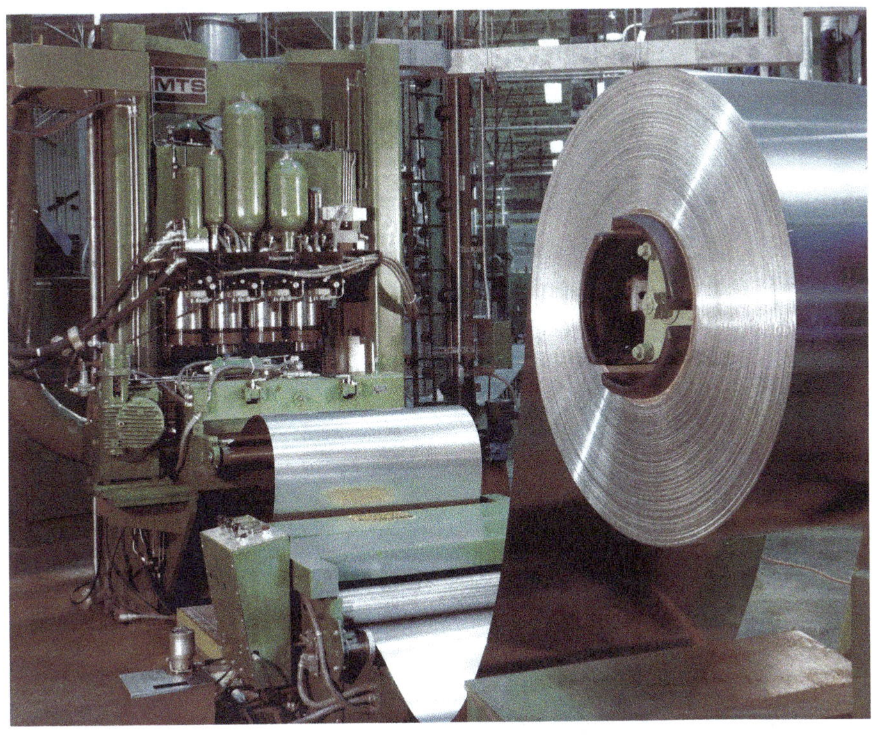

Rolls and rolls of sheet metal that would later become cans of XXX Pearl Beer. *Pearl LLC Archives.*

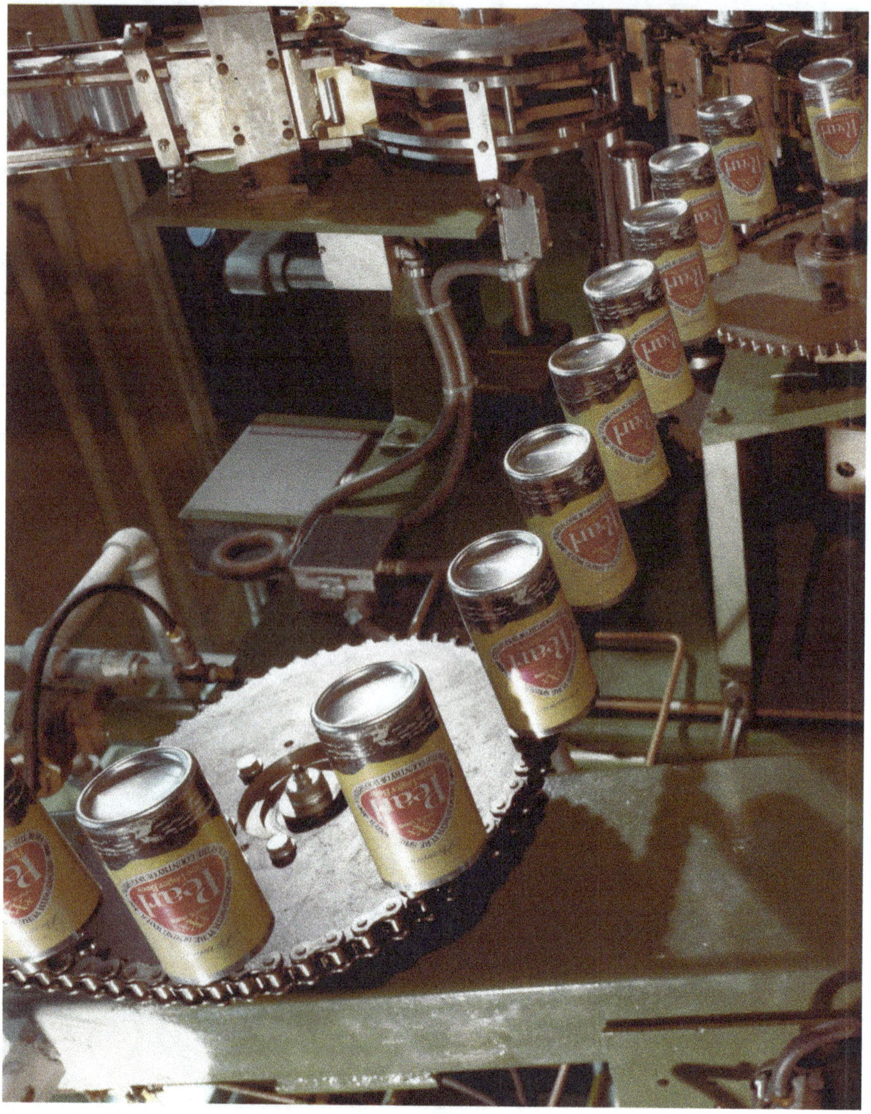

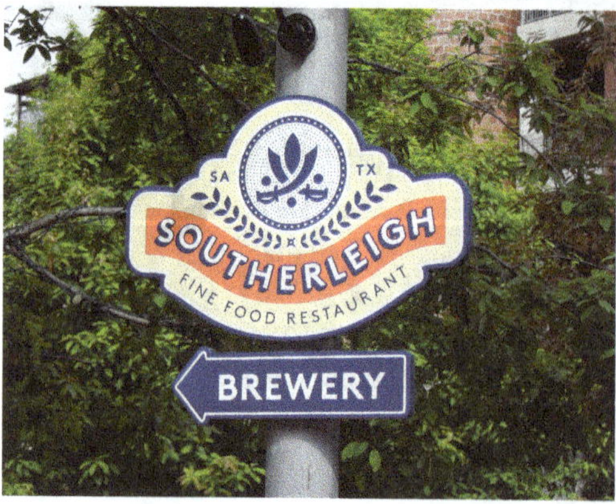

Above: XXX Pearl rolling down the canning line. *Pearl LLC Archives*.

Left: Southerleigh signage. *Jeremy Banas*.

Pearl Neon Clocks By Charlie Staats In the early 1930's Pearl came out with their first advertising clock. The Clock was a wooden art deco style with 4 different colors of neon, It is estimated that 50 or less were made. looking for a more standard clock Pearl found one in 1938 with the Octagon Neon Clock from the Neon Products Company of Lima Ohio,,,Pearl is the only brewery known to to use and continue to reuse this clock well into the mid 1970's..Thats 40 years! Whenever the brewery changed logos they would change out the faces when the clock came back to the brewery. Today these Pearl clocks can still be found in Texas bars and restraunts.....

There are two body styles Sharp or Rounded corners.

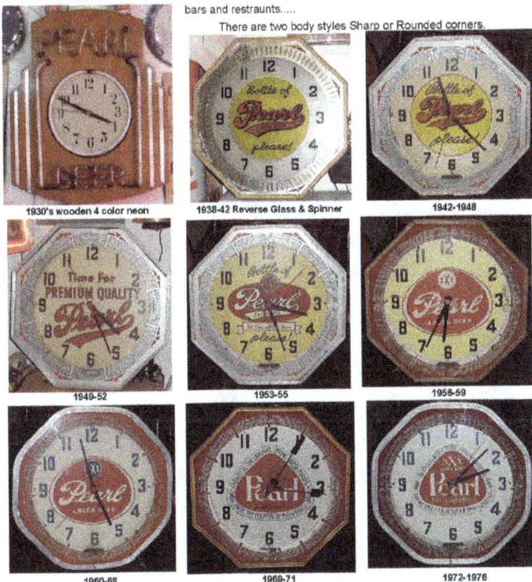

1930's wooden 4 color neon — 1938-42 Reverse Glass & Spinner — 1942-1948

1949-52 — 1953-55 — 1956-59

1960-68 — 1969-71 — 1972-1976

Things to know There are 8 different production known octagon clock faces..1.The neon ring is ALWAYS a light powder blue. 2.The front glass is always silver, silver with red or all red. 3.The first 6 faces are silk screened the last two are a total sticker dial face. There is a also 1 1969 proto type face and 1 custom 1960's black light neon octagon clock the brewery made for a restaurant

Left: Pearl clocks. *Jeremy Banas.*

Below: Neon Pearl signs lighting the way. *Jeremy Banas.*

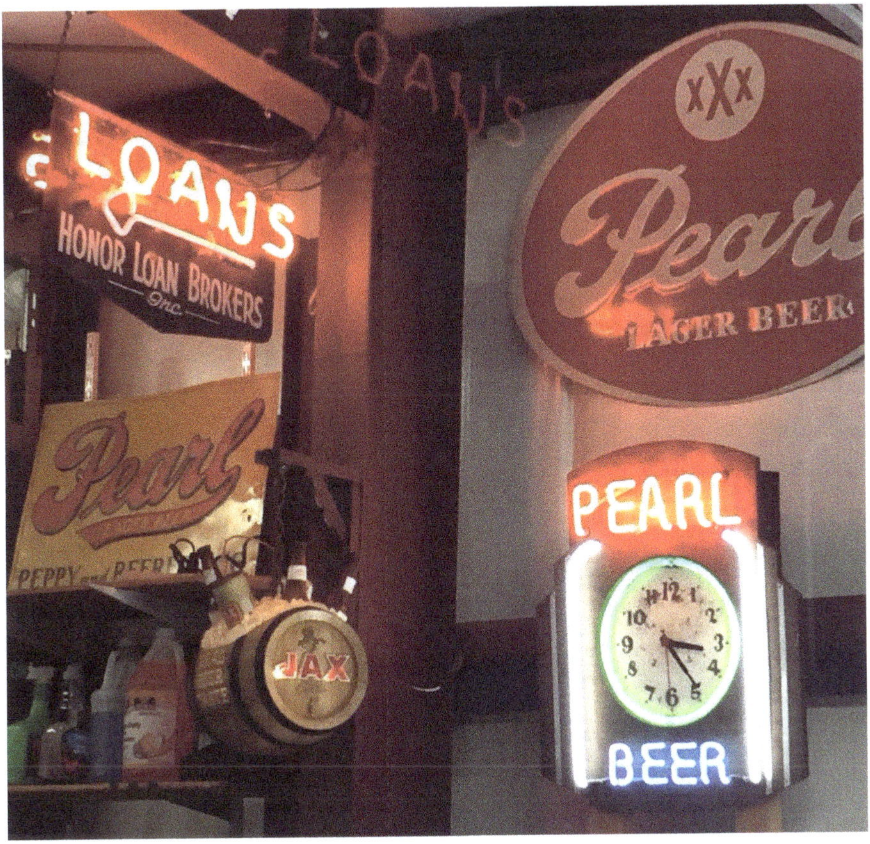

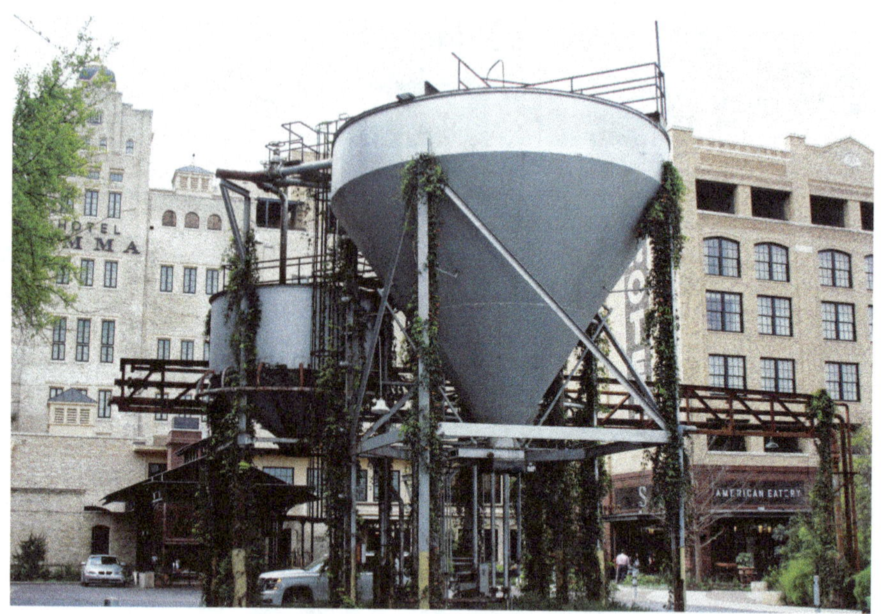

This repurposed fermenter from Pearl's bygone days greets visitors to the New Pearl complex. *Jeremy Banas.*

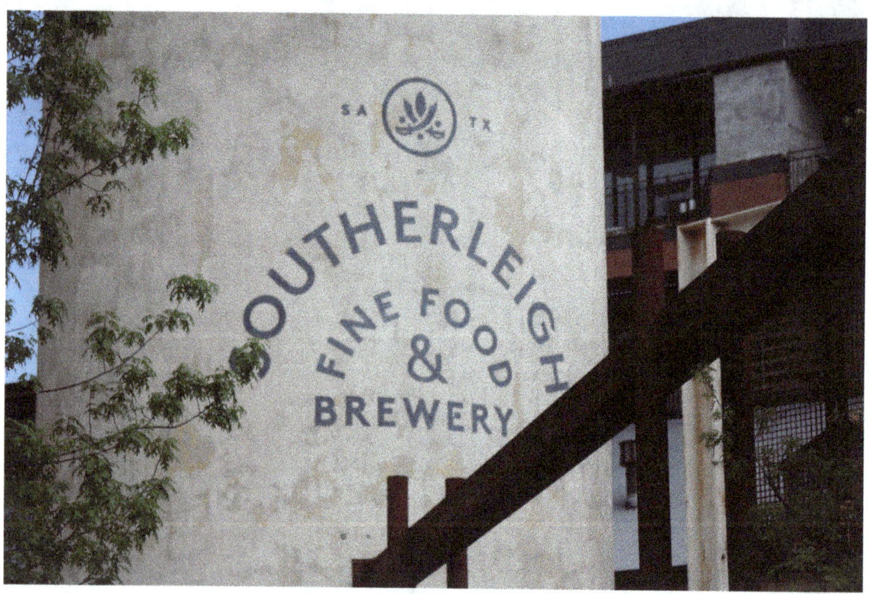

Southerleigh smokestack. *Jeremy Banas.*

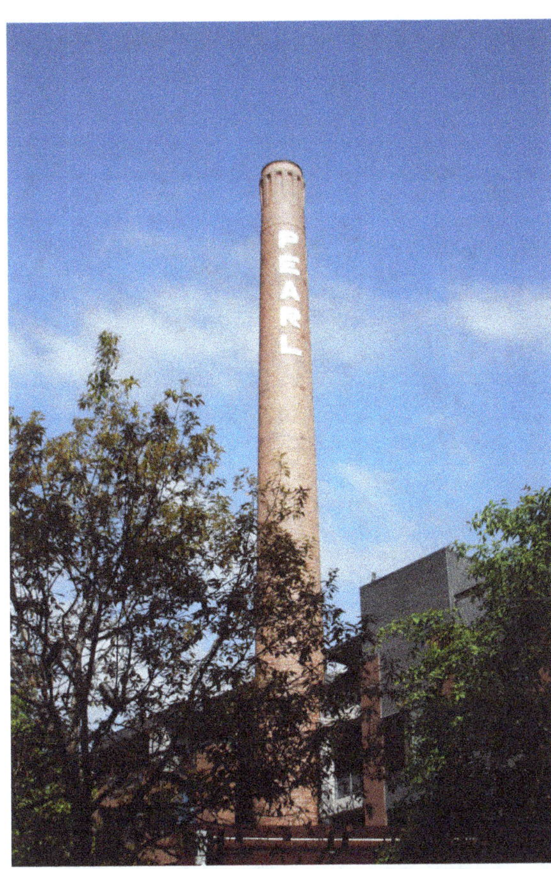

Left: Pearl smokestack dating back to the brewhouse construction in 1894. *Jeremy Banas*.

Below: Repurposed Pearl propane tank adorning the exterior of the Culinary Institute of America. *Jeremy Banas*.

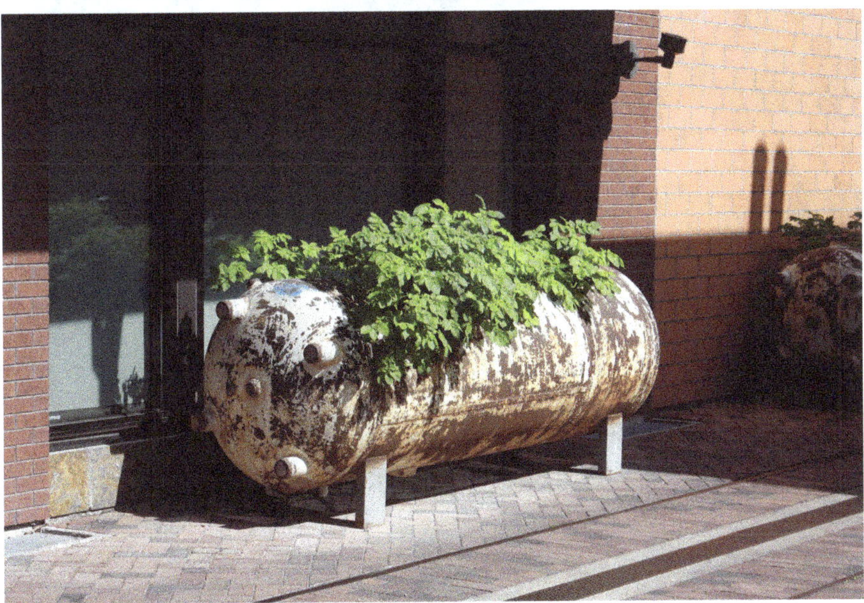

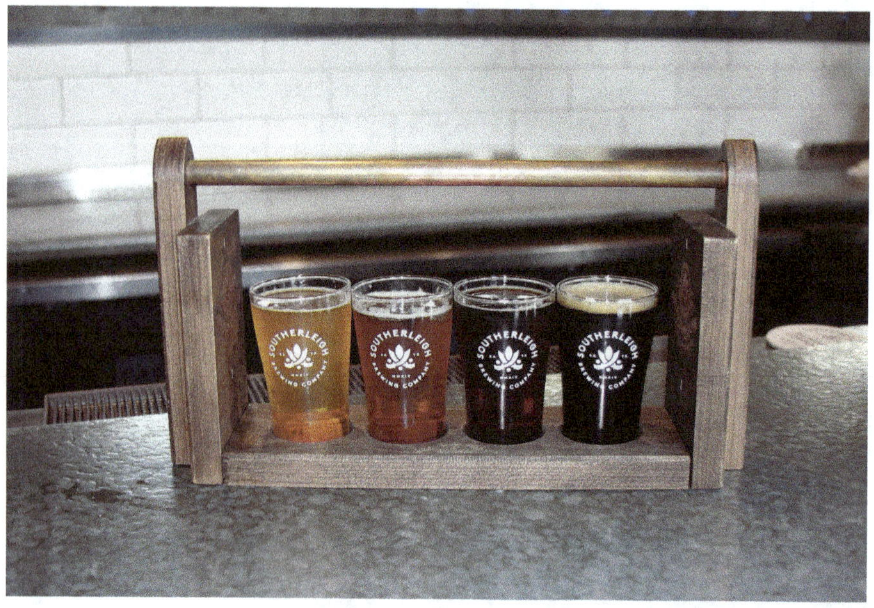

Flight of Southerleigh beers. *Jeremy Banas.*

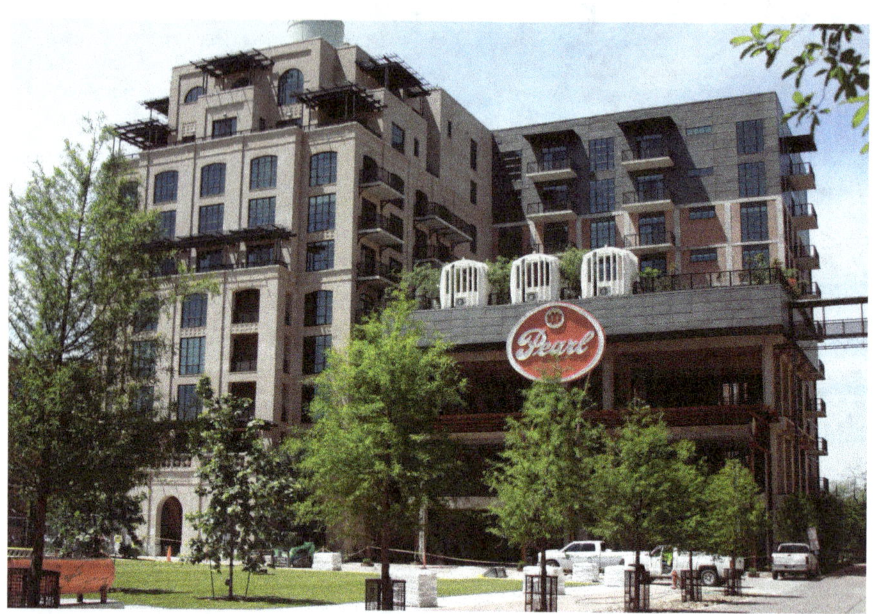

Pearl signage on The Cellars luxury apartments. *Jeremy Banas.*

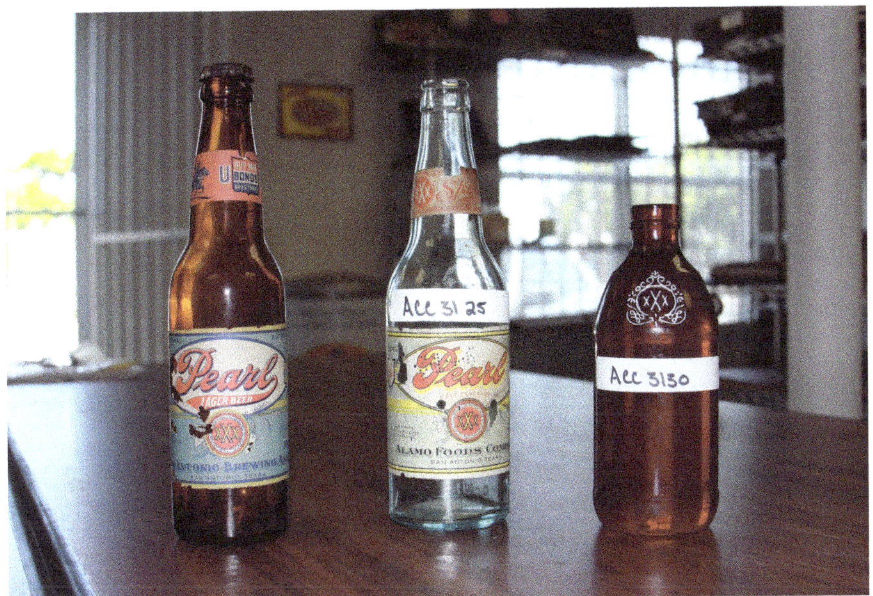

Above: A bottle of XXX Pearl Beer with a war bond label and a San Antonio Brewing Association bottle. *Jeremy Banas.*

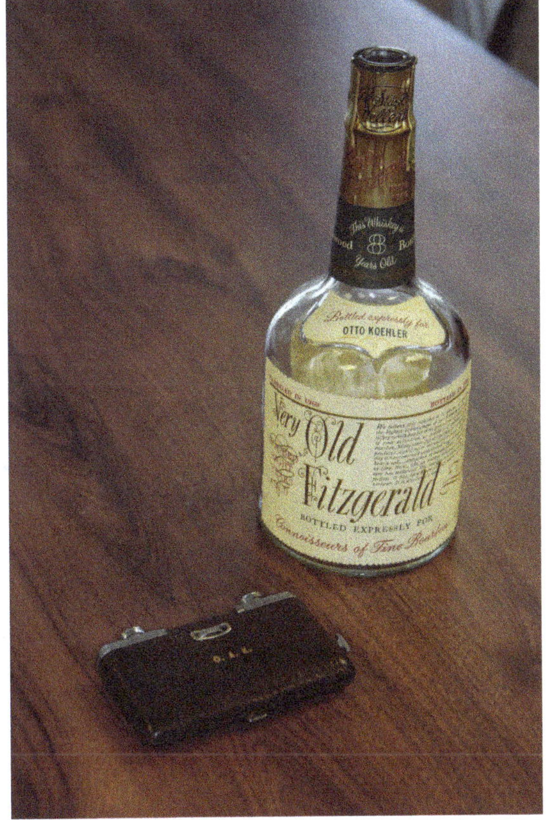

Right: A bottle of Otto A. Koehler's personalized whiskey from Old Fitzgerald. Otto A. had purchased his own barrels at the Kentucky distillery. *Jeremy Banas.*

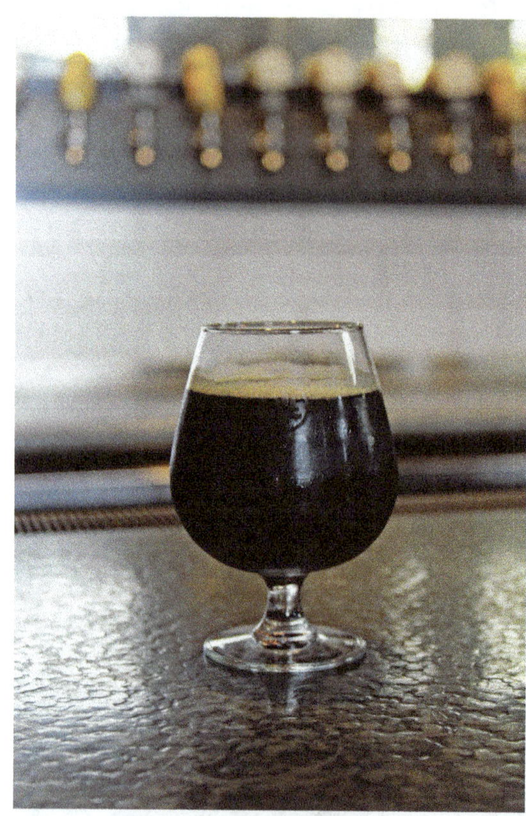

Left: Putin's Revenge Russian Imperial Stout from Southerleigh. *Jeremy Banas.*

Below: Texas Transportation Company railcar no. 2. *Jeremy Banas.*

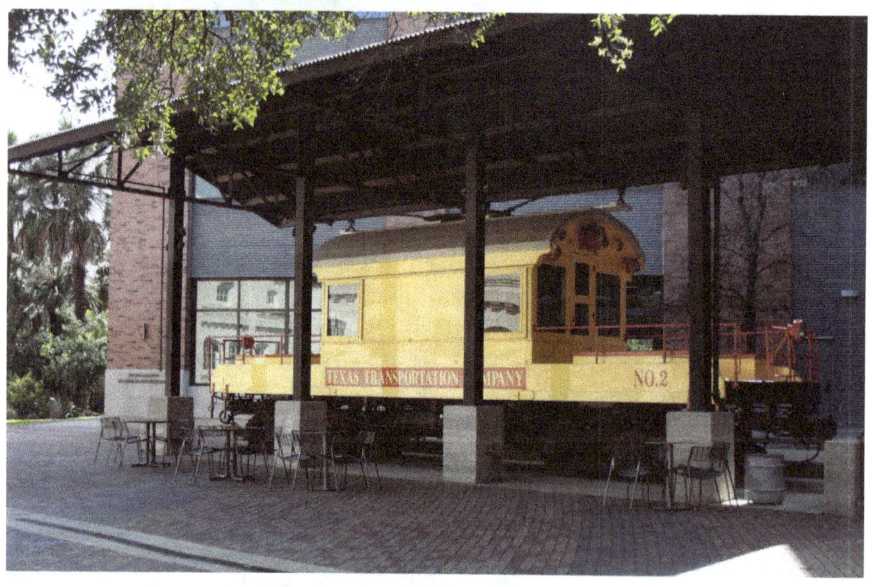

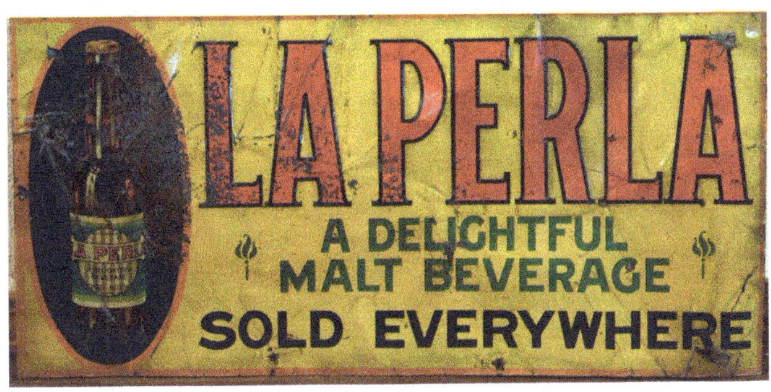

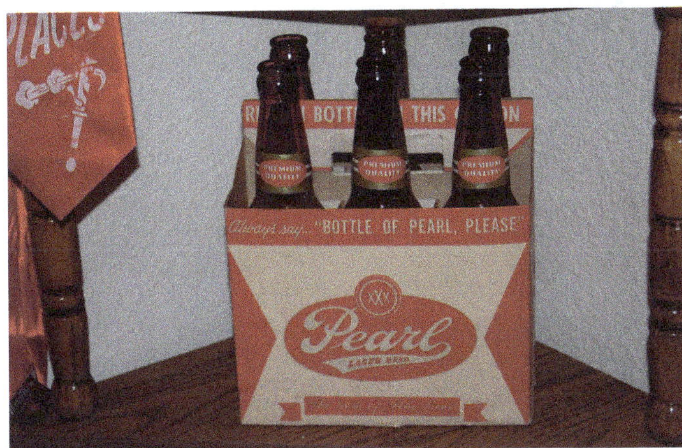

Top: A tin sign advertising La Perla. *Jeremy Banas*.

Left: A six-pack of XXX Pearl Beer. *Jeremy Banas*.

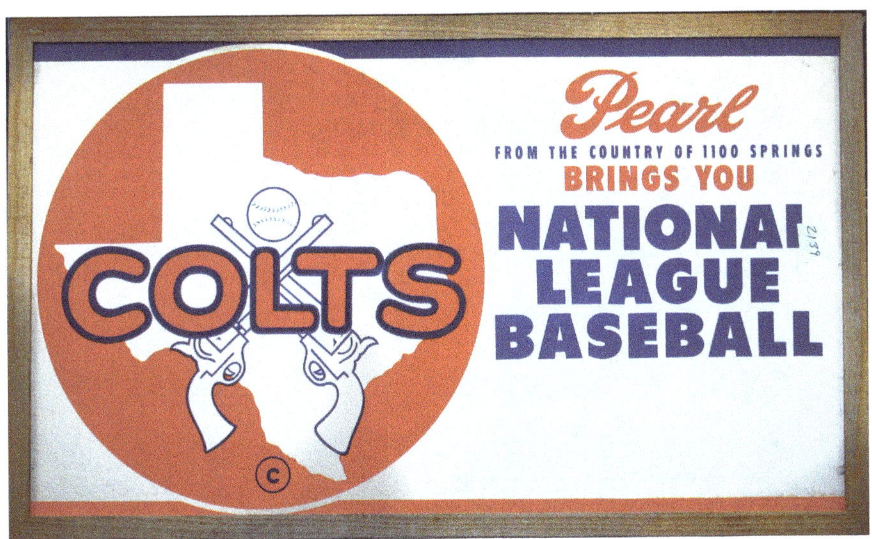

Pearl sponsorship of the MLB Houston Colt .45s of the National League. The Colts would later become the Houston Astros. *Jeremy Banas*.

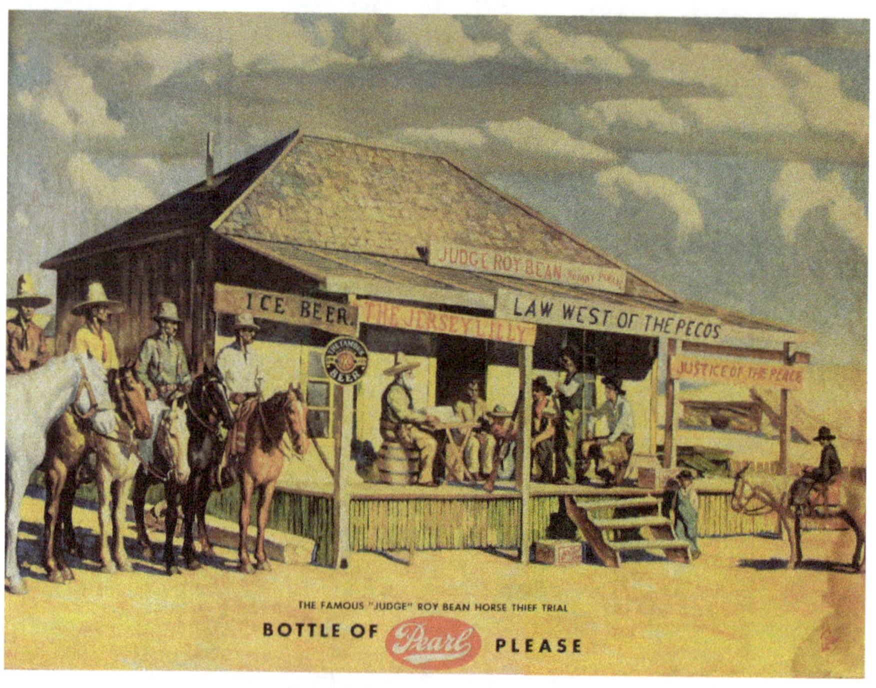

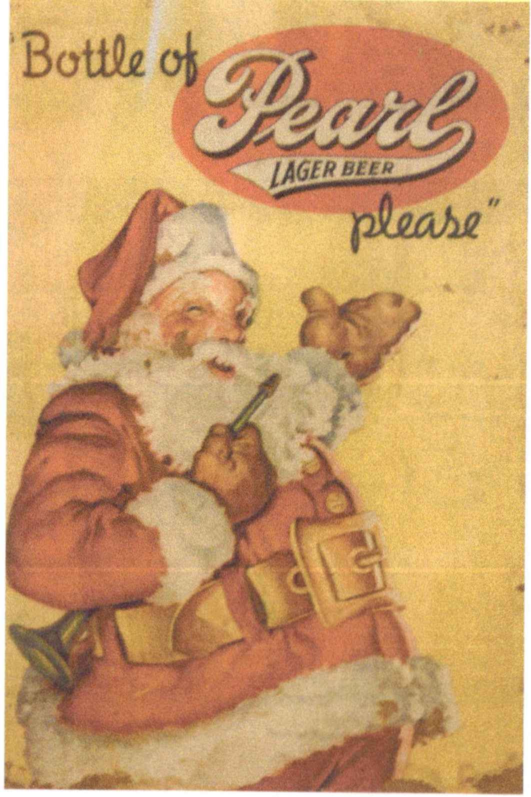

Above: A painting of the trial of a horse thief by Judge Roy Bean. The judge was famous for only serving XXX Pearl Beer. *Jeremy Banas*.

Left: A post–World War II Pearl ad featuring that jolly old elf himself. *Jeremy Banas*.

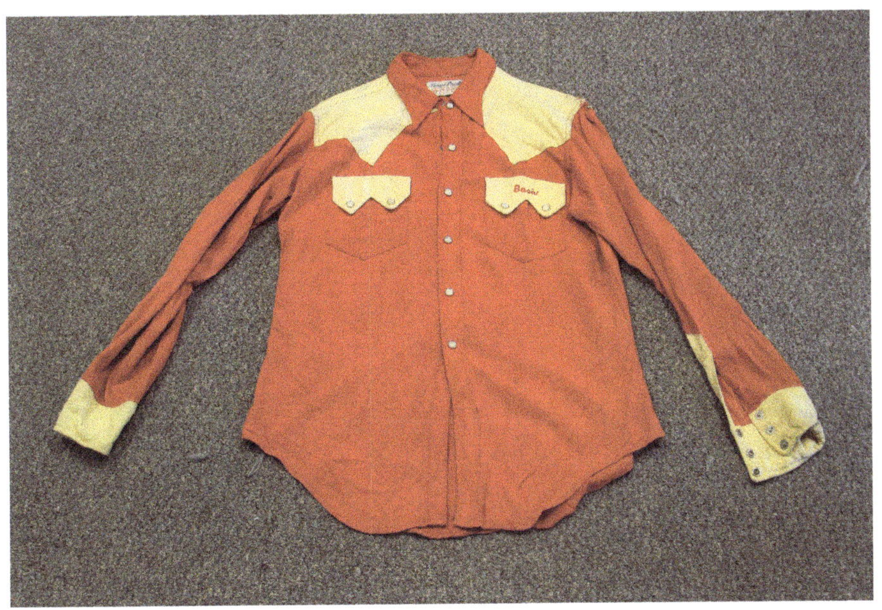

The stage shirt of Bash Hoffner, brother of Pearl Wranglers band leader Adolph Hoffner. *Jeremy Banas*.

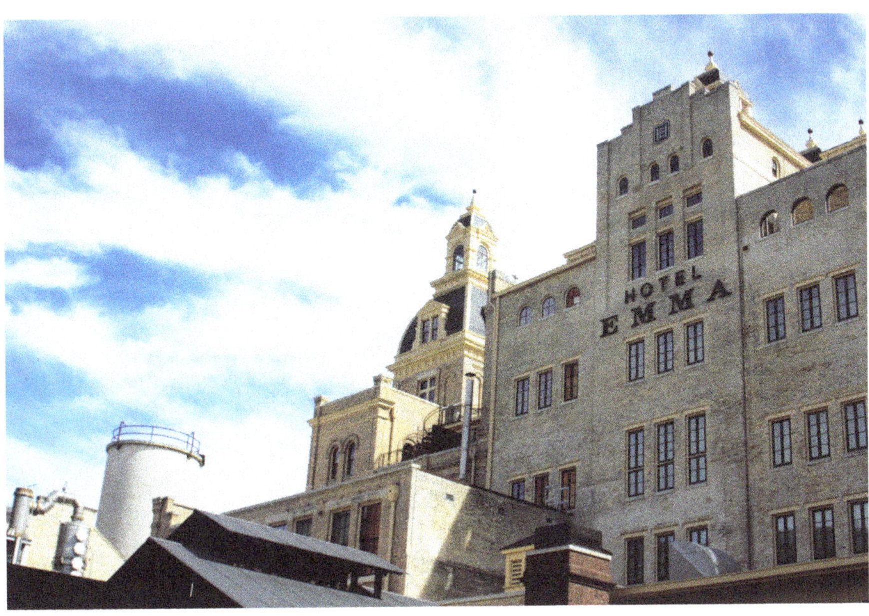

The back of the Hotel Emma. *Jeremy Banas.*

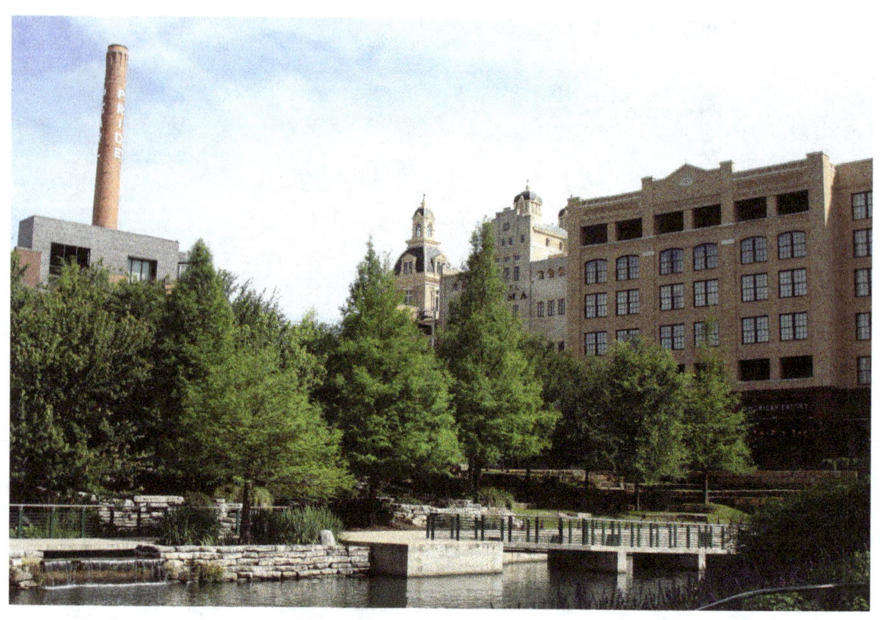

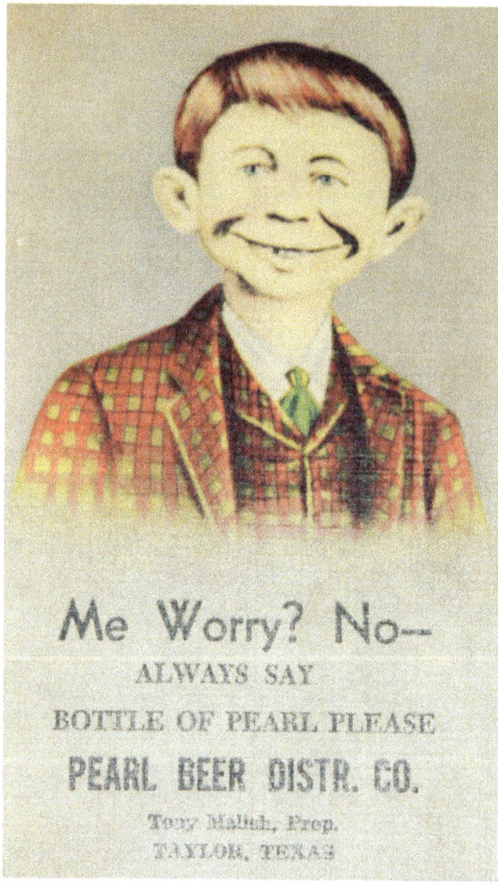

Above: A view of the Pearl Brewhouse and the Hotel Emma from the Riverwalk extension. *Jeremy Banas*.

Left: Before he starred in *Mad* magazine, Alfred E. Newman was Pearl's ad man. *Jeremy Banas*.

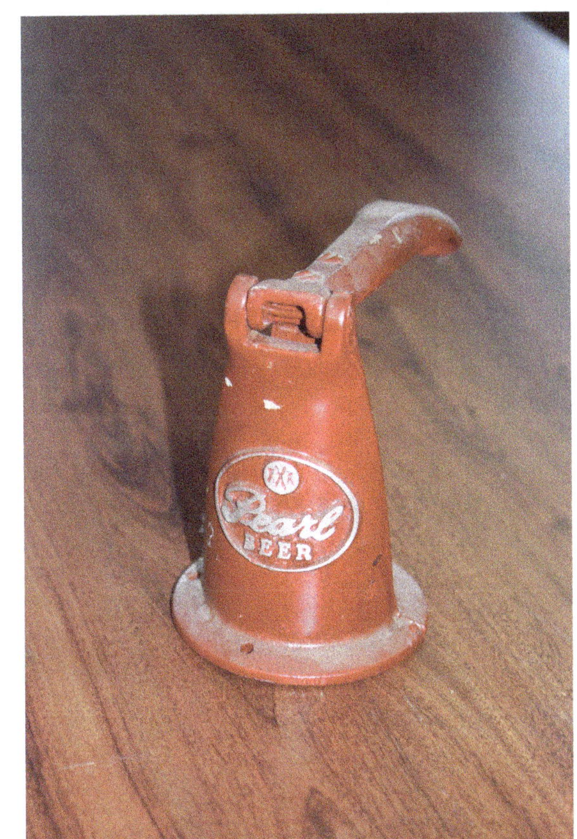

Right: The JC bar mount can opener. Designed by San Marcos, Texas resident James H. Crews, the patent was applied for in 1949. At the time, Pearl, Falstaff and Southern Select were using the JC. *Jeremy Banas*.

Below: Framed ads of the San Antonio Brewing Association, later 1890s. *Jeremy Banas*.

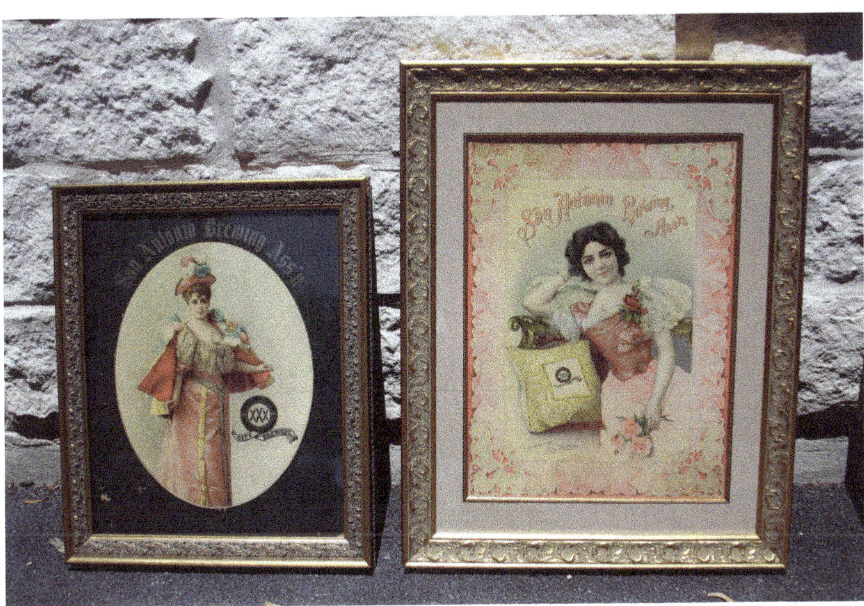

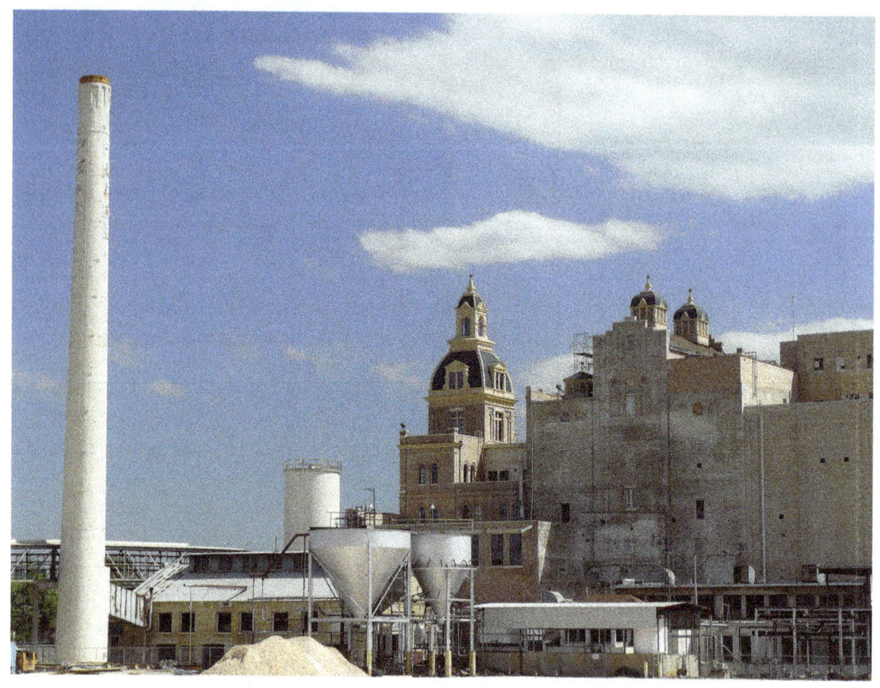

Above: It's all coming together! The New Pearl Complex takes shape, 2008. *Jeff Trei.*

Below: *Pearl Parade* magazine, 1952. *Jeremy Banas.*

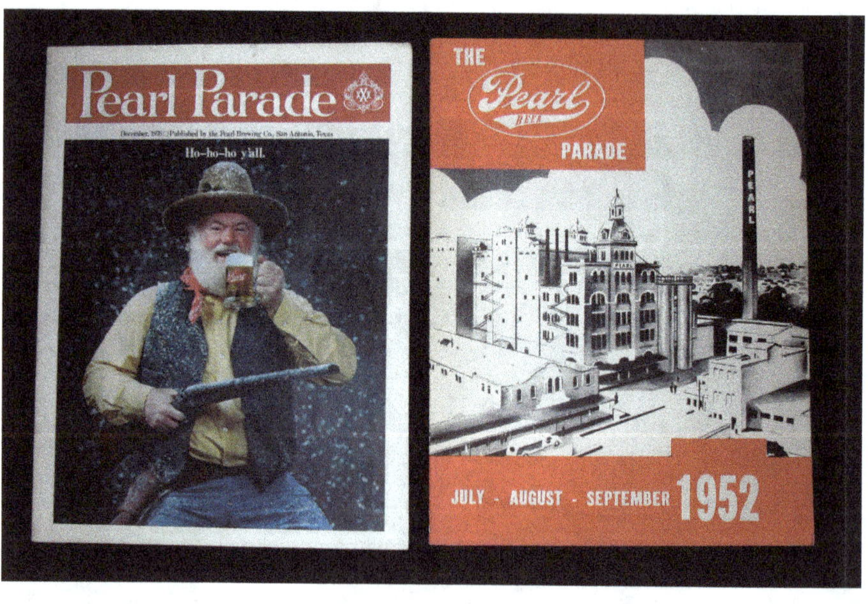

PERIOD IV

OTTO A. KOEHLER AND PEARL'S GOLDEN AGE, 1933–1969

PROHIBITION ENDS AND EMMA KOEHLER RISES FURTHER

In February 1933, many months before those first trucks rolled out of the brewhouse with beer at the end of Prohibition, Alamo Foods Company changed its name back to the San Antonio Brewing Association, with B.B. McGimsey as the general manager. Emma Koehler thrived in her tenured role as president, and along with McGimsey, they steered the San Antonio Brewing Association toward not only recovery but also prosperity.

Her tough and astute business sense was not earned overnight, though. Emma Koehler was born Emma Bentzen on February 25, 1858, in St. Louis, Missouri, to Ulrich and Helen Bentzen, who immigrated to the United States from Hanover, Germany, in 1837. The youngest of about seven children, young Emma Bentzen was not born with a silver spoon. Her father was listed as a horticulturist in the St. Louis census of 1870, although it is not known specifically what he did.

Little is known of how Emma Bentzen met Otto Koehler, although Martha Hix suggested that it may have been through Otto's brother August, who was employed by Julius Thamer, a local brewer, and whose wife, Dorothy, may have been a sister to Emma's mother, Helen. Regardless, Emma's story begins with her marriage to Otto on August 12, 1882, in St. Louis. Two short weeks later, Emma's father, Ulrich, passed away, and in 1883, the Koehlers moved to San Antonio so that Otto could start his job with the Lone Star Brewing Association.

Little is written of Emma's life while married to Otto Koehler, although she was thrust into the spotlight in 1914 when she was made a widow at the age of fifty-six. As the sole heir to the Koehler fortune, Emma set out to prove that a woman was more than capable of moving on, despite what was expected of widows of the time. Instead of wallowing in the embarrassment of what Otto had done, she preserved his name—even dedicating a park in his honor.

Although she had family and servants to help her the last several years, she continued to rely on help to get her through widowhood. Once such family member was Hedwig Koethe, the daughter of Emma's older sister, Anna. Hedwig's son, Lutz Issleib, would later factor prominently into the brewery.

After Otto's death, Emma seemingly regained her health. One might argue that without the specter of a cheating husband, she was invigorated. Emma was now determined to exert her influence on what she had inherited and helped build with her husband. She forced Oscar Bergstrom's hand in hiring Gregg and Company, and later, using her influence as two-thirds owner of the San Antonio Brewing Association, she was named its president officially in 1921.

Improvements were made at the brewery over the next ten years. In 1934, the famous Pearl smokestack next to the brewhouse was illuminated with neon lights. In 1935, McGimsey organized the Texas Brewers Association, of which he would remain president until 1951. The San Antonio Brewing Association's soda division was taken over by the Texas Dry Corporation. In 1935, it operated on the Pearl grounds until it went out of business, at which time the San Antonio Brewing Association bought the bottling equipment back.

Besides McGimsey, the San Antonio Brewing Association had two other hires who would see the brewery through Prohibition and beyond: Hiram B. "Pat" O'Brien and Aubrey N. Kline. The first of these larger-than-life men, O'Brien was hired in 1930 when the brewery was still known as Alamo Foods Company.

O'Brien's territory as a sales representative extended all the way to El Paso, as far east as Corpus Christi and as far south as the Rio Grande Valley. In 1933, just prior to the end of Prohibition, the brewery's output was only about 150,000 barrels. This was something that O'Brien sought to correct, and his ambition would help see him through. By 1937, he was promoted to general sales manager. By the time he retired in 1972, he would be senior

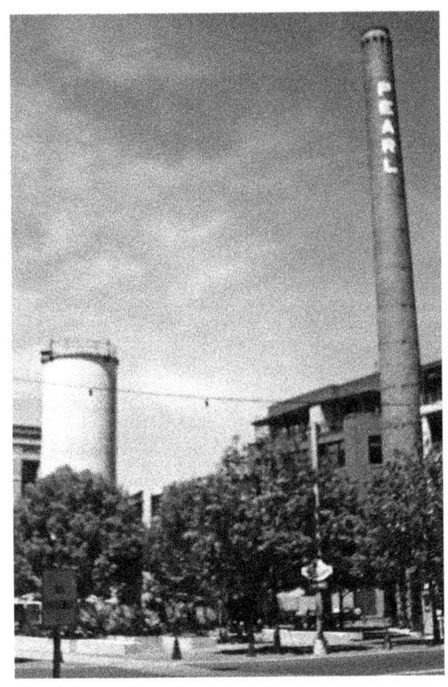

Southerleigh/Pearl smokestack. *Jeremy Banas.*

vice-president and marketing consultant, and the brewery's output would be about 2,200,000 barrels.

O'Brien was a genius marketer, having come up with one of the most successful advertising campaigns in the brewery's history, probably rivaling those of Anheuser-Busch and Miller. These campaigns included the famed "Country of 1100 Springs," a slogan that is still used today. In fact, this slogan inspired a billboard off Interstate 35 in Dallas that had a small waterfall with water running through it daily. He was the genius behind the famed Judge Roy Bean campaign, capitalizing on the Wild West judge's love of XXX Pearl Beer, as Bean served only that beverage. O'Brien had a slew of other advertising promotions and giveaways that in some ways would rival that of any macrobrewer today.

Perhaps one of the most successful campaigns was a local western swing band known as the Pearl Wranglers. O'Brien worked with Aubrey Kline, Pearl's genius of public relations, and recruited Adolf Hoffner, a local musician, to head up this band. Hoffner's South Texas band became Pearl's official musicians, the Pearl Wranglers. They went on to sing for nearly fifty years, all in the name of XXX Pearl Beer. At the end of each show, the bandleader always mentioned for folks to order "A bottle of Pearl please."

Over the course of his time with the San Antonio Brewing Association, H.B. O'Brien would help to build a distribution network from thirty-five wholesalers to four hundred distributors throughout forty states.

O'Brien's sometimes partner, Kline, was considered just as much a rock star at the brewery. Kline was one of the best public relations people in the business, with numerous awards supporting his success at Pearl. His work at Pearl began in 1936, when Otto A. Koehler, not quite president of the brewery, walked into a local family restaurant known as Boehler's that was not far from the brewery and met Kline. Boehler's was also the first place in San Antonio that received XXX Pearl when Prohibition ended. Otto A. took a shine to Kline and asked him to come work at the brewery as its public

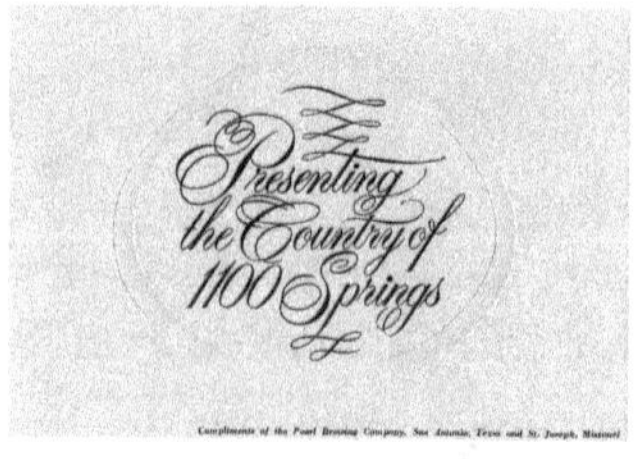

Pages 68–71: Country of 1100 Springs promo. *Pearl LLC Archives.*

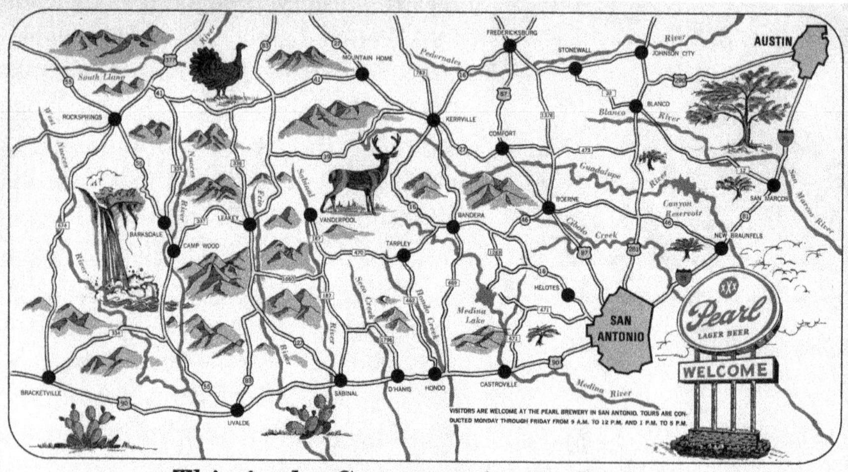

This is the Country of 1100 Springs

This big, lonesome land follows the general outline of the Edwards Plateau across more than 20 counties in Southwest Texas. It's changed very little since the Spaniards first saw it over 400 years ago.

In the air there's the crisp smell of juniper and cypress. Under foot, America's purest limestone. And flowing from 1100 springs, an incomparable water that forms the many streams and rivers in the Texas Hill Country. As the water flows over the limestone, much of it filters underground and is then tapped pure and clean a quarter-mile beneath the brewery by Pearl's own artesian wells.

This water is one of the finest natural brewing waters in the world and it gave the first brewers of Pearl Beer their original Spring Water Formula. With this water they were able to draw the finest flavors from their choice grains and hops — flavors often missing in other beers.

We stick to this formula today because it still gives Pearl Beer a noticeable edge in goodness and refreshment. Pour yourself a cold Pearl Beer today, and enjoy the delicate flavor this great water gives to beer. Every refreshing sip will take you back to the Country of 1100 Springs.

The photographs in this portfolio were all taken in the Country of 1100 Springs and are typical of the rivers and streams that flow through this rugged country. Although most of these locations are on private property, many beautiful scenes such as these can be viewed from the roads at stream crossings and public parks.

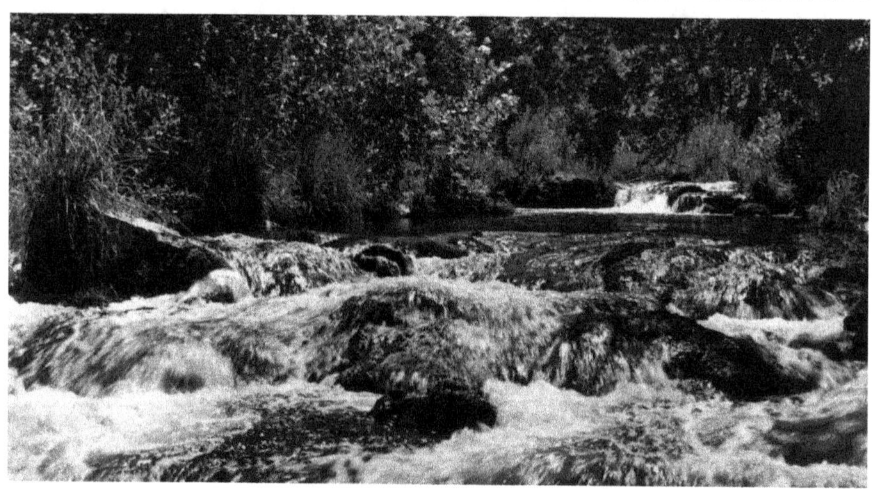

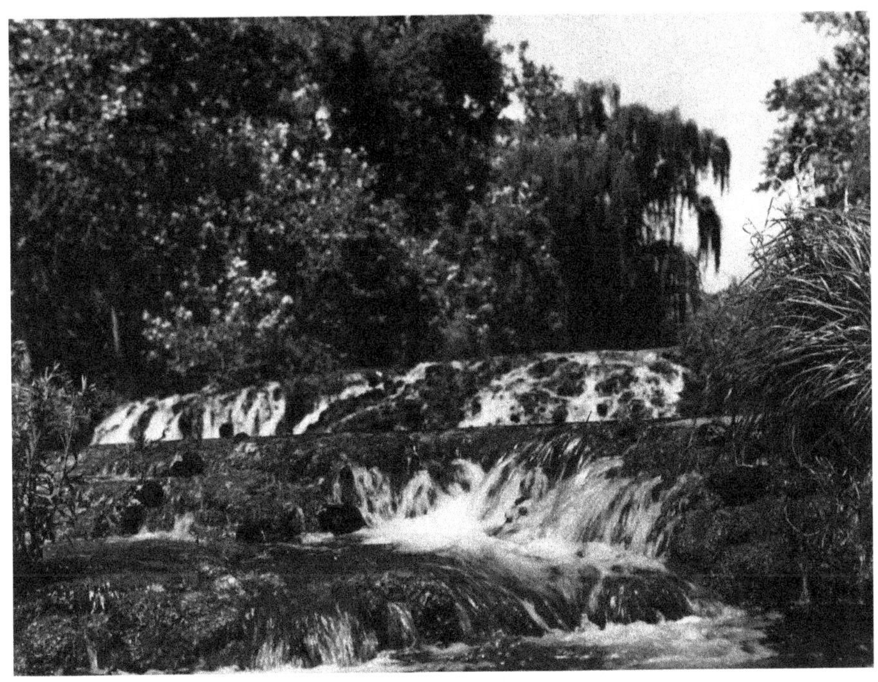

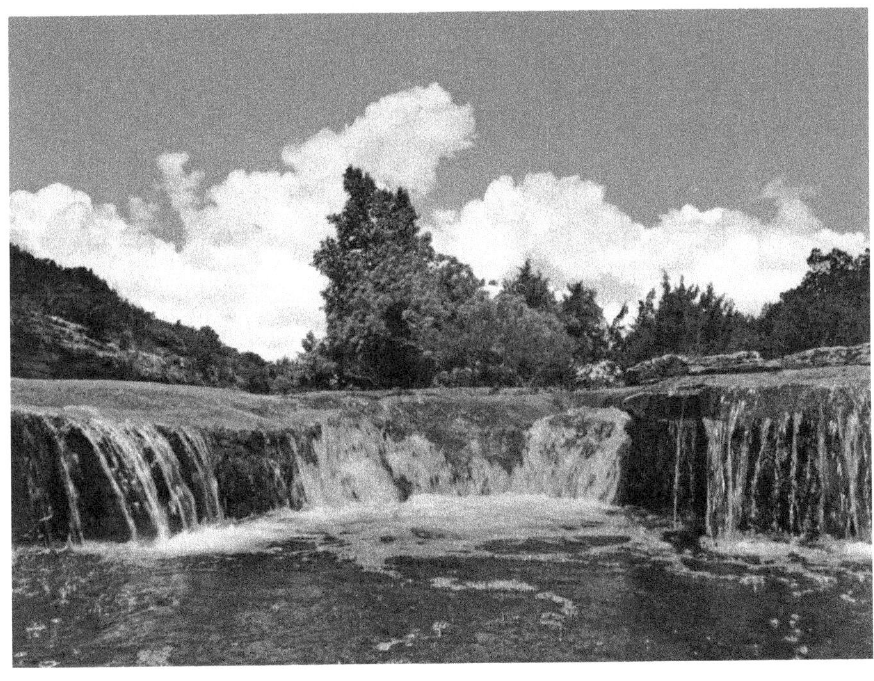

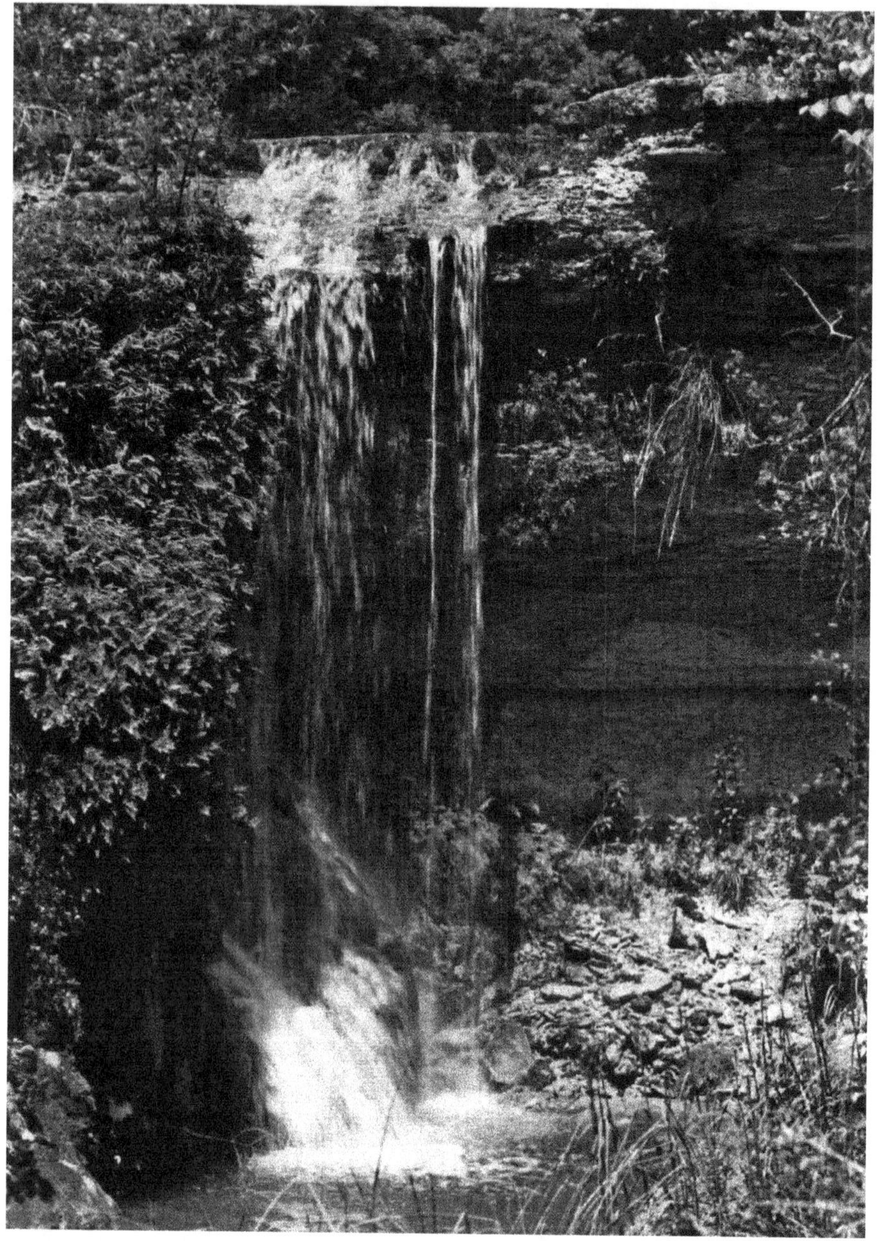

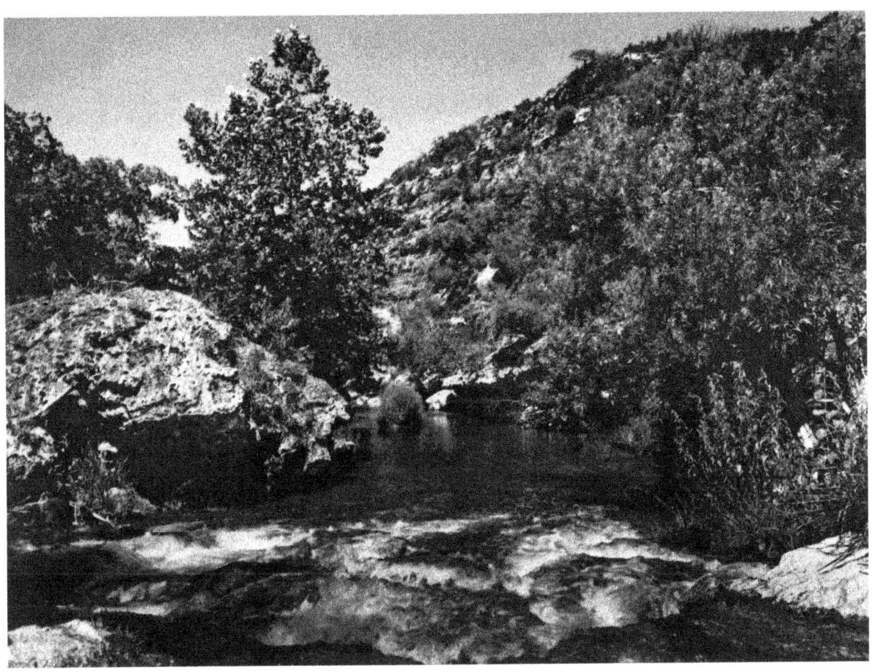

relations director. Not having any experience in the industry, Kline studied everything he could about public relations at the San Antonio public library and set out to work. He stayed thirty-six years and got to know politicians, governors and more. So popular was his style that he became something of a public relations subject himself, even picking up the nickname Mr. Pearl. He always greeted others with "Bless your heart."

Kline was very involved in the San Antonio community and served in several organizations. He was a participant in leadership with the March of Dimes, Golden Gloves boxing tournaments, the San Antonio Press Club Museum, the Texas tourism development board and the San Antonio Livestock Show. For many years, he was a committee chairman at the stock show and with Pearl's advertising dollars would buy young animals to give away at the auction, where the animals were donated to the Boys Club of San Antonio.

After retiring in 1972, Kline and his brothers went back to their roots and renovated Boehler's restaurant. They operated it for many years and changed the name to Boehler's Garden, running it in an old building that looked almost like the Leaning Tower of Pisa. For many years after Boehler's Garden closed down, it would become the famous Liberty Bar, a popular hangout for San Antonio residents.

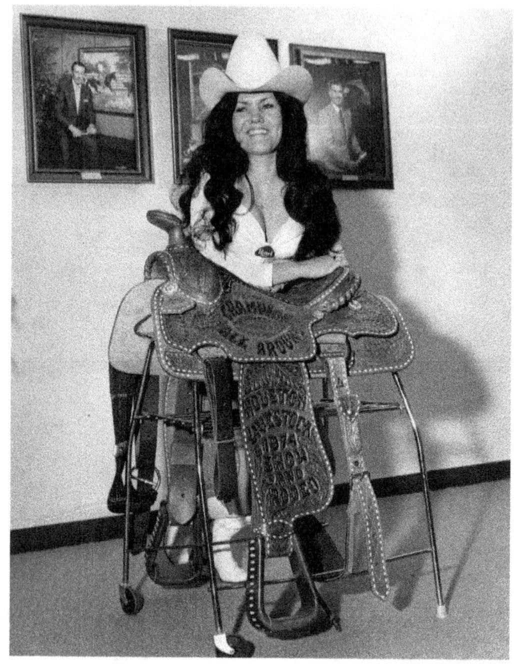

Miss Pearl 1974, posing at the Houston Stock Show. *Pearl LLC Archives*.

In the spring of 1935, new large pasteurization machines were obtained, as were high-speed fillers, increasing bottling by 80 percent. The year 1935 also saw the return of the Texas Pride beer, which would be brewed until 1938. The spring of 1935 also saw a little bit of fun for employees. In March 1935, San Antonio Brewing Association formed the brewery athletic club, organizing baseball, basketball and bowling teams. The men's baseball teams were known as the Prides, and the women's basketball teams were known as Brewettes. The bowling and baseball teams would continue on into the 1970s.

More changes and improvements were seen in the late 1930s and '40s as well. In 1936, Texans drank more than 1 million bottles of XXX Pearl and Texas Pride every nine days. San Antonio Brewing Association also introduced the new brand Cerveza Tolteca, with advertising all in Spanish. In the spring of 1938, the San Antonio Brewing Association became the first brewery in the United States to be completely air conditioned, and by summer of that year, it would get a large commercial neon sign, an invention known as the Neo-Rite system, that had a motion effect to it. By 1939, it had erected a more modern fireproof garage measuring 130 feet wide by 236 feet long, complete with shops to service its fleet of vehicles. It built a two-story addition to the bottling plant measuring 6,200 feet, doubling its previous size.

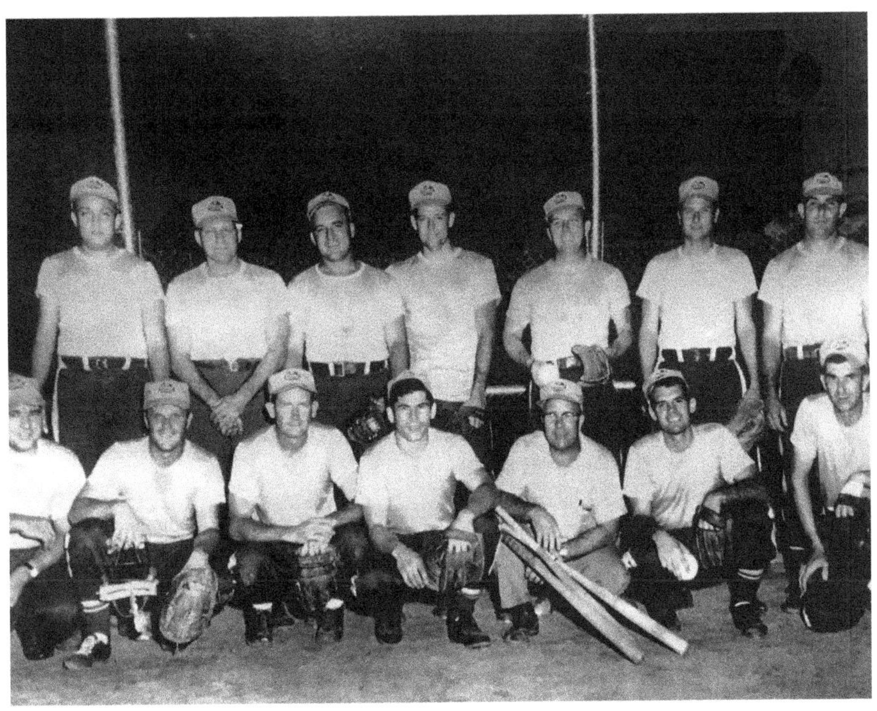

Pearl Pride baseball team, 1960s. *Charlie Staats.*

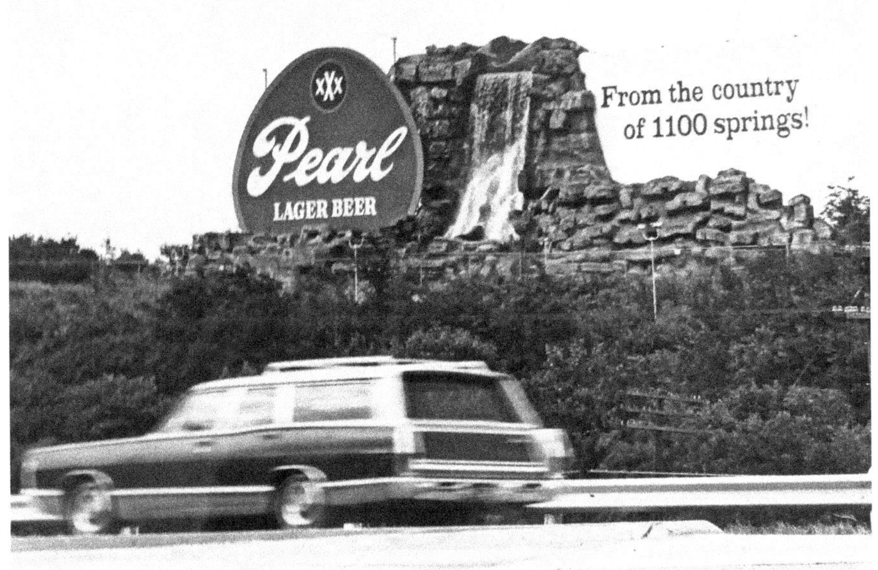

Pearl waterfall billboard. *Jeremy Banas.*

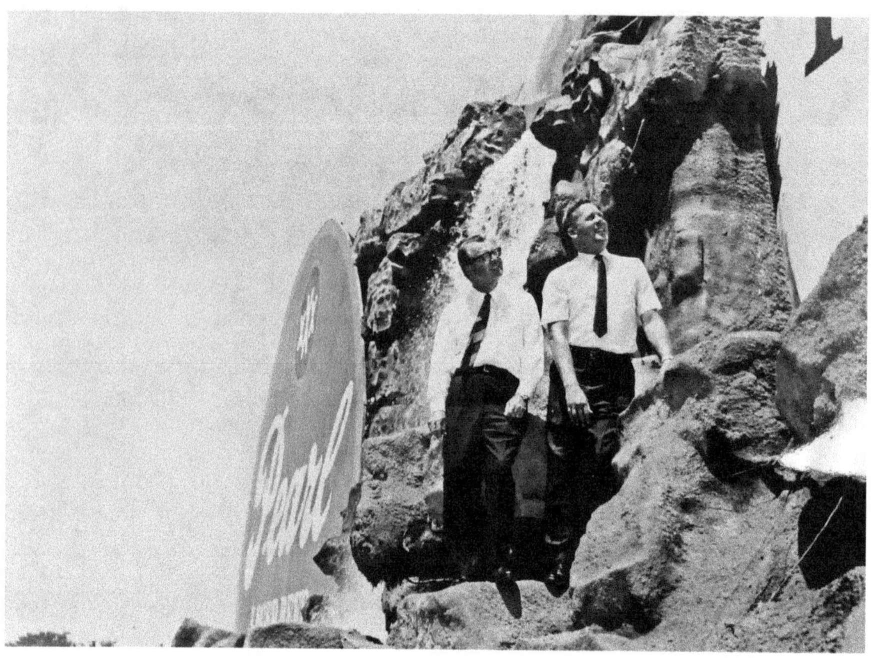

Pearl executives stand atop the Peal waterfall billboard. *Pearl LLC Archives.*

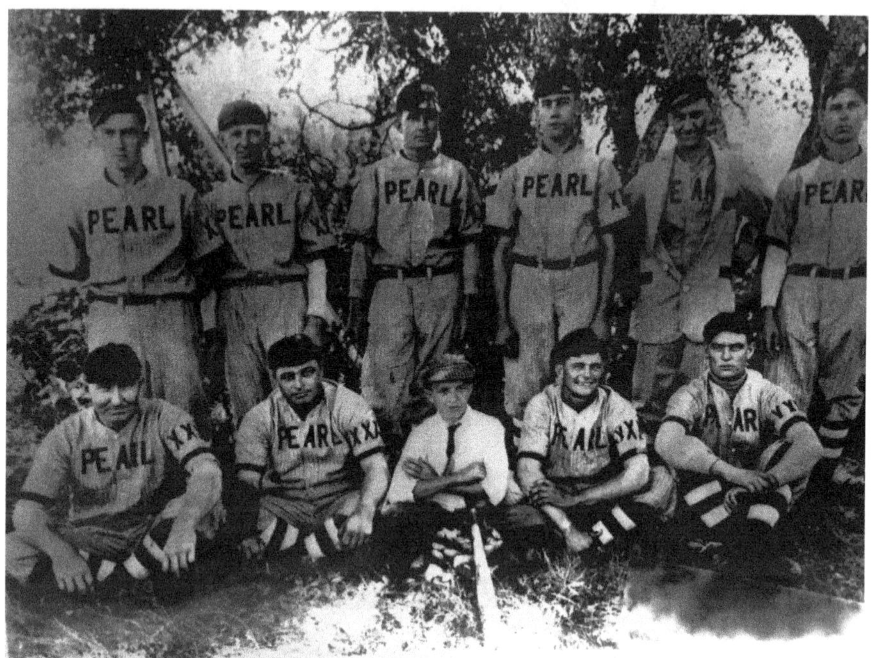

Players on the Pearl Pride baseball team, 1930s. *Charlie Staats.*

Other community involvement included a Miss Pearl Brewery contest that was held in 1941 and 1942. The year 1941 also saw Jinx Falkenberg working as an actress and model in the San Antonio Brewing Association's 1941 advertising. The year 1942 saw advertising changing to the image of Georgia Carol Wynn.

With World War II raging on, by April 1942 there was a metal shortage around the country. Otto A. Koehler, being the industrious man he was, invented a bottle cap salvaging machine that took used crowns and re-formed them to be used on new bottles, a practice that continued throughout the war. To this end, and to help with the war effort, the San Antonio Brewing Association donated its 200,000-pound ice machine that was installed in 1895 as scrap metal for the war effort.

EMMA PASSES AND OTTO A. RETURNS THE OTTO NAME TO THE BREWERY

In 1943, the venerable Emma Koehler passed away. A pillar of the community, the woman who had been here since the beginning, steering the ship through Prohibition and beyond, would be sorely missed. Almost immediately, the board of directors elected Otto Andrew Koehler as president of the San Antonio Brewing Association.

Otto A. ushered in what many would later call the brewery's golden age—Otto A. himself was often referred to as a beloved employer and close friend over the next twenty-six years while he was head of the San Antonio Brewing Association. More than anyone else, Otto A. seemed to embody the original Otto's ability to relate to pretty much anyone.

The young Otto A. was born to Karl Koehler and his wife, Lina Unverzacht, on July 24, 1893. The couple, along with Otto A. and their eldest son, Charles, was living in North Warren, Pennsylvania. Sometime before the turn of the twentieth century, Karl took his entire family back to Germany to visit extended family. It would not be as pleasant of a trip as planned, for Karl became sick and passed away in Germany. In about 1909, Otto Andrew was brought to San Antonio to stay with Otto Koehler and his wife, Emma. Although Otto A.'s brother, Charles, would later come to San Antonio as well, it was Otto A. who arrived first.

Now that the Otto name had returned as president of the brewery, many saw a very bright future for the San Antonio–based brewery, although it was a slow and methodical growth that Otto A. presided over. This allowed much time to cultivate a variety of interests and eccentricities. Otto A. was well known for his love of fishing, the outdoors and big game hunting. Many of his prizes were prominently displayed in the Pearl's Safari room at the brewery, as well as at a private club at the home he inherited from his uncle and Aunt Emma on West Ashby Place, aptly called the Zebra room. His many conquests filled the walls of both rooms and are still observed with fondness today.

Otto A. was not content to merely run the brewery that had been a part of his family for so many years. He wanted to know all aspects of the business intimately, and to this end, he went so far as to attend brewing school in Chicago in about 1934 so that his technical skills would improve. He attended the Wahl-Henius Brewmaster School along with future Pearl brewmaster and friend Harry Haeglin, who would also be plant manager around the time of the 1953 expansion of the brewery.

Despite his well-known love of hunting and fishing, one little-known fact was his love of machines and inventing. During World War II and the well-documented shortage of metal, the ability to make crowns and bottle caps became increasingly difficult. Not one to let such a problem defeat him, Otto A. found a solution. As metal was certainly short in San Antonio, he devised a machine that would take old bottle caps and re-crimp them onto new bottles. The brewery instituted a policy with its distributors: if they did not return each case with all of the caps, the distributors would be shorted one case of beer on the next delivery. To ensure that this did not happen, the distributors passed this on to the restaurants and bars, advising them of the same. This worked wonders, as they were always out of crowns. For the workers at the Pearl, though, these crowns proved to be troublesome when they were reused. "Those crowns had two liners, aluminum foil and cork," said Al Marmor, a superintendent of the bottle shop. "It was a mess, those crowns. The foil kept coming loose and clogging the re-crimping machine."

The San Antonio Brewing Association also took a more direct approach in the war effort. During part of World War II, bottles of XXX Pearl Beer carried labels on the neck of each bottle recommending customers purchase war bonds—quite ingenious when you think about it. I'm sure supporting the troops was near and dear to Otto A.'s heart, but the benefit to the company was the goodwill and faith for Pearl drinkers, something that would carry on for years to come.

The San Antonio Brewing Association got involved in the local community in other ways too. The brewery sponsored broadcasts for local radio station

WOAI AM 1200, and on October 15, 1943, WOAI celebrated its 2,000th Pearl-sponsored broadcast. This was not the only radio station where the San Antonio Brewing Association sponsored programs, though, for in March 1950, the brewery sponsored a thirty-minute news program entitled *Your Radio Newspaper* on local station KTSA.

CHANGE CONTINUES AT A RAPID PACE

Changes became commonplace at the San Antonio Brewing Association over the next twenty years. In May 1948, it broke ground on an eight-story addition and purchased new brewery equipment, in addition to a new bottling unit, pasteurizer and washer. In April 1949, it added a filling machine. This expansion led to quite a growth by the end of 1948. For San Antonio's largest brewery, there were 340 employees producing two thousand barrels per day, with trucks delivering them to thirsty Texas residents. A few years later, in 1951, the San Antonio Brewing Association introduced the Pearl pick-up pack, six twelve-ounce bottles of Pearl beer, hoping that this added convenience would boost sales.

In 1949, Pearl entered the canned beer market, releasing its first beer in a can on September 29. One year later, in the fall of 1950, more improvements came to the buildings themselves. All the brewery buildings were freshly painted, taking twenty-five to thirty men using two thousand gallons of paint two and a half months to complete. This was a much-needed upkeep of the brewery and its grounds. The improvements would not end there; the old stables, long since out of use other than for storage, got an extreme makeover of their own.

The Pearl Stables were renovated and updated to become the Pearl Corral Hospitality room, which contained the famous Safari room. Decorating the interior of the former stables was a mural painted by James Buchanan Wynn of Wimberley, Texas, standing 8 feet high and 280 feet long. It became the United States' longest continuous mural depicting Texas ranch life—clearly falling right in line with Otto's love of animals.

It was likely this passion that saw the San Antonio Brewing Association purchase its first animal at the San Antonio Livestock exposition in February 1951. A grand champion steer known as "Shorty" was purchased for $21,000 from Andrew Tatsch. The San Antonio Brewing Association had never before bid on any prize animal. The record-breaking purchase price was as much a story as the animal's subsequent donation after the livestock exposition so that the brewery could help with funds for a building program for local family charity Boysville, which still exists today on North 1604. The general director of Boysville, Armin F. Bahnsen, was shocked and overjoyed by the unexpected generosity and indicated the time that the prize steer might be sold again to raise funds.

B.B. McGimsey, executive vice-president at the time, said the San Antonio Brewing Association's purchase of the grand champion was to help the Livestock Exposition obtain a new record. In addition to that, he said the brewery had a large interest in helping with programs for boys throughout Texas who could raise better cattle for the following year's stock show. McGimsey went on to say that Boysville was "a fine organization, backed by fine men, which is doing a great job in the education and non-denominational character training of orphan boys."

However, the biggest changes in the brewery's history came in 1952 and 1953. Recognizing that many people around San Antonio and Texas often confused the name San Antonio Brewing Association with an organization that might be representing breweries around San Antonio, the board of directors elected to change the name of the brewery to that of its flagship XXX Pearl Beer, becoming the Pearl Brewing Company. The year 1952 also saw the very first issue of *Pearl Parade*, an employee magazine that came out between July and September of that year.

Otto A. and the board of directors were just getting started with improvements and changes. Expansion at the brewery and equipment upgrades were in order so that it could stay competitive, increase production and put out the same quality product for which it was known.

By 1953, much of the expansion had been completed, and a special issue of the *San Antonio Express* declared Pearl the largest brewery in the Southwest. This expansion, one of the crowning jewels of Otto A.'s reign with the brewery, gave it a more than 50 percent increased capacity, raising its annual production to almost 1,225,000 barrels. The new buildings also created room for new and desperately needed equipment. This included a very large beer storage area, adding fifty-seven glass tanks, each holding 880 gallons, on just the first three floors. On the fourth and fifth floors, increased space for fermentation was now available. The brewery also added a canning shop that could package six-packs or cases of XXX Pearl Beer at a rapid pace of eighteen thousand cans per hour, with room left over for expansion down the road. Add to all of this a payroll that by the end of 1953 had hit the $2,200,000 mark,

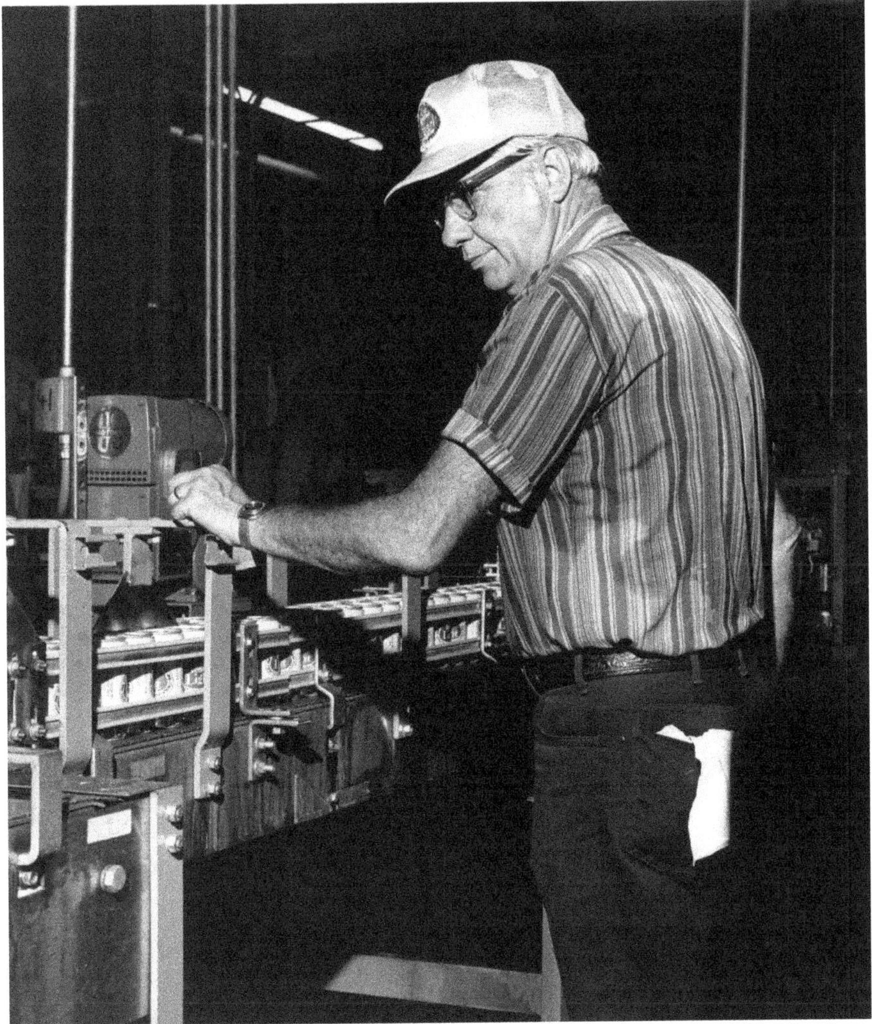

Pearl canning employee, 1970s. *Pearl LLC Archives.*

Pearl Brewing had begun to be the force in the San Antonio community it had always hoped to be.

Although this expansion was one of Otto A.'s triumphs, he was actually not present for the kickoff. No, our dear Otto A. was in Africa as often as he could to hunt anything he could find. In fact, he had just recently killed the largest elephant that Kenya had seen in the past fifteen years before that point. His African safaris would become the stuff of legend even at that time. A film exists even today of several of his African safari

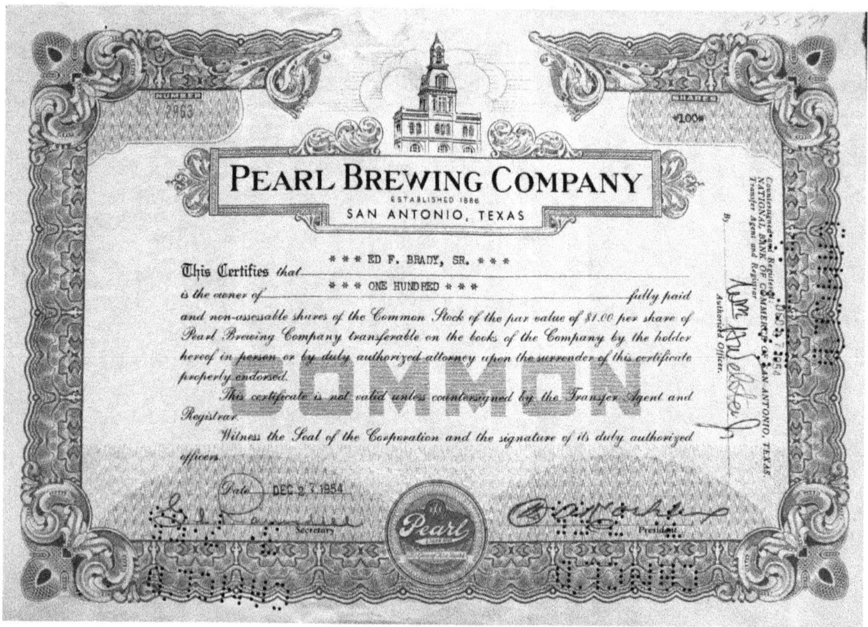

NUMBER 2963

SHARES *100*

PEARL BREWING COMPANY

ESTABLISHED 1886

SAN ANTONIO, TEXAS

This Certifies that *** ED F. BRADY, SR. ***

is the owner of *** ONE HUNDRED *** fully paid and non-assessable shares of the Common Stock of the par value of $1.00 per share of Pearl Brewing Company transferable on the books of the Company by the holder hereof in person or by duly authorized attorney upon the surrender of this certificate properly endorsed.

This certificate is not valid unless countersigned by the Transfer Agent and Registrar.

Witness the Seal of the Corporation and the signature of its duly authorized officers.

COMMON

Secretary

President

NATIONAL BANK OF COMMERCE OF SAN ANTONIO, TEXAS

Transfer Agent and Registrar

By

Authorized Officer.

Certificate of Pearl common stock. *Jeremy Banas.*

adventures, as well as a book called *Ku-Winda*, a kind of how-to book for conducting a safari.

In 1954, Pearl Brewing sold 117,696 shares of common stock to the public for about eighteen dollars each, but only to Texas residents. This brought an influx of cash that would allow the brewery to continue to grow and also give San Antonio and Texas residents a piece of their own brewery.

PEARL BREWING COMPANY DOMINATES THE COMPETITION

By 1955, Texas Pride would see its third return, as well as the introduction of XXX Pearl Beer in quart bottles. Alas, though, Texas Pride would last only until around 1956. The remainder of 1955 saw quite a lot of promotion and experiments for the brewery. Pearl Brewing sponsored bullfights, a show on KCOR TV channel 41 and a sponsorship of the television show *Passport to Danger*, as well as a championship bowling tournament, both on WOAI TV channel 4. Before 1955 was over, though, Pearl would try an experiment that would not end in success: the introduction of twelve-packs of its bottles,

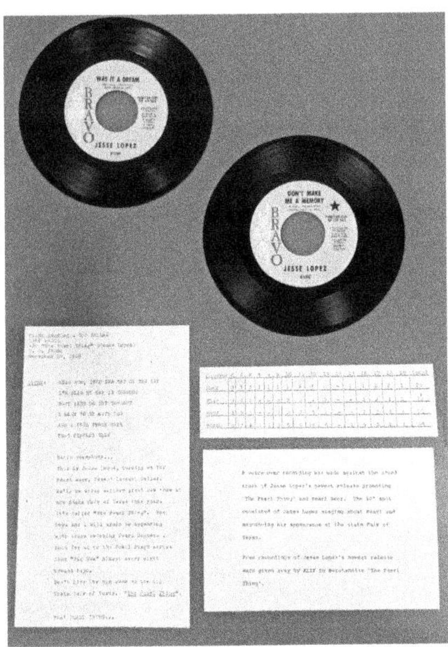

A .45 recording of "That Pearl Thing" by Jesse Lopez, a song about Pearl beer that aired on a Dallas radio station, December 10, 1968. *Jeremy Banas.*

although it merely amounted to two six-pack containers put together in a hand carrier. Perhaps consumers weren't ready to purchase that much at once or they did not much care for the carriers falling apart if they became damp.

Continuing to try and diversify, Pearl brought back Pearl Bock, which had been sporadically available in the '30s and '40s; it made its full return in 1958. In January 1959, Pearl laid claim to the first oversize billboard in San Antonio to flash the time and temperature. The billboard was a popular feature at the intersection. More promotions would be seen later in 1959 with two inventions from a Pearl employee that carried the Pearl logo: the "Pearl-O-Lure," a three-pronged lure using leftover tin from the brewery, and the "Hook Jacket," a protector for hooks on the lure. Other promotions included small packs of hand lotion, insect repellant and a snake bite treatment kit and were quite the gimmicks for local residents, who proudly carried these around.

Clearly Pearl was not resting on its laurels. The '60s came in big for the brewing company. The James Street entrance to the brewery was renamed Pearl Parkway, likely to fall in line with the brewery's recent name change a decade earlier, and included a new sign on Broadway Street. A version of the sign can be seen today in the exact same location. Pearl Brewing also introduced glass cans, a non-returnable stubby beer bottle and a zip-open pack carton, hoping to give consumers another option to carry their beer home. In 1960, Pearl also became the first brewery in Texas to sell 1 million barrels of beer that year.

There would be a lot of excitement the rest of the decade. Perhaps the most significant business decision for the brewery in 1961 was its acquisition of the historic Goetz Brewery in St. Joseph, Missouri. This gave Pearl Brewing an additional brewing facility in a part of the country that would allow it to reach a wider audience outside of its southwestern dominance.

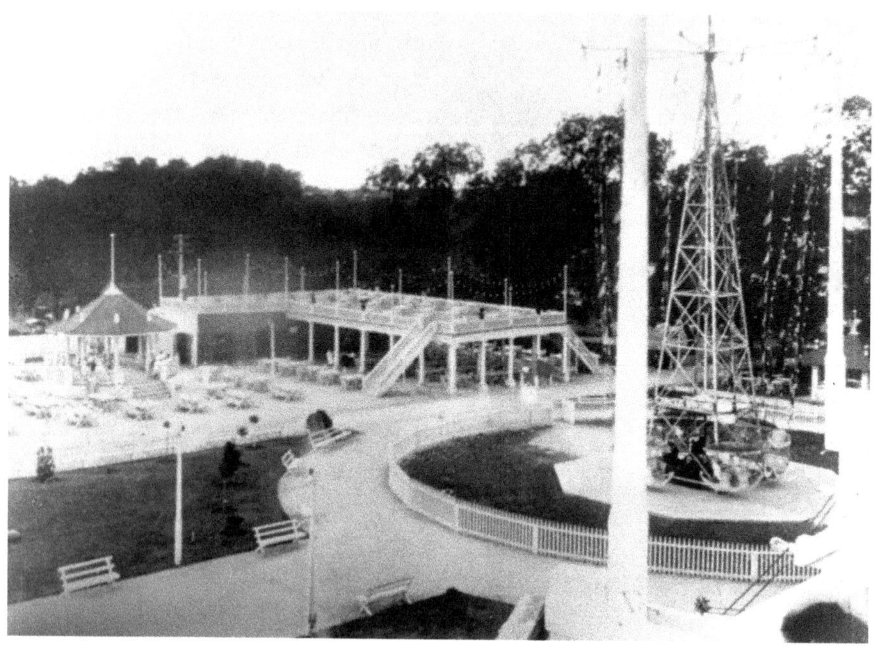

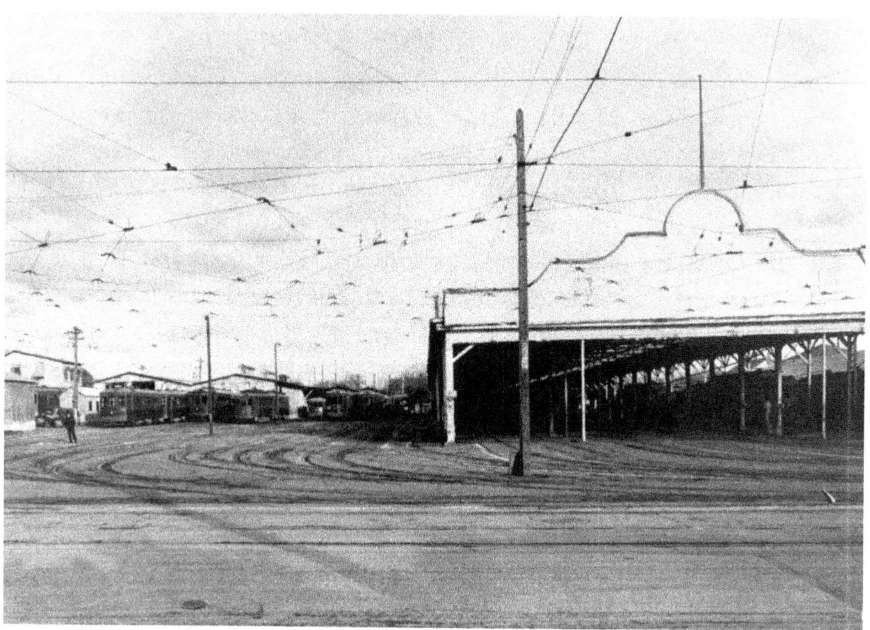

This page and opposite: Pearl Light Park. *San Antonio College and the Alamo Colleges District Foundation.*

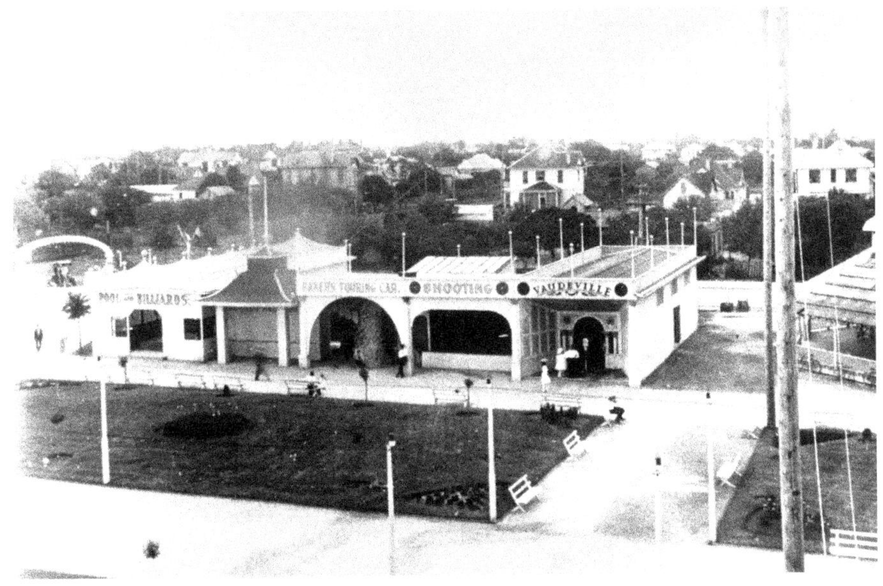

To give a little context to this purchase, we must look back to 1951 for a moment. After numerous offers from larger breweries around the country to purchase Pearl had been turned down, Pabst Brewing out of Milwaukee came calling, and B.B. McGimsey was interested. He saw it as a way for the brewery to grow and for an investor such as himself to reap huge profits. Pearl's vast dominance in Texas and around the Southwest had not gone unnoticed by larger brewers around the country.

Not everyone on the board, including Otto A., was interested in this. In fact, the narrowly defeated vote to sell Pearl would drive a deep wedge in McGimsey's relationship with Pearl and the Koehler family. This division continued over the next few years and would lead to McGimsey's exit from the brewery. However, McGimsey did land on his feet, having made a tidy sum over the last few decades that helped open Kelly Field National Bank in San Antonio in 1956. He would go on to have several other business interests in San Antonio; he also became a thirty-second-degree mason.

Pearl's need to grow and diversify was soon satisfied by another historic regional brewery. After a lot of research, Goetz Brewing in St. Joseph, Missouri, fit the bill. Although it would not see monetary savings until later, it was able to begin brewing Pearl soon after the purchase at the St. Joseph facility (while also brewing the Goetz brands at the San Antonio location). Some jobs were eliminated that were duplications of efforts, but Pearl Brewery treated the former employees of Goetz exactly like its own,

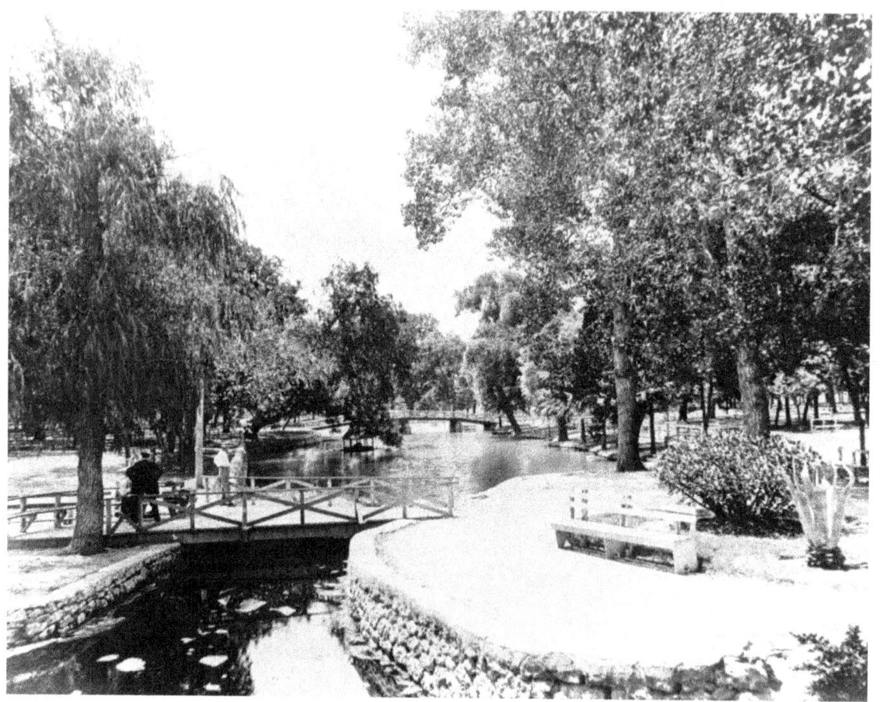

Koehler Park, 1920s. *San Antonio College and the Alamo Colleges District Foundation.*

with some Goetz employees coming to San Antonio to work at Pearl. A.J. Range became vice-president, with H.J. Eickenrot handling the PR work.

The remainder of 1961, as well as subsequent years, saw many additional sponsorships and new products introduced. Pearl Brewing wanted to continue to have an edge over the competition. It sponsored a Wild West performance troupe known as the Pearl Gunslingers in 1961, and in March 1962, Pearl purchased the radio and television rights of the Houston Colt .45s, the Major League Baseball expansion team that would go on to become the Houston Astros. Pearl sponsored a total of 162 radio broadcasts and 14 telecasts of away games in 1962. When the John Wayne movie *The Alamo* premiered in 1963, the Duke himself was on hand for the showing at the Pearl Brewery.

The year 1965 saw Pearl introduce Pearl draft beer in cans and quart bottles, as well as a home draft beer system known as "Pearl Port-A-Tap," essentially a boxed draft system that was placed in a refrigerator. There were also ring pop top–style cans that required no opener and the purchase of the Judson Candy Company. Why Pearl entered the candy business is something that has puzzled many for decades. Pearl was profitable in 1965, and although its business interests varied, the candy company still seemed rather "out of the box" for the brewing company.

The Judson Candy Company had already made a name for itself in Texas and throughout the Southwest. Although it was clearly not the largest candy company in the country, its presence was well known. Three sons and their father, George Eugene Judson Jr., founded the Judson Candy Company, which produced cherry sours, pralines and peanut brittle, as well as other candies, at its long-standing factory on South Flores Street. At one point, Judson Candy Company made more than one hundred different varieties. In fact, it was a popular destination for school field trips in the San Antonio area. Pearl ran the Judson Candy Company from 1965 until 1983, when Atkinson Candies purchased Judson from Pearl. Despite Pearl owning 20 percent of the popular candy company, Pearl's name was never listed on any advertising for candy boxes. The only evidence of Pearl's ownership rested in signs and office supplies around the company's plant.

One could speculate that Pearl Brewing Company's purchase of the Judson Candy Company had much to do with its bitter rivalry in the beer industry with the Lone Star Brewing Company. The purchase of Judson Candy Company may have had something to do with Lone Star's president, Harry Jersig, who became president in 1949. Jersig had worked at Judson Candy Company for quite a number of years before his tenure at Lone

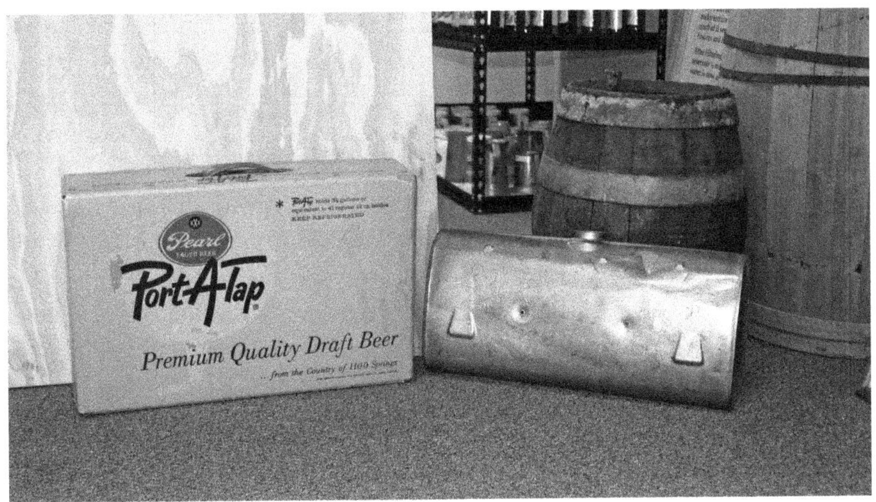

"Port-A-Tap," a home draft system. *Jeremy Banas.*

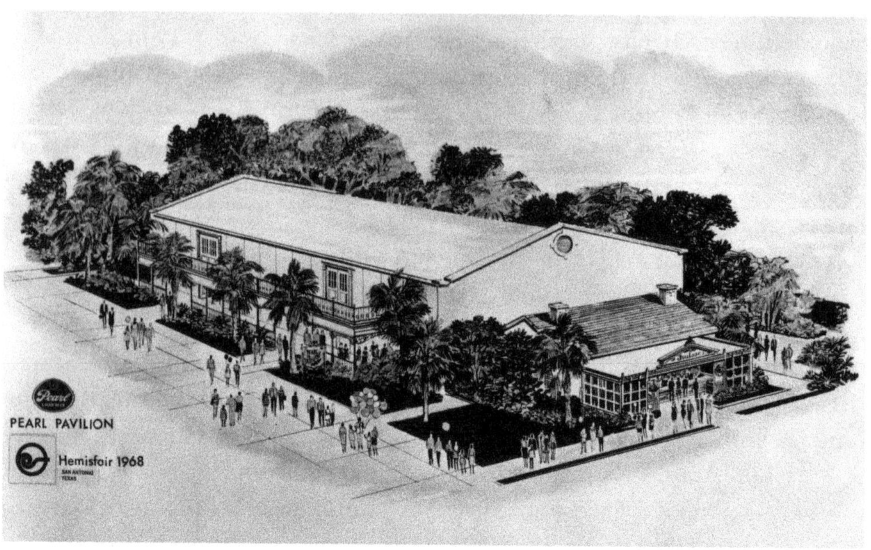

Pearl Pavilion at the 1968 World's Fair. *Pearl LLC Archives.*

Star and still thought fondly of its employees when he left. In addition to it being a business opportunity, Otto A.'s purchase of the Judson Candy Company may have been about knocking Lone Star.

Many more changes would occur over the next few years. In 1966, Pearl Brewing became the first company to contract for exhibit space at the 1968 World's Fair held at Hemisphere Plaza. Later that year, it introduced twist-off caps on all twelve-ounce non-returnable bottles. With all this promotion and increased sales, another update to the brewery was needed. In 1967, more than $1 million worth of fermentation tanks, a new filter and grain mill were added. By December 1967, Pearl Brewing had purchased RC Cola bottling plants in Houston, Beaumont and Galveston, Texas. When Hurricane Beulah hit, Pearl donated fifty thousand quarts of bottled water to victims that likely came from these bottling plants.

More self-promotion in 1967 was seen in the form of the Pearl Beer Country Music Spectacular in September, starring Faron Young, Porter Waggoner and the one and only Willie Nelson. The Pearl Brewing Company went on to sponsor events such as Saturday night boxing on local television, and in 1968, the Pearl Brewing Pavilion premiered at the 1968 Hemisphere World's Fair.

In 1969, Otto A. Koehler's involvement in the former San Antonio Brewing Association, now the Pearl Brewing Company, came to an end when the beloved leader passed away. Things would never be the same at the brewery. Since its humble beginnings in 1886, the Koehler family helped steer the Pearl Brewery into statewide and regional dominance, as well as had a profound effect on the San Antonio community.

PERIOD V

THE DECLINE OF THE PEARL, 1969–2001

FOR EVERY UP THERE IS A DOWN AND THE STRANGE TALE OF OTTO A. JR.

With the death of yet another Otto Koehler, Pearl Brewing faced a similar void in leadership as it did with the first Otto Koehler. Vice-President A.J. Range became president after Koehler's passing.

With new leadership in place, Pearl set out to continue its growth. One of its first changes was buying the RC Cola bottling plant of El Campo to add to its three other RC Cola bottling plants. Pearl also continued its sponsorship efforts with the sponsorship of a Formula One race car. The year 1969 would continue to be a transitional one for Pearl, although it also served to revisit certain business-related plans that were initiated by B.B. McGimsey and shot down by Otto A. Koehler. After Otto A.'s passing, the Koehler family soon saw that it would be increasingly difficult to compete with larger breweries around the country. The year 1969 saw a giant change in the purchase of Pearl Brewing Company by the Southdown Corporation of Houston, thus ending independent ownership of the brewery for the first time in more than eighty years.

The death of Otto A. would not be the last anyone would hear the name Otto A. Koehler. In a strange turn of events, his son Otto A. Koehler Jr.'s name began to hit the news. In January 1964, Otto A. Jr. was committed to Emory John Brady Hospital in Colorado Springs, Colorado,

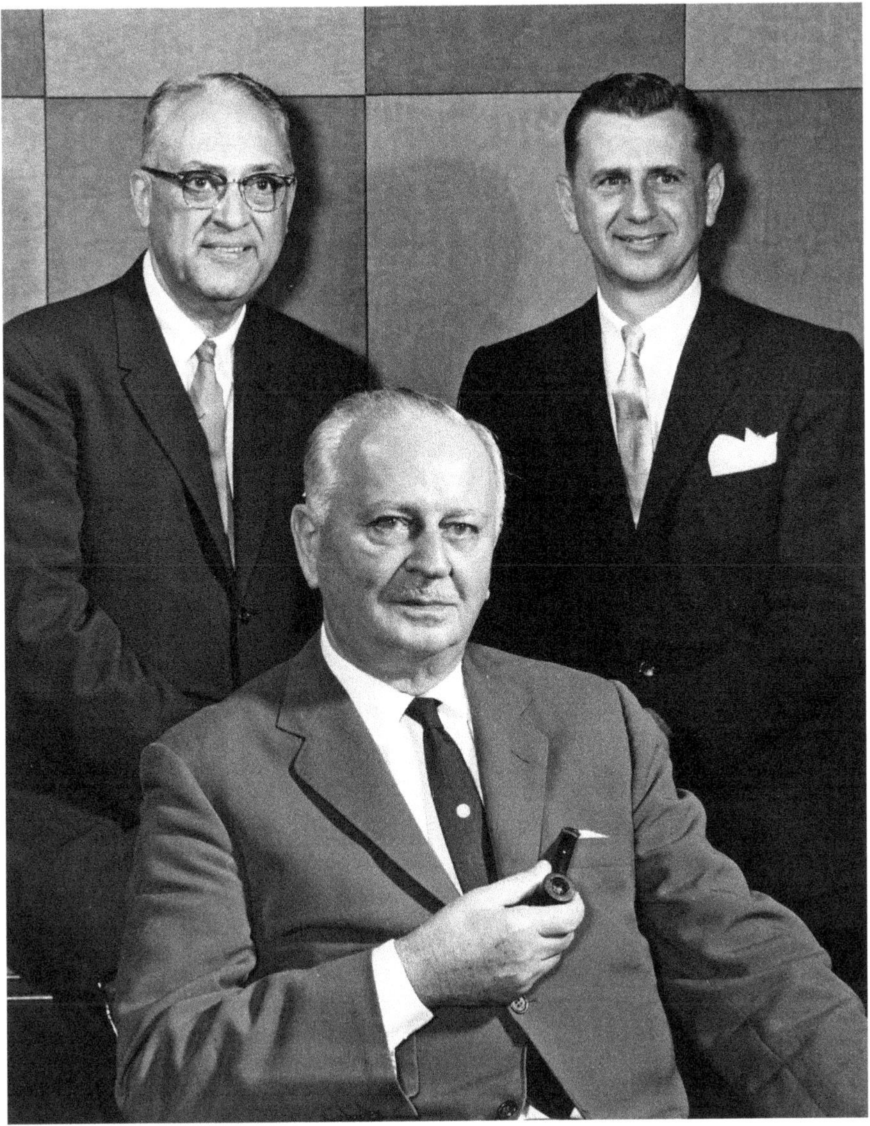

Otto A. Koehler (*sitting*) and Pearl's board of directors. *Pearl LLC Archives.*

for "mental issues." Although there is speculation, the exact reason for the confinement is unknown. Consider that Otto A. Jr. was heir to the Koehler fortune when, in 1969, his mother, Mrs. Otto A. Koehler, obtained a court order upholding her son's confinement. This was after Otto A. himself had passed and prior to the sale to Southdown. Here Otto A. Jr. sat for ten years, until 1974, when he hired an attorney to start a court action to have himself released from the sanitarium, arguing that his confinement had been executed against his will.

His attorney first cited that his client needed more in-hospital freedom and then later sought Otto A. Jr.'s outright release from the hospital. Later, in May 1974, U.S. District Judge Hatfield Chilson ruled that Otto A. Jr. had been given many freedoms when he was transferred from Brady Hospital to Mount Airy Psychiatric Center in Denver, Colorado. It is against Mount Airy that Otto A. Jr.'s suit is filed. It seems Otto A. Jr. had been given open freedoms to wander around, including being allowed to leave Mount Airy for up to two hours at a time. Rumors of Brady Hospital having a habit of confining wealthy people began to surface, and later in 1977, a Senate subcommittee heard allegations regarding the hospital and mistreatment.

Otto A. Jr. would get his freedom from confinement only to go missing. Mrs. Otto A. Koehler then filed a petition to be made conservator of her son's reported $10 million estate. This petition was denied. Otto A. Jr. was found and released six days later, only to die a year later in 1975.

The deal to purchase Pearl Brewing was large enough that it made the newspapers around the country, especially in Texas and Louisiana. The *Monroe News-Star* announced on July 15, 1969, that the board of directors for each company had agreed in principle to a merger of Pearl with Southdown on a tax-free basis, subject to approval. Southdown's board had already approved. The deal worked out well for Pearl's acting president, A.J. Range, who would end up with a seat on Southdown's board, as well as a spot on the College of Engineering Foundation advisory panel at the University of Texas–Austin.

Range indicated that the merger would be good for Pearl, as Southdown also had rice farms in addition to sugar, with rice being a key ingredient to Pearl's recipe and sugar able to be used for Judson Candy Company. Each of the 1,451,476 shares of stock from Pearl would receive 1 share of Southdown preferred stock in return. From there, each of Southdown's preferred shares would receive eight-tenths of a share of Southdown common stock. Each share of Southdown stock would receive a vote toward any matters that came up. A condition of the sale would also allow Pearl stockholders to sell if they wished—and at an exorbitantly high forty-five dollars per share.

The Southdown corporation began as a sugar cane company in the 1930s and later diversified itself into a multitude of other businesses as it reorganized in later decades. In addition to acquiring the Pearl Brewing Company, the Southdown Corporation of Houston also acquired its 179

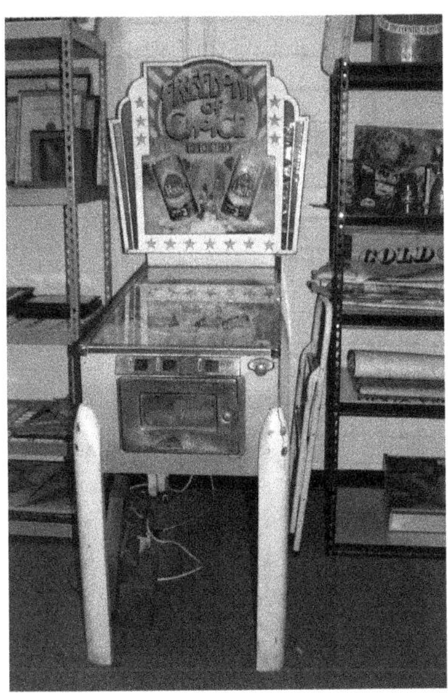

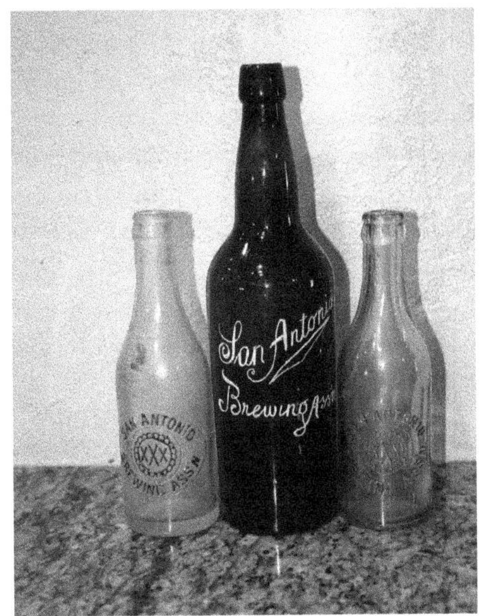

Left: Pearl pinball machine converted sometime in the 1960s. *Jeremy Banas.*

Right: Various San Antonio Brewing Association bottles of XXX Pearl Beer. *Jeremy Banas.*

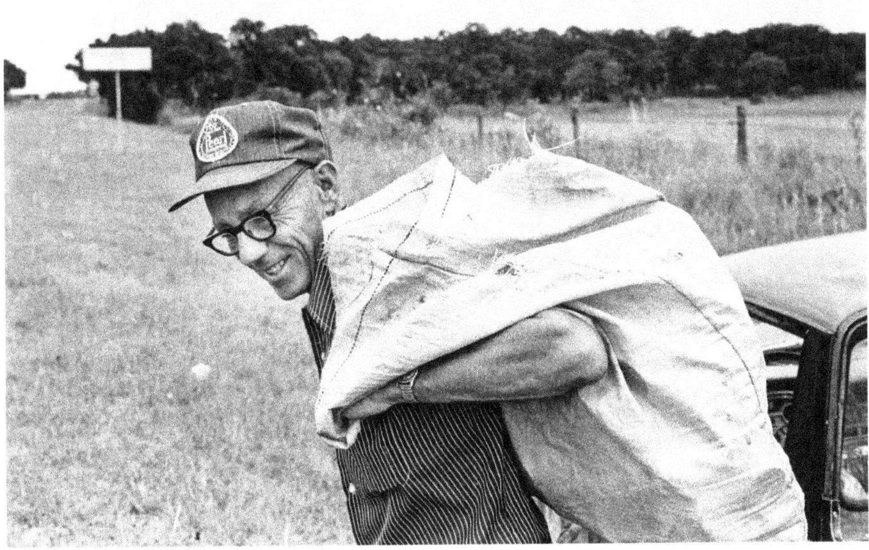

A Pearl recycler smiles while holding a bag of XXX Pearl cans headed to a recycling plant. *Pearl LLC Archives.*

trucks, the Judson Candy Company business, all of Pearl's RC bottling plants and both the Pearl Brewery and the Goetz breweries in St. Joseph.

In 1971, Frank Horlock, who had the largest Pearl distribution center in Houston, Texas, was appointed acting president of the Pearl Brewing Company by Southdown ownership. In the same year, Horlock and Pearl filed suit against Anheuser-Busch and Schlitz for antitrust violations, including selling beer below market cost. Despite all this, the move was pretty good to most. Pearl beer was sold in nine states, and Country Club Malt Liquor was sold in forty-two states and was, in fact, the highest-selling malt liquor in the United States.

In 1972, Lee Birdsong was installed as president of Pearl Brewing, and he would oversee many changes that year. Pearl became the first national sponsor of the Mutual Black Network, purchasing thirteen weeks of one-minute radio spots for Country Club Malt Liquor. The Pearl Coral and Safari

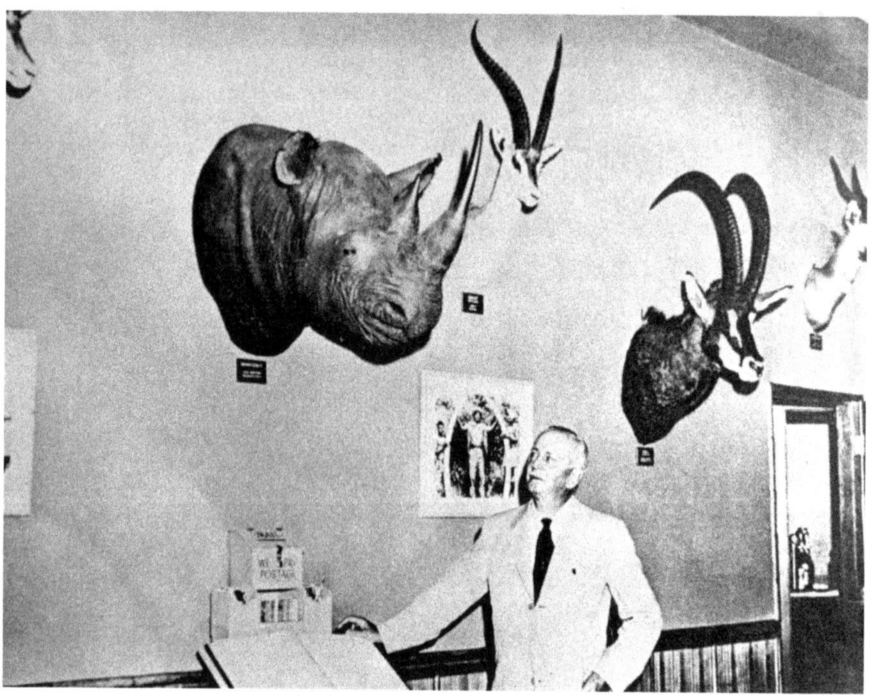

Above: Otto A. in the Safari room. *San Antonio College and the Alamo Colleges District Foundation.*

Opposite, top: Frank Horlock at the press conference for Jersey Lilly. *Pearl LLC Archives.*

Opposite, bottom: Pearl president Horlock (*second from right*) and the Pearl Can Club. *Pearl LLC Archives.*

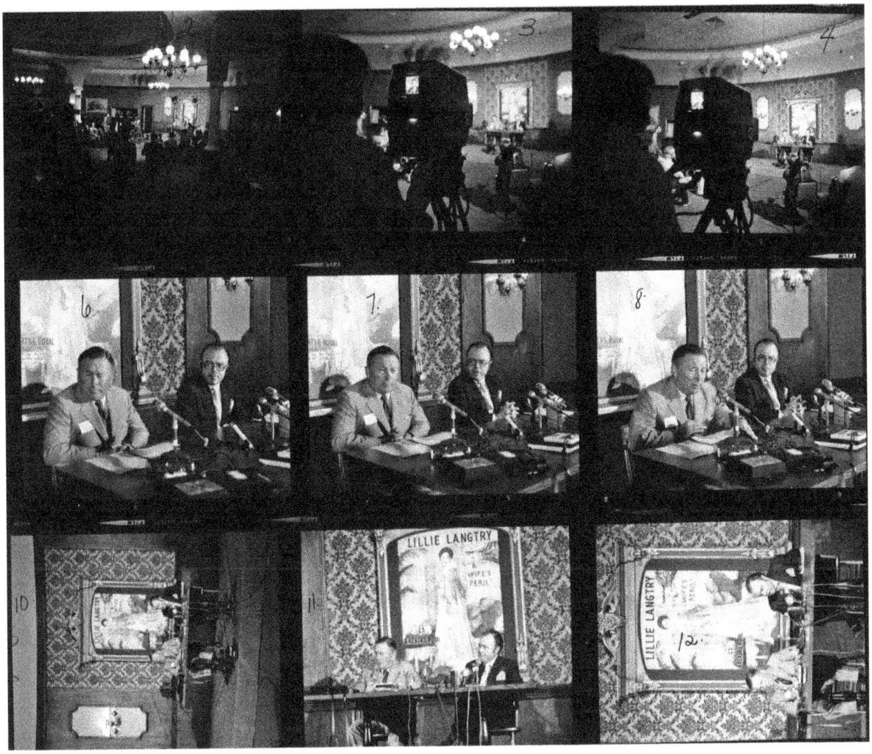

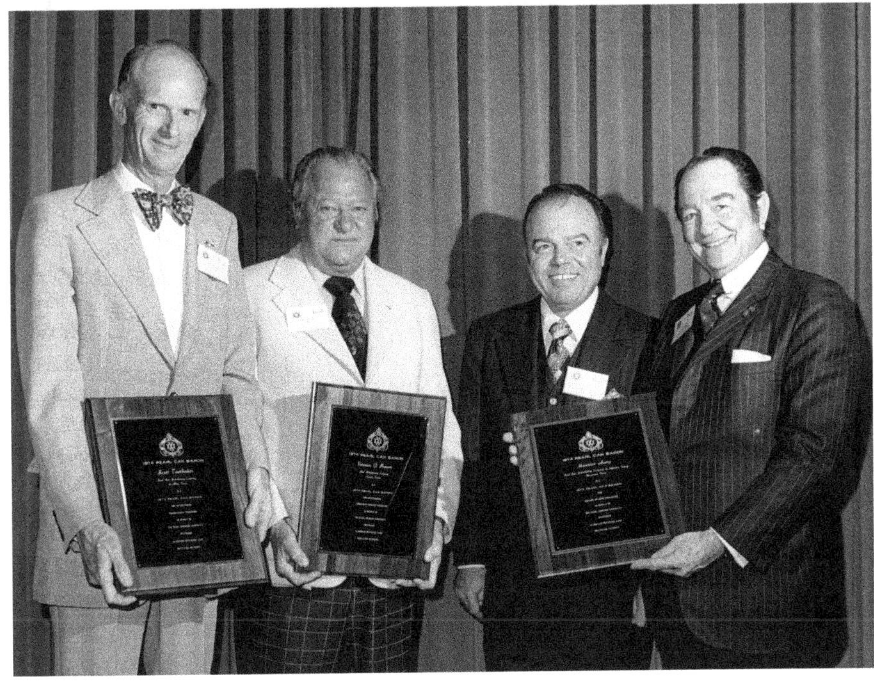

rooms would be renovated as the Jersey Lilly and 1886 rooms, harkening back to Pearl's beginnings. The year 1972 would also see a wooden replica of the Judge Roy Bean Saloon, which would double as the brewery's gift shop, as well as the fourth return of Texas Pride. Pearl Light was introduced for the first time in addition to Kassel Beer, a house brand for local San Antonio Handy Andy grocery stores.

In 1973, Frank Horlock became CEO of Pearl, with Lee Birdsong remaining president. Pearl would also become a major sponsor of the San Antonio Spurs, a new ABA basketball team. Pearl aluminum recycling centers opened, and an extension to the San Antonio River was proposed that would run right behind Pearl. The Pearl would also complete a German beer garden that would serve Pearl Beer to river barge traffic that would come by on the future extension.

PEARL BREWING JOINS THE PABST BREWING FAMILY

The next few years saw little change. Between 1974 and 1976, Pearl bought the Jax Beer brand and formula, opened an aluminum can manufacturing plant and closed the St. Joseph, Missouri brewery. The year 1977 would see a major change for Pearl Brewing with Southdown Inc. divesting itself of Pearl to the General Brewing Company of San Francisco, owned by Paul Kalmanovitz and his S&P Company, which would go on to acquire other brands as well, including Pabst. It would take more than a few attempts for Kalmanovitz to acquire Pabst, as the nation's third-largest brewer resisted for a while.

In the same year that saw an ownership change with the purchase by General Brewing Company, Pearl introduced a few new items. The brewery, now on its second corporate owner, introduced Billy Beer and Pearl Light, which boasted sixty-eight calories, around 50 percent less than regular XXX Pearl Beer. Billy Beer would not prove to be a sound business decision and flopped in production.

In 1979, Lutz E. Issleib was promoted from plant operations manager to executive vice-president and manager of Pearl, ushering the old brewery into its tenth decade. Pearl Brewing would go on to sponsor Boy Scout Explorer Post 840, led by Tom Nichols, the brewery's director of environmental affairs. Issleib would also see the introduction of Pearl Light Genuine Draft and Pearl Cream Ale and see Pearl Light sent to

Mexico, along with the return of Texas Pride, which would see distribution to Saudi Arabia and China.

Lutz Issleib had a bit of the Koehler/Pearl influence when he came on board with the brewery. Issleib's mother, Hertha Koethe Issleib, was niece to Emma Koehler and had come back with her on one of Emma's trips to Germany with an eight-year-old Lutz in tow.

As the company tried desperately to find its identity as a corporate brewery, it would see Pearl Light Genuine Draft and Pearl Cream Ale bomb in the eyes of consumers, almost as if these were merely attempts to take up shelf space—or perhaps they were brewed only for profit and not for the love of it. In fact, outside of records in local papers of various corporate parties and the flop of Select Special 50, the 1980s were rather bland. Upgrades were merely an afterthought during this time, as more money would be spent on advertisements to promote the brewery's products, including an ill-fated Pearl Light roller derby–style television ad.

Another poorly conceived idea to save money was the "leaking beer keg" policy. At times, Pearl allowed distributors to return unused leaking kegs to Pearl, with the beer then sucked out of the kegs and put back into storage tanks to be reused. Although it was not a formal policy, such a practice would prove to hurt Pearl's long-standing reputation for good quality.

Despite the failure of several other advertising campaigns, as well as newly introduced beers, one marketing campaign and one new beer saw fairly large success. Capitalizing on the popularity of the evening soap opera *Dallas*, Pearl Brewing created J.R. Ewing's Private Stock, a beer that was marketed to those who either identified with or appreciated the sneaky and conniving J.R. Ewing character himself. In 1980, when the campaign was in full swing, the brewery claimed to have orders for more than 500,000 cases of the beer, which was already available in many parts of the country.

Pearl vice-president Frank Spinosa gave the quote that defined corporate Pearl: "People today buy an image, not a beer, but a lot of people like a lot of JR's image, a man will buy J.R. Ewing's Private Stock because it says a lot about him without even opening his mouth." J.R. Ewing's Private Stock's packaging was even a gimmick, placed in what were known as six-shooter six-packs, with twelve-ounce cans that featured a western-style belt. Advertising even featured a quote from J.R. Ewing himself: "If you have to ask how much my beer costs, you probably can't afford it."

This carefree and relaxed attitude even extended to many brewery employees. Drinking among employees who worked on the canning line or cleaned the tanks was not uncommon. "Some of the employees even had their own mugs that they would bring to fill up throughout the day," said Grant Wood, current head brewer for Revolver Brewing in the Dallas area. Wood was a Pearl plant employee and brewer from 1985 to 1989 before leaving for the Lone Star Brewing Company.

Grant Wood originally interviewed for a position at the brewery, a lab position as microbiologist. Prior to that, he had been working at Vandewalle farms doing odd jobs. At Pearl, Ed Robby, who was head of quality control at the time, hired Wood. Two years later, plant manager Ed Mueller sent him to brewing school at the Siebel Institute in Chicago, with Wood returning to Pearl as a third-shift brewer.

Wood was in charge of tank analysis, package approval and approval for brewing. "I worked with a bunch of old Germans at the brewery," said Wood, "guys who had already been there for decades. I remember one guy would come in early around four in the morning, clean four tanks and then head home." Wood also described one employee, Howell Parker, who hand-cleaned the tanks by crawling into them despite tales of hauntings in those tanks and the brewery itself, including from an old brewer. There were areas in G cellar that would lend one to think they were haunted, with odd noises and shadows spooking employees.

Wood also described Pearl as one heck of an interesting old brewery. It still employed a cereal cooker, and its mash tun was undersized. It employed direct steam injection with two lauter tuns, a copper kettle and stainless steel kettles. Grits and malt were used in the recipe, along with corn syrup and six-row malt. Pearl yeast was mixed from three different strains, but it was a stable mixture. The original Pearl strain had been used from the very beginning in 1886, although it died out a few years before the Pabst purchase of Pearl, at which point it switched to Pabst yeast.

Wood noted that they were still using the recipe brought back from Germany by Otto Koehler, but things changed after Prohibition. Many breweries, including Pearl, were looking for ways to produce cheaper and lighter beer. It was a specific corn syrup that it used, a high maltose corn syrup that mimicked the sugar profile of malt. During this time, it ran waste beer through the vacuum still that was built just outside the brewhouse, sometimes selling the alcohol or using the base for near beer.

In the early '80s, Pearl had as many as 535 employees and introduced just shy of 2 million barrels of beer that were available in forty-five states, lending Pabst use of the San Antonio brewery for many of its other brands. By 1985, Kalmanovitz had consolidated his holdings as the Pabst Brewing Company, making him the fourth-largest brewer in the United States.

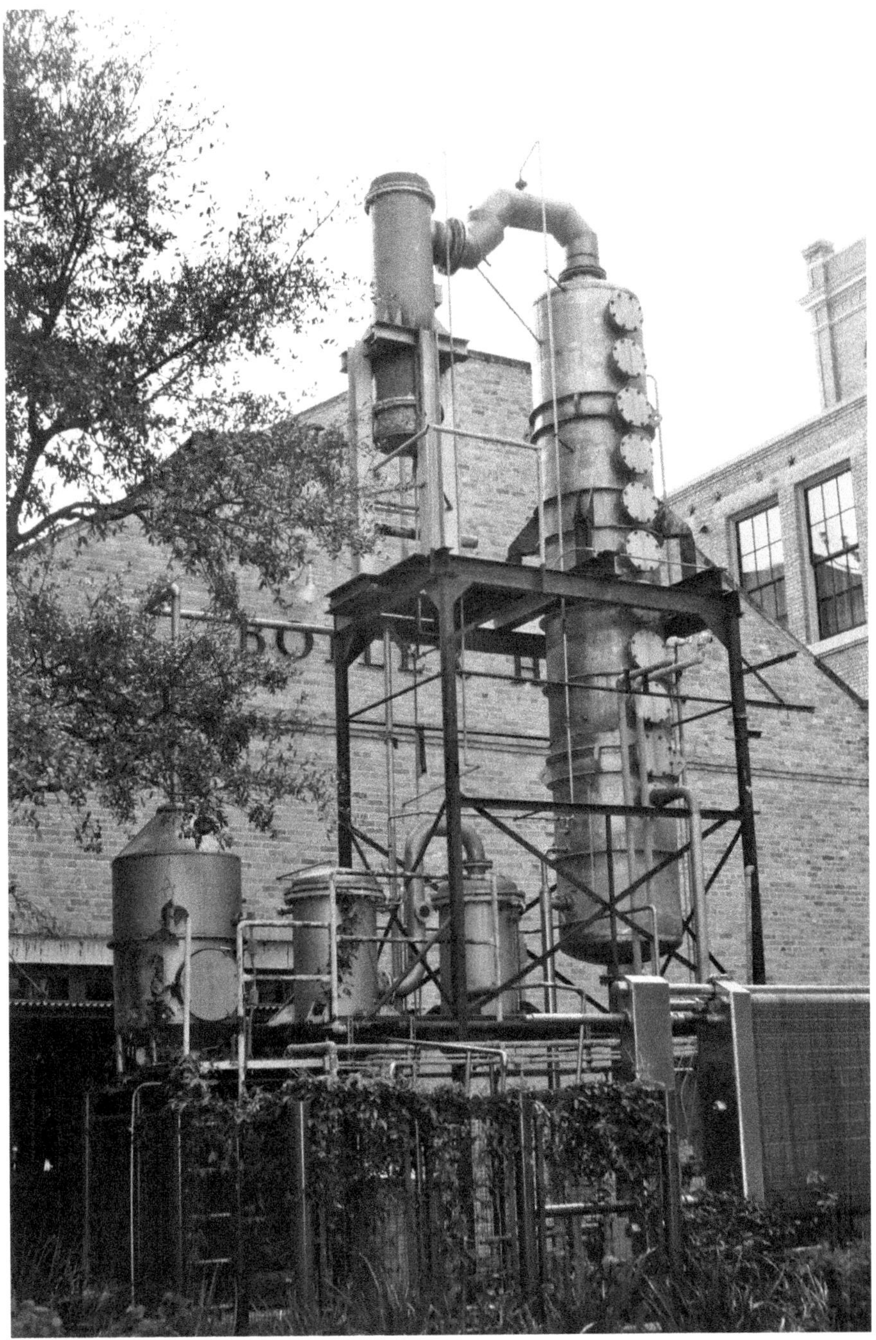

Close-up of the Pearl still. *Jeremy Banas.*

PEARL STRUGGLES TO KEEP UP WITH THE JONESES

In about 1990, competition increased, with large brewers and many business practices in the process of changing. Many of the breweries that Kalmanovitz had acquired over the years were not able to keep up, whether due to lack of upgrades or lack of care. Kalmanovitz passed away in 1987, and his company was put into a trust. This trust was definitely not going to spend money on any improvements. Problems were manifesting, and employees who were part of the Teamsters Union Local 1110 decided to take a four-dollar-per-hour pay cut in order to keep the brewery going. By the mid-1990s, Pearl was producing barely over 1 million barrels, around the same number it did in the 1950s.

With Kalmanovitz's other consolidations, including purchases of brands such as Rainier, Olympia, Schlitz and Lone Star, by 1999 the Pearl Brewery was the only site left open that was still brewing brands owned by Pabst, while all others were brewed at various Miller plants around the country. Lone Star returned to its brewing roots in San Antonio at the same time, thus bringing this icon back—labels would include the phrase "Certified brewed in San Antonio." In early 2000, Pabst Brewing officials announced that they would close the Pearl Brewery—just before the city's famous ten-day celebration known as Fiesta—with Pabst officials advising that the closure meant a loss of almost three hundred jobs by June 2000.

Pearl union members even offered management a pay and benefits freeze for two years, showing just how much love these employees had for the brewery that had been their home for decades. Unfortunately, the offer was rejected, and CEO Bill Biting advised that although they appreciated the gesture of a wage and benefit freeze, it was not going to be enough. In April 2000, Pearl executives met with union leaders to discuss the closure. Biting again rejected trying to save the brewery, stating that the overhead to keep the brewery running was just too much. Production of Pearl, Lone Star and even Pabst itself and its other brands was to be contract-brewed by Miller Brewing in Fort Worth.

These changes were hard on the employees, many of whom had been there for decades. "The brewers had their own personalities that carried over to their work ethic, as well as the character and personality of Pearl Brewing Company," said Bill Jones, who was Pearl's last brewmaster from 1984 until its closing in 2001.

Although the Kalmanovitz purchase of Pearl in 1977 did much to bring Pearl back to a focus on its brewing operations, first by the divesting itself of its other businesses and breweries, Kalmanovitz also kept tight control of any money. A lack of upgrades to the brewery was only part of it. Money spent on advertising dropped as well, leading Pearl to have difficulty keeping up locally and nationally with Anheuser-Busch, Miller and Coors. In many ways, it is almost as if it liked the idea of owning breweries but cared nothing for the history and traditions of these breweries. This approach did not sit well with many Pearl employees. Pearl employee David Mahaffey was not about to let a possible closing stop him from putting out the best product he could. "Until the last day we're producing a product, we'll put out the best quality we can because we take pride in our jobs. We make the best beer in the world right here. We want to keep the place open," Mahaffey said with passion.

Pearl employees even made a bid to buy the brewery that had been such a large part of their lives and that of San Antonio. The famed Teamsters Local 1110 made a bid to purchase the brewery using money from its national pension fund, the national union and traditional financing.

Pabst executives and the union came to a deal in May 2000 to keep the brewery open another three years with 50 employees and production dropping to 500,000 barrels. On June 30, 2000, more than 260 Pearl employees walked out of the brewery gates, never to return. After these layoffs, Pabst officials advised the remaining employees, all 80 of them, that production would move completely to Miller Brewing in Fort Worth by April 2001, almost raising a finger to the three-year deal with the union. What began in 1886 with a takeover of City Brewery and evolved into 115 years of grand brewing tradition simply faded into the history books. Throughout its history, Pearl had a lot of drama but also a lot of love, tradition and involvement in San Antonio's history.

With Pabst having already moved its headquarters from Milwaukee to San Antonio a few years earlier, it maintained its headquarters in the former Pearl administration building for at least a few more years. By 2005, Pabst had moved its headquarters closer to Chicago, wanting to be closer to its old-style beer brand, although the company still maintains a small office in San Antonio. These days, a Russian American with ties to Russian investment funds owns Pabst. Pearl is still brewed to this day, although Pearl and Pearl Light are brewed in much smaller quantities at the Miller Brewing's Fort Worth brewery.

The grounds lay abandoned and were in great disrepair for almost a year before they were put up for sale. For those who were able to attend a public auction of Pearl equipment, it was as if those last days of Pearl were held in suspension, almost frozen in time. It was as if everyone who worked there

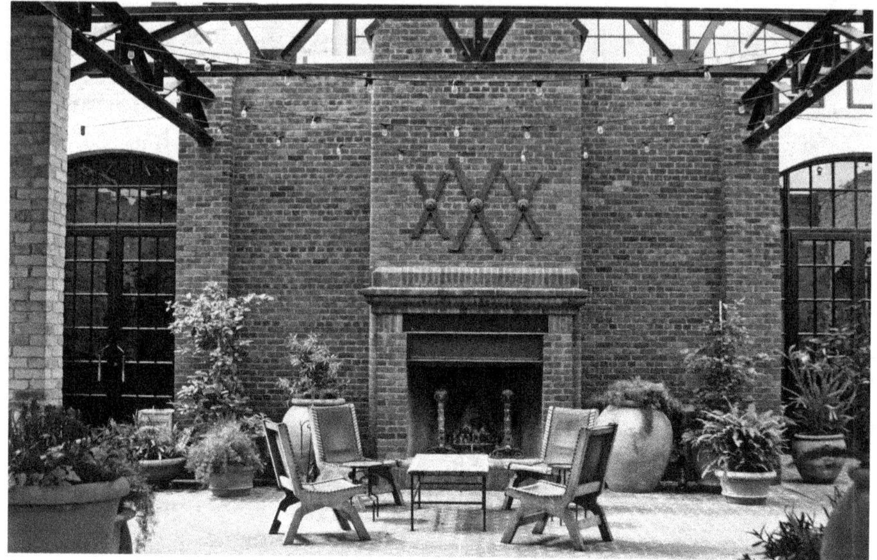

The XXX adorns the fireplace at the entrance of the Hotel Emma. *Jeremy Banas.*

on the last day just got up and left, taking nothing with them. Said Silver Ventures in a recent case study, "All of the brewing equipment, much of it original, was in place. Laboratory equipment sat on tables, ready for use. The advertising warehouse was stocked with promo materials, both current and past. The administrative offices were fully furnished, with file cabinets housing reams of records dating back to the early 1900s. Historic photos and memorabilia were stored and protected, including hand-drawn ink-on-silk architectural drawings from the 1800s." Brad Farbstein, owner of Real Ale Brewing in Blanco, Texas, remembered the auction. "People were running all over the place grabbing whatever they could find," said Farbstein. Farbstein himself picked up many nuts and bolts that he later incorporated into his own brewing equipment, although some of his Pearl finds were incorporated as handles in the bathrooms at the Real Ale taproom.

In 2002, local businessman Christopher "Kit" Goldsbury purchased the property through his Silver Ventures development company. Goldsbury had the vision to turn the Pearl grounds into a mixed-use development, restoring the area to prominence. This vision has been realized, as the Pearl is now home to many companies, nonprofit organizations, restaurants, bookstores, the Culinary Institute of America and the iconic brewhouse itself, which is being developed into Southerleigh Fine Food and Brewery and the Hotel Emma, rated the third-best hotel in the world.

PERIOD VI

THE NEW PEARL, 2002–2017

PEARL RISES FROM THE ASHES

In most redevelopment communities, an abandoned property such as the Pearl was not an attractive prospect. It's very risky to even think of trying to make something of it. On one hand, the facility sat at the crossroads of two highways, was adjacent to a soon-to-be-revitalized Broadway Street, served as a bridge between downtown San Antonio and affluent areas such as Alamo Heights and bordered an unimproved area of the San Antonio Riverwalk. The iconic and historical buildings of the facility were intact as well, despite some needed renovations. In so many ways, this property was bursting at the seams with possibilities, although it was going to take someone unconventional to step up or the facility would likely fade away as fast as a Texas thunderstorm.

The area around the Pearl complex was overrun with crime, including assault, murder and prostitution. The unimproved area of the rivers was overgrown and served as a hangout for those with no homes. The groundwater itself was tainted by a nearby fuel storage leak, not to mention there was a large amount of asbestos and lead on the site.

The grounds stayed closed and abandoned for all intents and purposes until 2002, when local resident Christopher "Kit" Goldsbury purchased land as well as all of the buildings. He has repurposed this regional brewery facility with its thirty-six original buildings, measuring 500,000 square feet

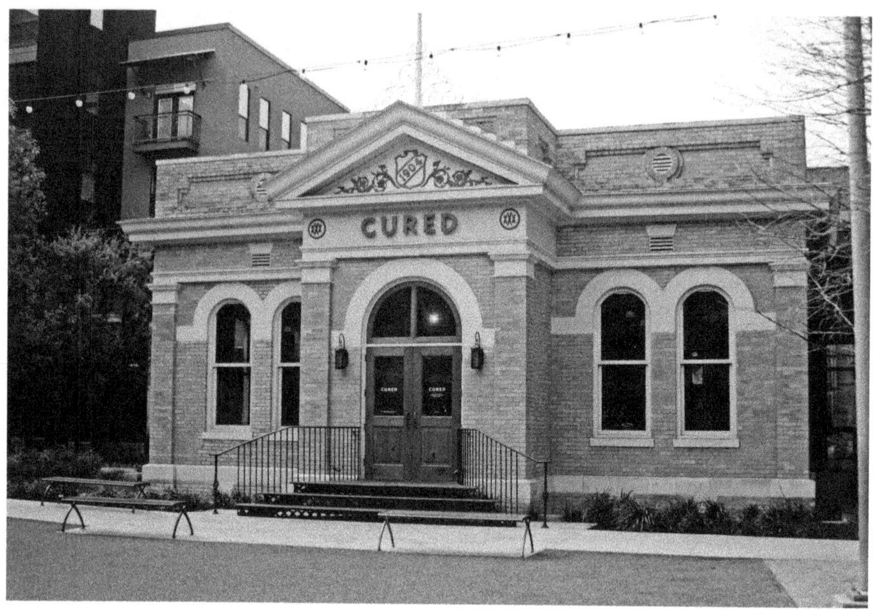

Cured at Pearl, a Chef Steve McHugh–led restaurant, now resides in the former Pearl administration building. *Jeremy Banas.*

over twenty-one acres, into a mixed-use complex. Goldsbury was known to most as the former owner of Pace Foods, beginning his career there soon after high school. He married owner and founder David Pace's daughter, Linda Pace, and began to work at Pace. Goldsbury quickly moved up in the company and proved that he had a head for business, helping build Pace Foods into a multimillion-dollar company that dominated the condiments market. After a time, Goldsbury and Linda purchased Pace Foods from David Pace and expanded the company even more. In the early 1990s, Goldsbury and Linda parted ways, with Goldsbury buying out Linda's shares. By 1995, Goldsbury had sold Pace Foods, makers of Pace Picante Sauce, to Campbell Foods, netting him $1 billion and making him San Antonio's first billionaire at the time. Goldsbury used the proceeds from the sale to form a new company, Silver Ventures, through which the purchase of the Pearl property was made possible.

Goldsbury had been looking around town for many investment opportunities and settled on the Pearl facility. Purchasing the complex and its buildings, along with any items still in the brewery, as well as intellectual property such as names and previous charters, Goldsbury has invested quite a lot of funds into developing the New Pearl into what it is today. Pabst

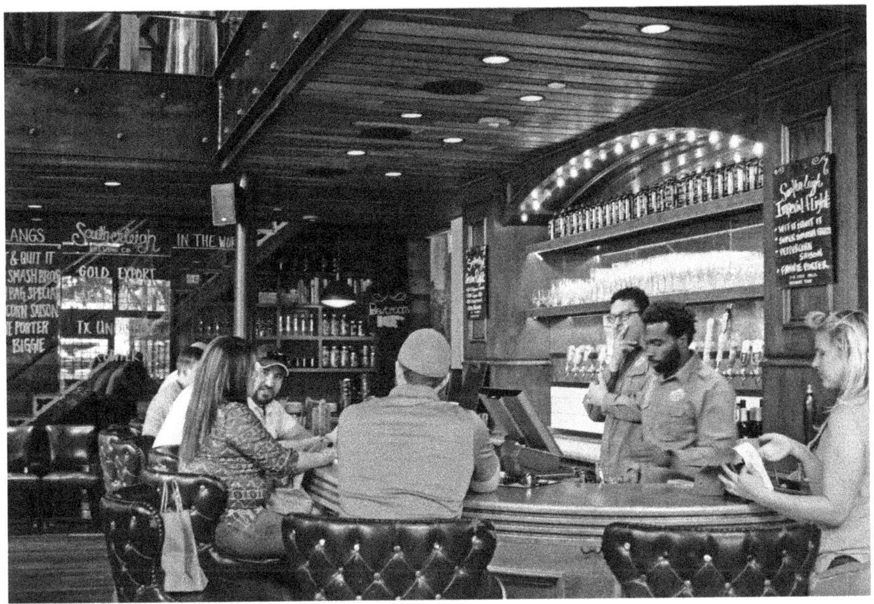

Thirsty San Antonians enjoy Southerleigh's wares at its bar. *Jeremy Banas.*

retains ownership of the Pearl brand itself, though. The growth has been slow and well thought out, allowing for success and honoring the history of the Pearl. Today, there are numerous shops, restaurants, apartments and nonprofit organizations that take up residence at the Pearl facility.

Ironically enough, Goldsbury's former spouse, Linda, and her brother, Dr. Paul Pace, are descended from the Koehler family themselves, with a direct line to Otto and Emma. Linda's mother, Margaret Emma Bosshardt (later Margaret Pace Willson), was the daughter of Anna Juliana Adelheid Hedwig, a niece to Otto and Emma Koehler. Frank Bosshardt, Margaret's father and a local attorney, also worked at the brewery and was part of Emma Koehler's inner circle during her run of the brewery. As a young girl, Anna lived with Otto and Emma, a tradition that would extend to Margaret, who spent much of her childhood around her Great-Aunt Emma. Both Linda and Dr. Pace also spent time at the Koehler mansion, getting to know the second Otto, Otto A. Koehler, and spending many holidays there. The irony lies in that Goldsbury eventually purchased that which Linda's family used to own.

To realize this vision for the Pearl would take Kit Goldsbury and Silver Ventures a lot of planning, commitment and money. Silver Ventures had

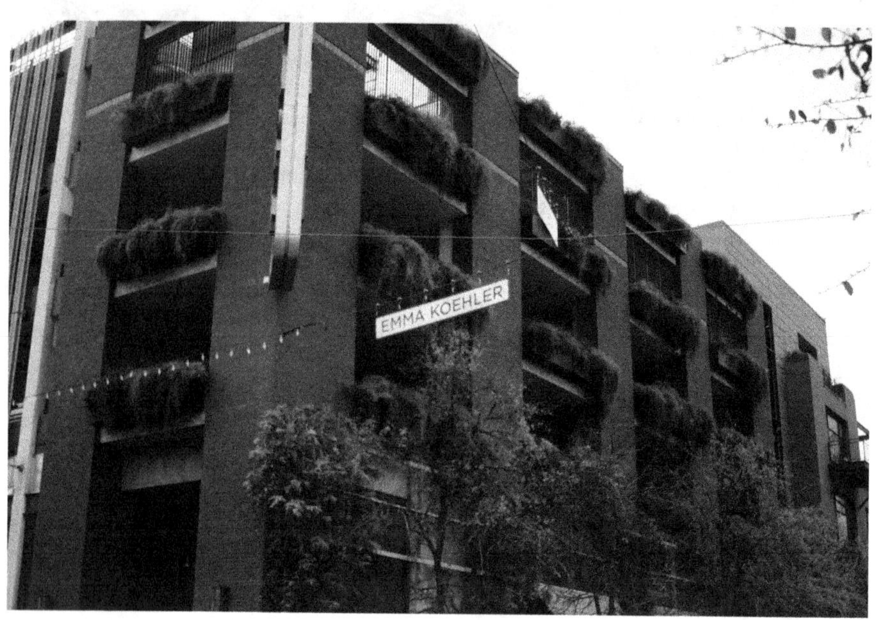

The Koehler garage at the Pearl complex. *Jeremy Banas.*

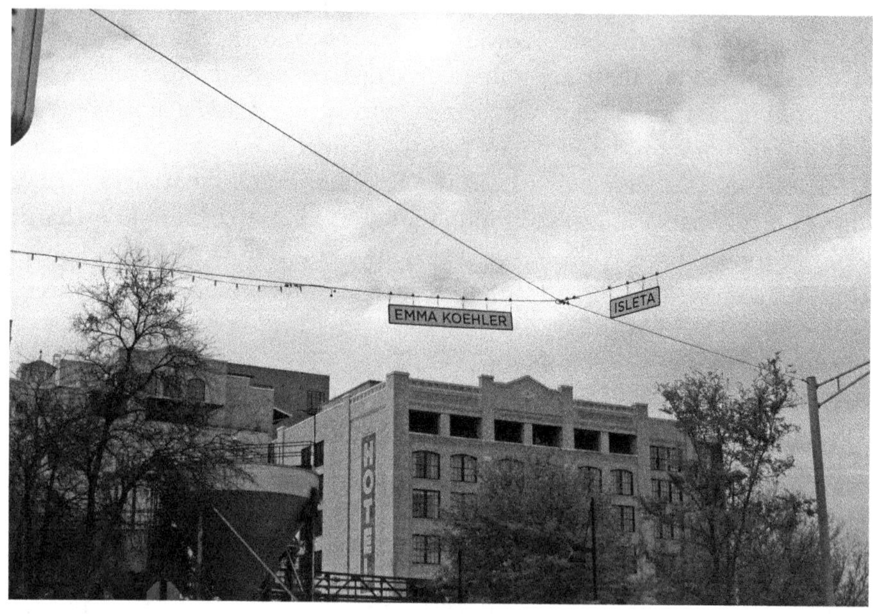

Emma Koehler Street at the Pearl complex. *Jeremy Banas.*

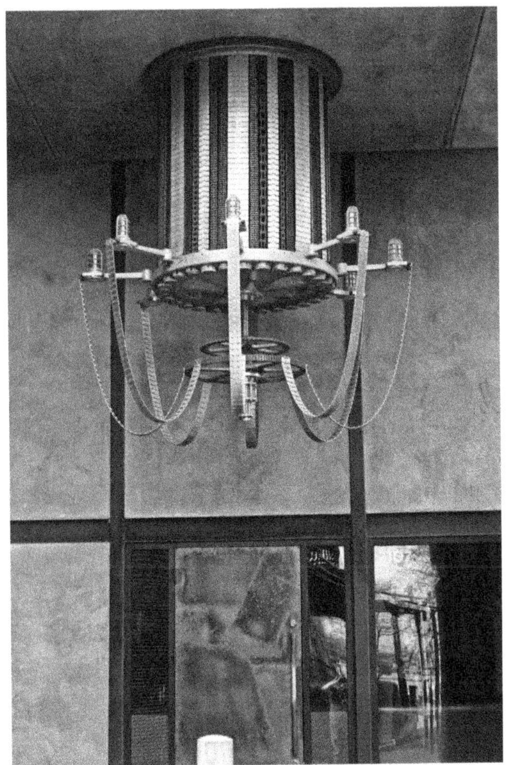

Left: Canning equipment chandelier. *Jeremy Banas*.

Below: Hotel Emma and the Pearl Brewhouse, forever linked. *Jeremy Banas*.

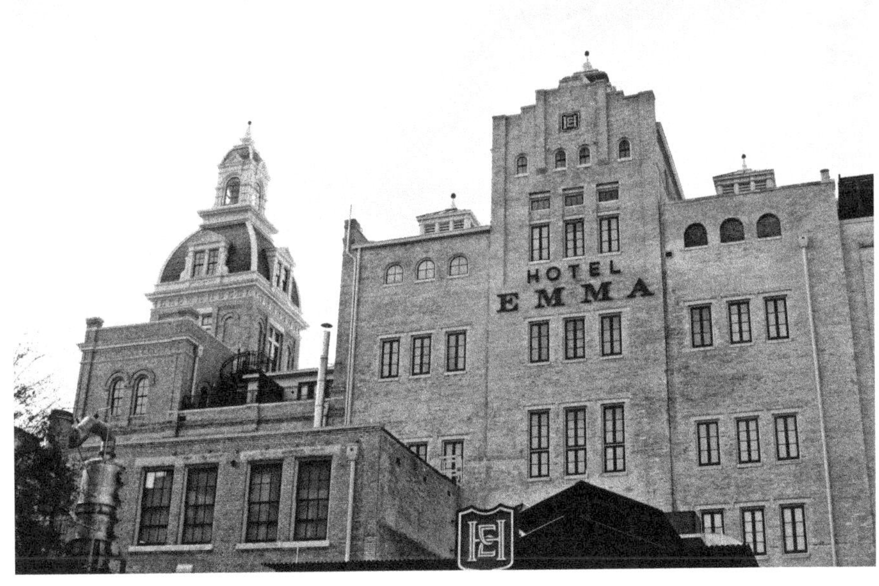

started out investing in area real estate, and there was no branch of the company established to handle the redevelopment of properties. That did not seem to stop Goldsbury from seeing what others did not: an opportunity to protect a historic and iconic complex that gave the city part of its identity and bring it back to life with an eye on the past, as well as the future, even if he was not sure at the time what exactly he would do with the property.

Once purchased, Goldsbury and his team at Silver Ventures set out to develop their vision for the future of the complex. First, though, they would need to rifle through all of the buildings, equipment, papers and the like to see what could be done away with and what was historically important enough to keep and use in the redevelopment. The contents that would be kept were moved to warehouses for safekeeping. Contractors were hired to remove the tanks and other brewing equipment from the brewhouse and adjacent buildings. The asbestos and lead were cleaned up, and Silver Ventures partnered with the city to install new drainage systems that took them out of the floodplain.

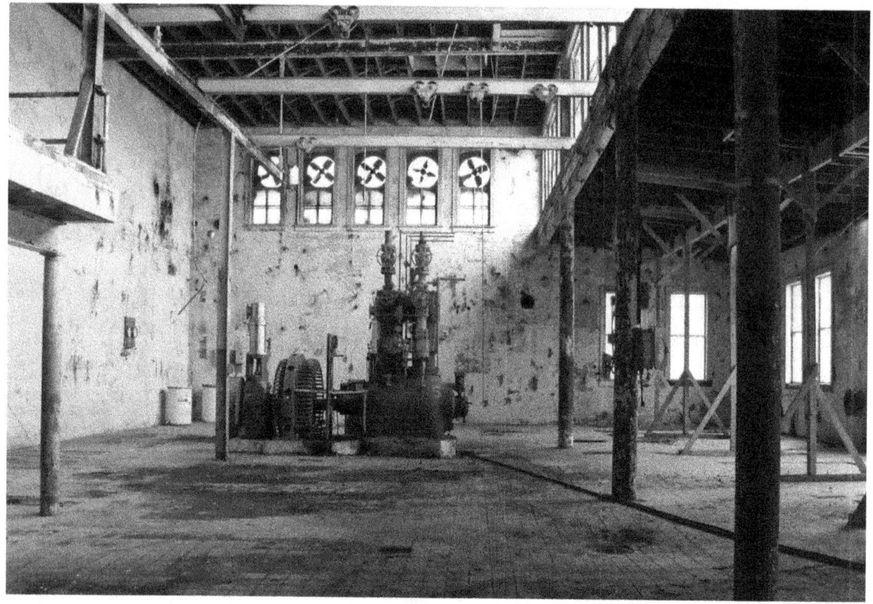

Above: Renovation of the Pearl Brewhouse interior, 2007. *Jeff Trei.*

Opposite, top: Getting a makeover, the brewhouse interior is almost ready, 2007. *Jeff Trei.*

Opposite, bottom: These old valves stand ready for someone to use them once more, 2007. *Jeff Trei.*

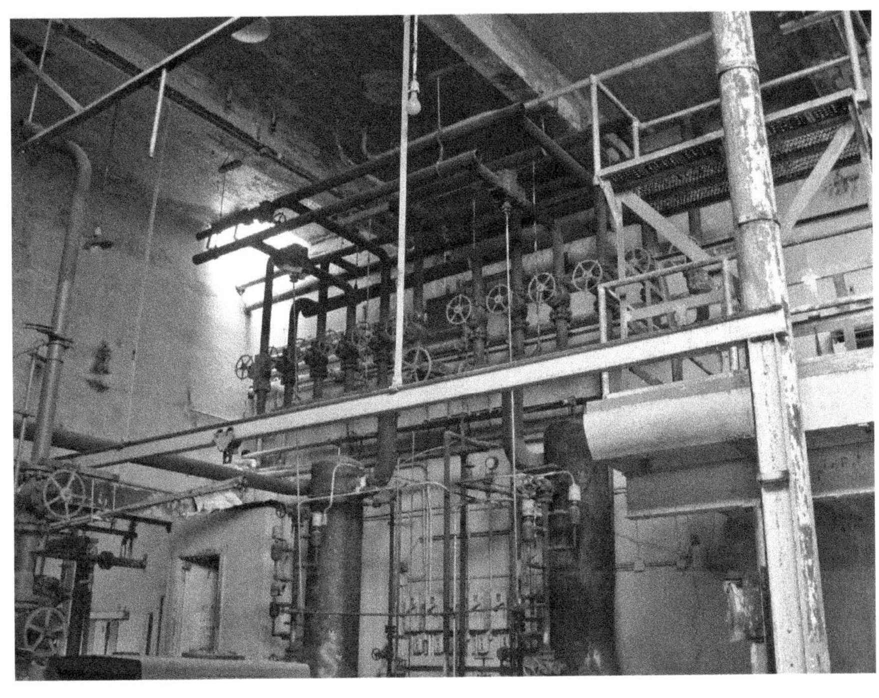

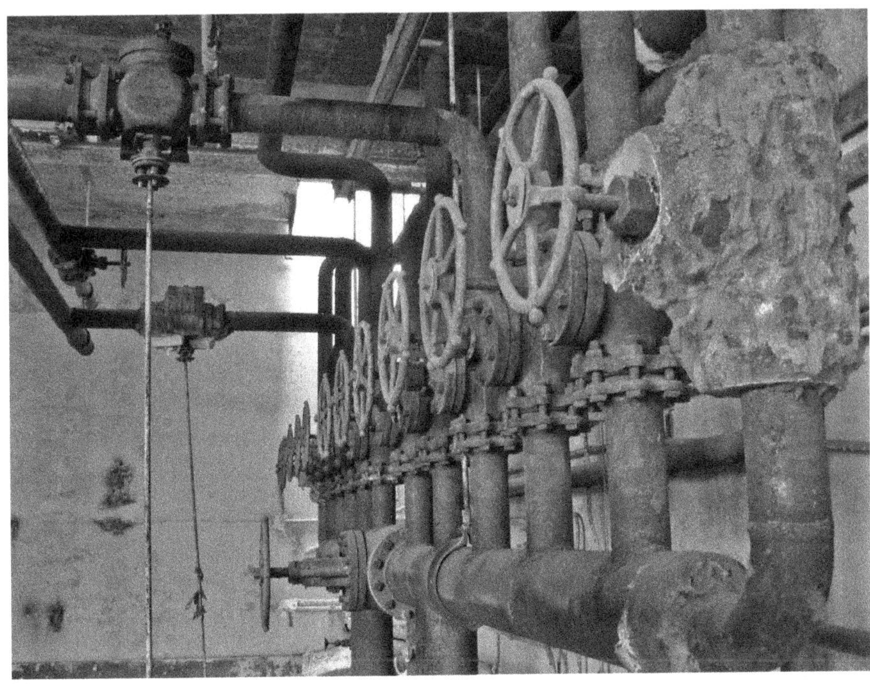

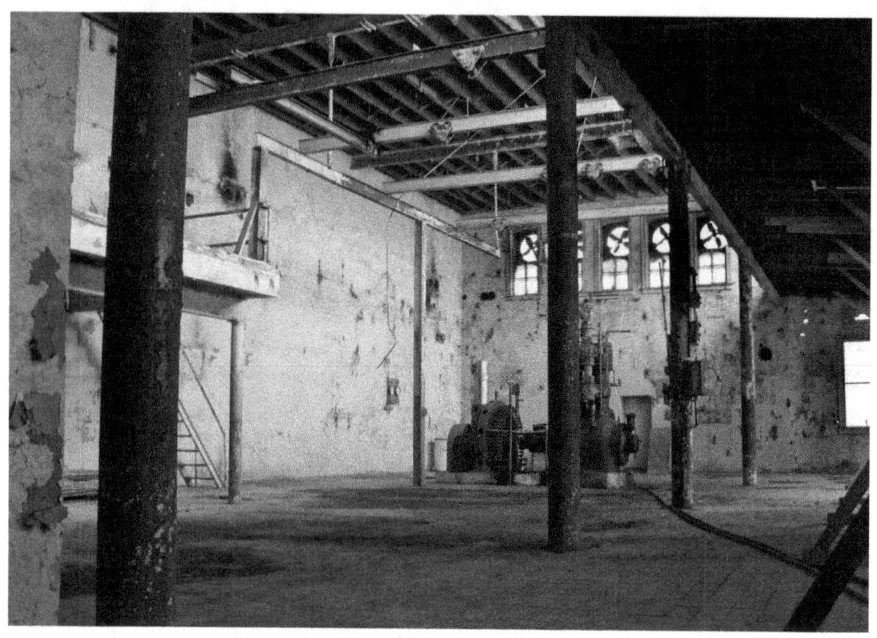

A section of the brewhouse that would become Southerleigh Brewing, 2007. *Jeff Trei.*

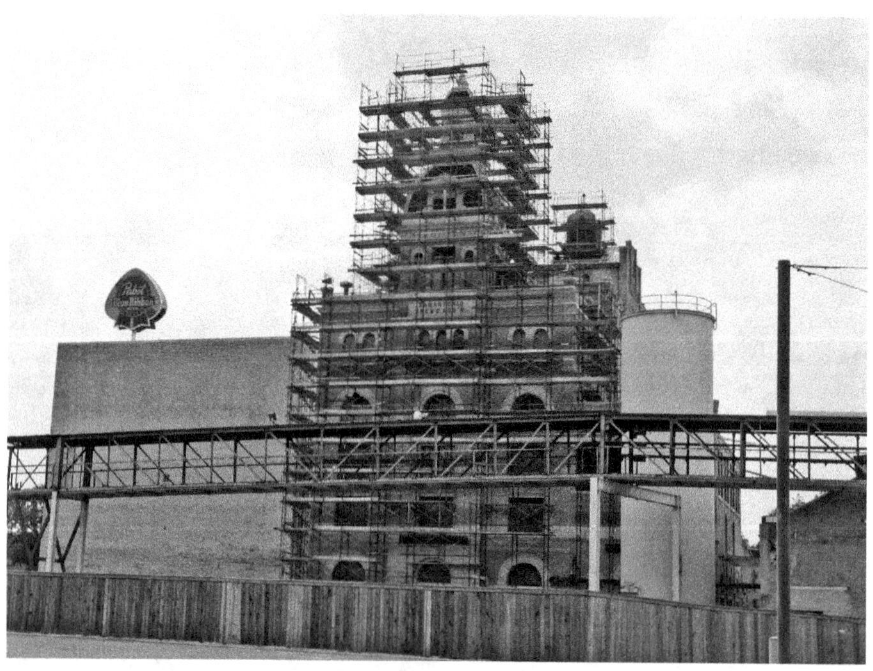

Restoration of the brewhouse exterior, 2007. *Jeff Trei.*

During the three years that this cleanup would take, Silver Ventures began to formulate its vision for the Pearl complex. In 2002, several developers and urban designers with experience in similar projects got together with Goldsbury and Silver Ventures to hammer out a plan. That plan would entail integrating the Pearl back into the community and turning it into a place where the community could once again gather. These brainstorming sessions produced a very specific framework and guidelines for the project. The Silver Ventures case study reflects that the complex would need to "be a primary gathering place for San Antonians; with a focus on local talent—chefs, retailers, designers, architects, artists, craftsmen and businesses; it must preserve and celebrate Pearl's history and attention to detail in all aspects of the endeavor—built environment, tenants, operations, etc.; and let food be central to the entire undertaking and raise the local level of culinary awareness and excellence."

PEARL REBIRTH GETS MORE ROBUST

Silver Ventures has approached every aspect of the redevelopment by keeping its core goals in mind, from building design to function and its impact on the community, although market constraints were still taken into consideration. Once the vision was solidified, architects, contractors and the like were brought in to get the party started, and only those with a proven track record were used in the initial development and every single one afterward. From the Can Plant apartments to the recent purchase of the nearby Fox Motel, Silver Ventures has had a plan for everything.

As the development of the complex began to take shape, the year 2004 saw the New Pearl's first tenant move in. Silver Ventures coaxed Minnesota-based Aveda into establishing its San Antonio Institute at the Pearl, just a few hundred feet from the Pearl Brewhouse. Although this marriage would last only eight years, Aveda moved its school into the building that had previously housed the Pearl Brewery's garage, built in 1939. Today, it is home to the Iron Yard, a computer coding school.

Not long after Aveda moved in, more tenants arrived. Il Sogno, a modern take on Italian cuisine, and Sandbar, a seafood restaurant, arrived with great expectations. Since then, more have moved in as new buildings were erected to house businesses that aligned with Silver Ventures' vision of protecting history while creating an entirely new identity. The old Pearl Administration

Building was refurbished and modernized and is now home to Cured, a restaurant owned by Chef Steve McHugh. The old building that housed the boilers for the brewery was reborn as the trendy Boiler House restaurant and is adjacent to the brewhouse building.

In 2009, Pearl launched a year-round farmers' market, the first such market in the San Antonio area, and it now operates twice a week, on Saturdays and Sundays. In 2010, the famed Culinary Institute of America opened its third campus at the Pearl, bringing students from around San Antonio and the world to attend. From there, the progression continued with the opening of the Park at the Pearl in 2011, a one-thousand-person-capacity amphitheater devoted to art, music and family events on Sundays, as well as a park next to the brewhouse complete with a geyser aptly named "Gustav's Geysers" after the late brewer, continuing to bring about Silver Ventures' vision of the Pearl becoming a community center once again. Helping with this community spirit was the introduction of bike sharing in San Antonio. The popular bike share company B-Cycle installed locations around San Antonio, with the station at the Pearl being one of its busiest.

What the New Pearl was missing was the thing that launched its history all those decades ago: brewing. This was one of the main goals for Goldsbury and Silver Ventures when the Pearl revitalization began a decade previously. The answer to this would not be far away. Brothers Tim and Alex Rattray came to the rescue with their idea for a barbecue-themed brewpub on the Pearl grounds. After being shown several properties as possibilities by Silver Ventures, the Rattray brothers settled on a quite historic location. What became known as the Granary 'Cue and Brew opened in November 2012 in the former home of Ernest Charles Mueller, who arrived in 1890 from Germany to take over as chief cooper at the San Antonio Brewing Association. Mueller had come to San Antonio by way of St. Louis, Missouri, where he worked as a cooper for Anheuser-Busch alongside Ignatz Hrovat. After Hrovat moved to San Antonio and became brewmaster at the San Antonio Brewing Association, he convinced his friend Mueller to follow him.

The home stayed in the Mueller family until 2004, when it was sold to Silver Ventures and the Pearl LLC. Fast-forward almost a decade and the Rattray brothers were bringing brewing back to the Pearl for the first time since 2001. The Granary became a massive part of the effort to revitalize the Pearl and this historic area of San Antonio. Chef Tim Rattray was no stranger to restaurants, having been involved in the Pearl's first two restaurants, Il Sogno and the Sandbar. His brother, Alex, who gained a deep

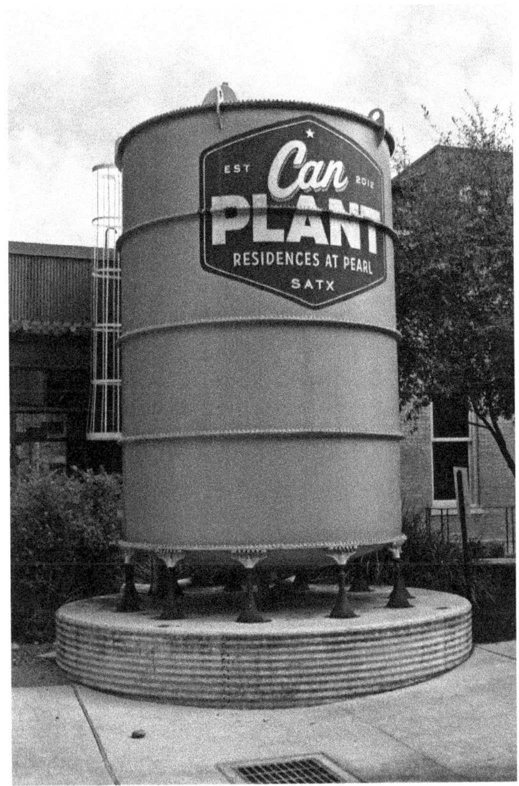

Left: Can Plant apartments at the New Pearl complex. *Jeremy Banas*.

Below: B-Cycle station provides locals and visitors to the Pearl an option to get around the area. *Jeremy Banas*.

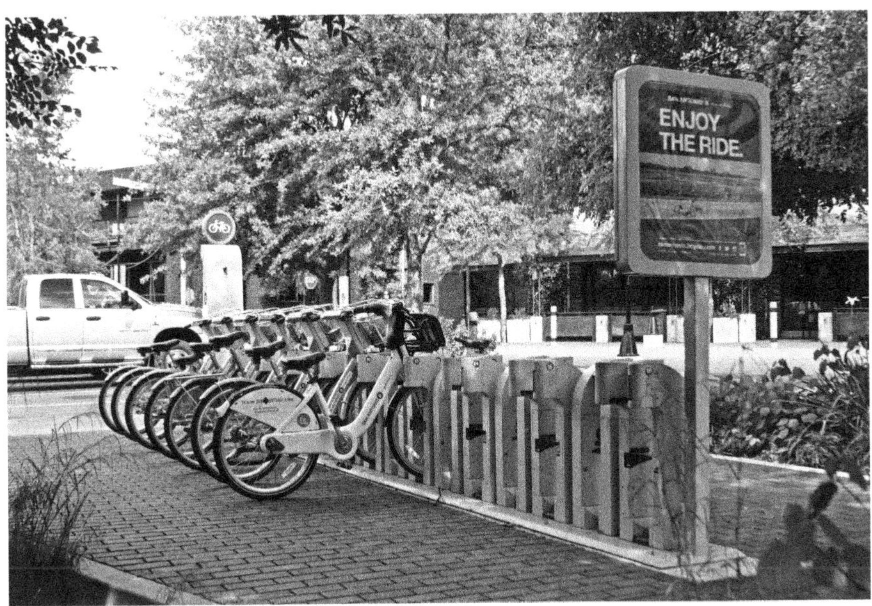

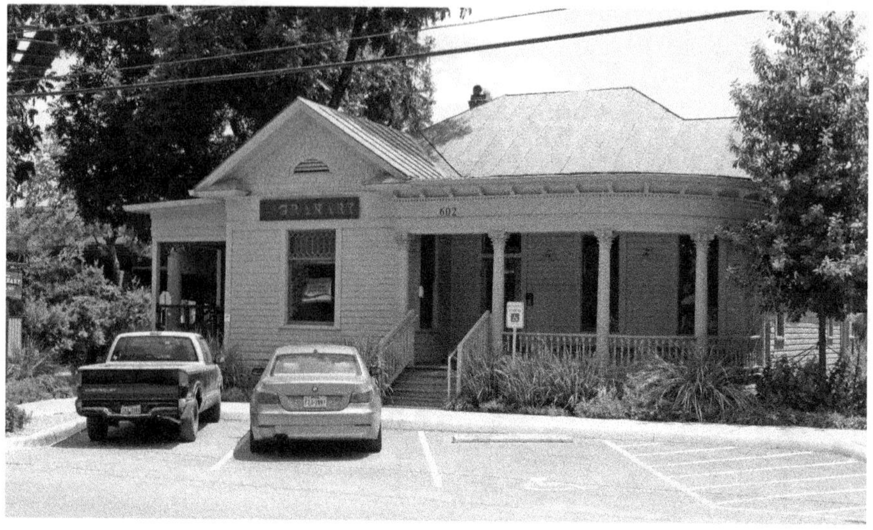

The Granary 'Cue and Brew. *Jeremy Banas.*

love of brewing after spending time in England, had begun homebrewing several years earlier and set out to master his craft before the brewpub opened by attending brewing school at the respected Siebel Institute of Brewing in Chicago, thus giving him some production brewing experience. Alex Rattray now heads up brewing at Freetail Brewing's brewpub off Loop 1604 in San Antonio.

Oddly enough, the Rattray brothers had little idea about the historical significance of the home they would soon remodel into their restaurant and brewery, although it was hardly lost on them once they found out. Even with having expanded the historic home to include a massive outdoor smoking pit, things are tight in the old home. The Granary houses a seven-barrel brewing system, as well as fermentation and serving tanks carefully placed in the smallest of spaces in the old structure. Despite this, the brewpub is easily able to accommodate patrons, as well as multiple taps serving beer from guest breweries, including brews served from two old-school beer engines.

On the food side, the brewpub serves traditional American barbecue via counter service, with meat by the pound from St. Louis, Texas and Memphis during the day. The evening fare is a little worldlier, with barbecue represented from around the world, a more formal setting, wait staff and food pairings but with a relaxed feel. Why the two different approaches? The brothers wanted to make lunch efficient and

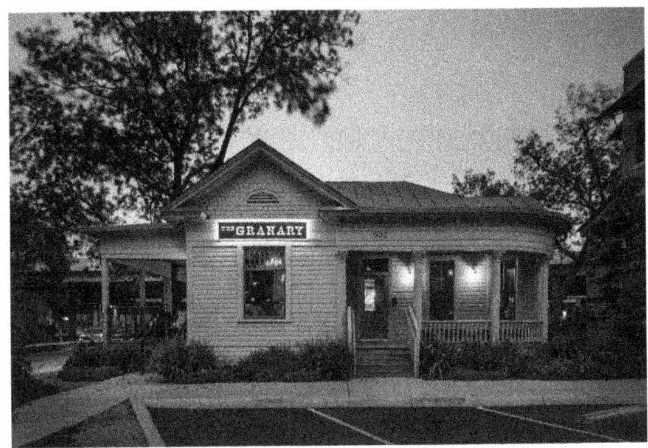

The Granary at night. *Nan Palmero.*

approachable for those on the go but have a refined and relaxed feel in the evening. Both the beer and food are all artisan and elevated in approach, with a focus on getting local ingredients as often as possible. The meat is sourced from local ranches that humanely raise their animals. The brewpub approaches operations in the best possible way, with a huge focus on service, taking care of employees and only doing business with those who feel the same way. Sounds like the Granary fits right in with Silver Ventures' philosophy just fine. The brewpub's website sums up this philosophy perfectly: "We are a globally inspired barbeque restaurant, rooted in Southern hospitality, hand-crafting our own beer."

After the opening of the Granary, another restaurant moved into another historic Pearl building. Local celebrity chef Steve McHugh opened his restaurant Cured in the 114-year-old former business office building of the Pearl. Much like the Granary, McHugh had a lot of remodeling to do in order to transform the former offices into a restaurant and bring the building up to code. Cured's location almost makes it as much a centerpiece of the New Pearl as the iconic brewhouse. McHugh utilized local branding school SCAD to help create his brand identity. On SCAD's website, Cured's focus is described perfectly: "This multi-layered and many-faceted project incorporated both the historical elements of the Pearl and the Chef's personal narrative. An expert in Charcuterie, Salumi and all forms of preserves Steve is also a cancer survivor. As he cures, is cured, and continues to cure the needs to the community with his cooking and charitable work, it was not hard to determine a name and a path forward."

BREWING RETURNS TO THE PEARL BREWHOUSE

The Granary and Cured were only the beginning of Silver Ventures' and New Pearl's determination to bring brewing, as well as the brewery's historic buildings, back to life. There was still the matter of the iconic brewhouse. Enter another local celebrity chef, Jeff Balfour. Balfour hailed from Texas's Gulf Coast area, specifically Galveston, and had made quite a name for himself in San Antonio as the head chef at Citrus in the Valencia Hotel. Balfour was also looking to open a brewpub in San Antonio and saw the Pearl as an option. After Balfour and Silver Ventures discussed ideas, Southerleigh Fine Food and Brewery was born. The new brewpub would occupy the former Pearl Brewhouse, bringing brewing back not just to the Pearl area but also to the former brewhouse itself.

Southerleigh is on point, with its master chef and brewer extraordinaire William Les Locke (Locke was also the first head brewer at Branchline Brewing in San Antonio) paying homage to the Pearl's past while looking forward to the future with its own identity. Balfour had been looking to open a brewpub for a while prior to getting in contact with the Pearl group in 2011, and he felt that the original brewhouse was optimal. "When you look

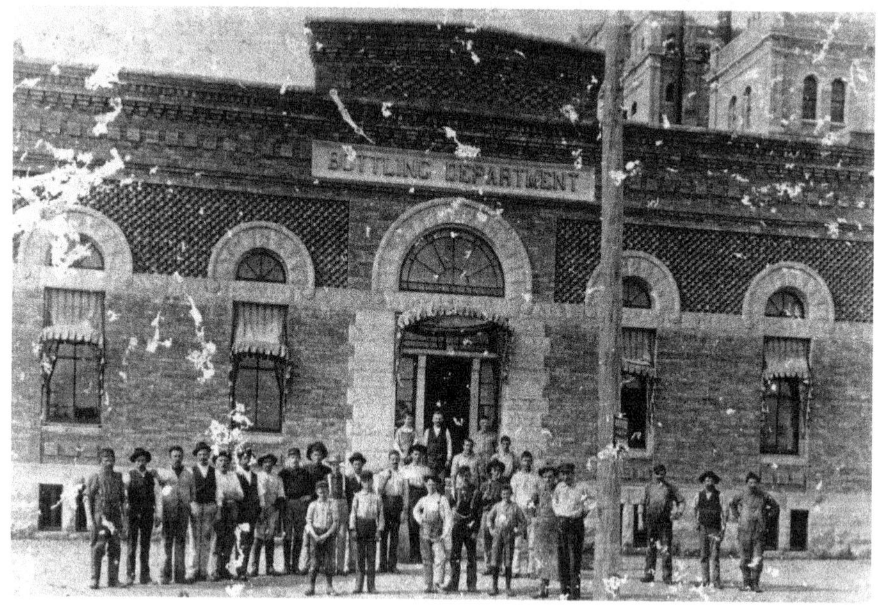

San Antonio Brewing Association employees in front of the original Pearl bottling building, early 1900s. *Pearl LLC Archives*.

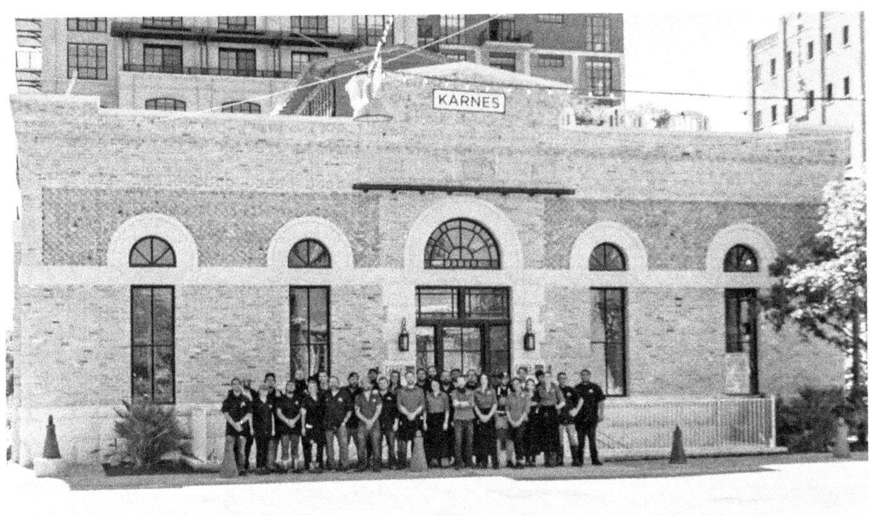

Southerleigh Brewing employees (current occupants of the Pearl brewhouse) in front of the rebuilt Pearl bottling building, 2017. *Jeremy Banas.*

at the space and the artist's renderings, it's just perfect," said Balfour, who along with Locke sat down with me to discuss Southerleigh.

"The Pearl group had always wanted brewing to return to the brewhouse," said Balfour, who had looked at a few other locations prior to the Pearl. With this revitalization of brewing tradition, both Balfour and Locke hope that it serves as a model for other defunct regional breweries. "We're excited to continue the Pearl tradition with Southerleigh," said Locke. "It's a feeling that can't be put into words."

Southerleigh does more than just continue the brewing tradition of the area. Most of the building incorporates a large amount of the original brewery. Much of the original equipment has been incorporated as part of the brewery's motif. Four fermenters, original to the Pearl, are kept on the upper level, visible to patrons of Southerleigh's south dining room, and serve to cover many of the serving tanks. The building's original arches have also been kept, in addition to some of the original pumps and firkins. The brewpub's north wall features an artist's rendering of the original brewhouse blueprints along with a timeline of its history.

Southerleigh features a menu that adjusts with the season, reflecting Balfour's upbringing in Galveston, Texas, and traditional southern dishes. Some menu items include hand-rolled pretzels, Texas Longhorn jerky, wood-fired meats, traditional shellfish boils and beer-braised meat, among

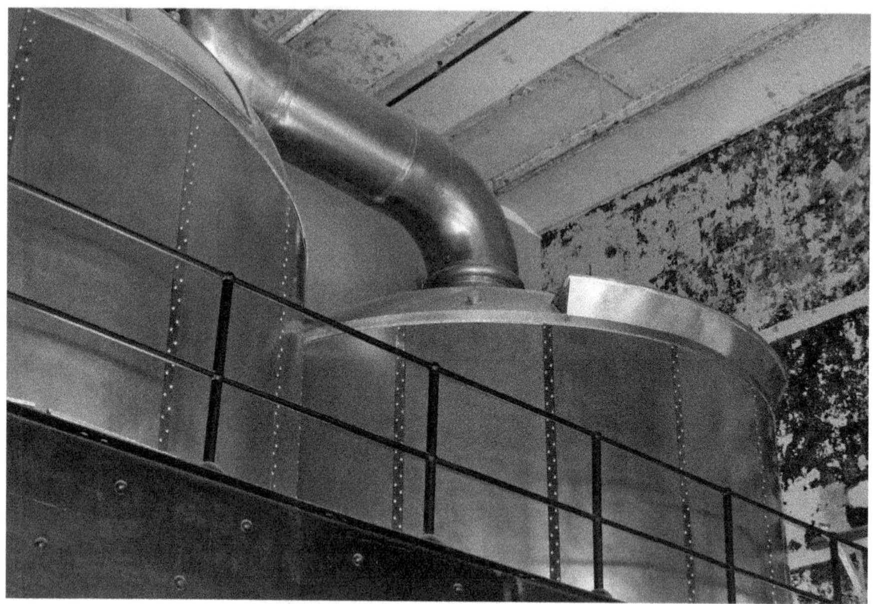

Original Pearl kettles used as a façade for serving tanks at Southerleigh Brewing. *Jeremy Banas.*

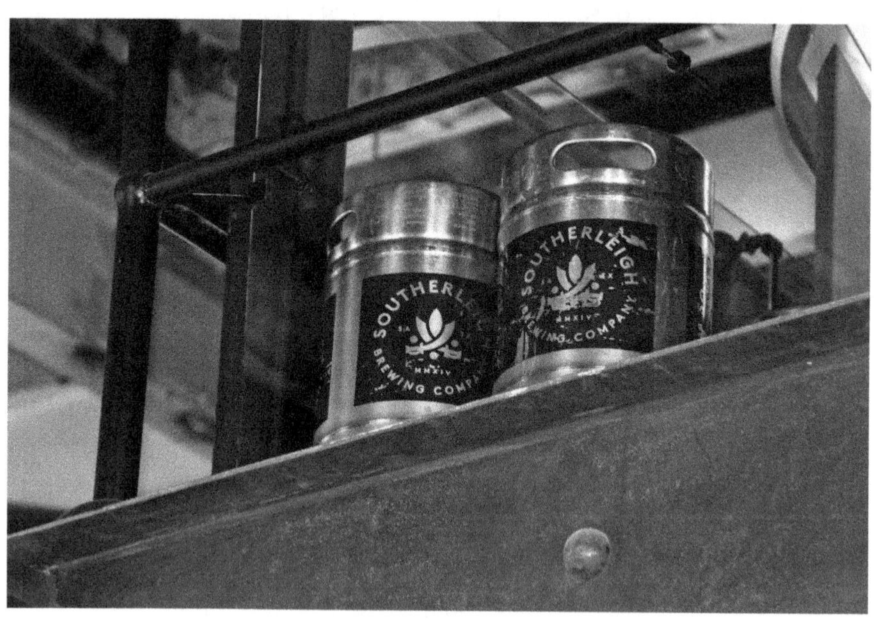

Kegs full of malted goodness sit at Southerleigh waiting for distribution. *Jeremy Banas.*

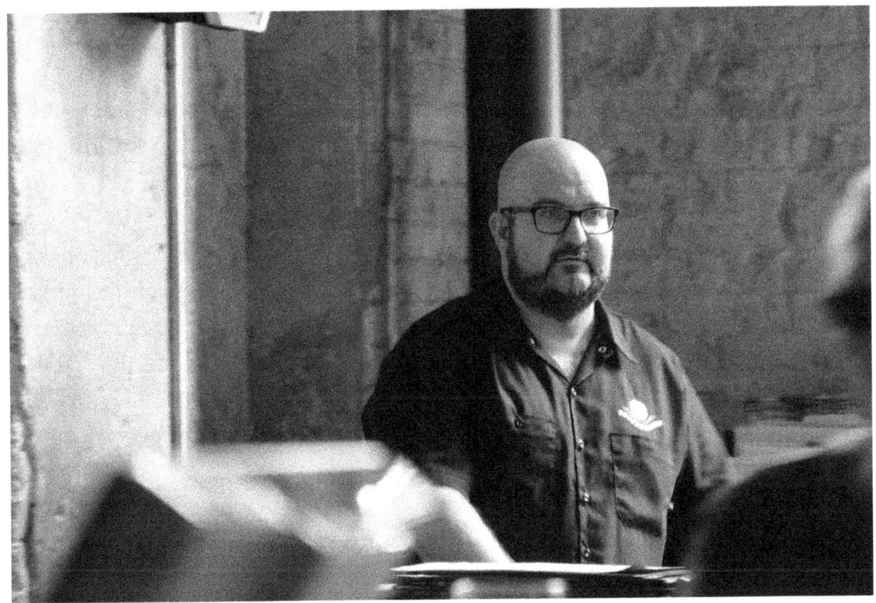

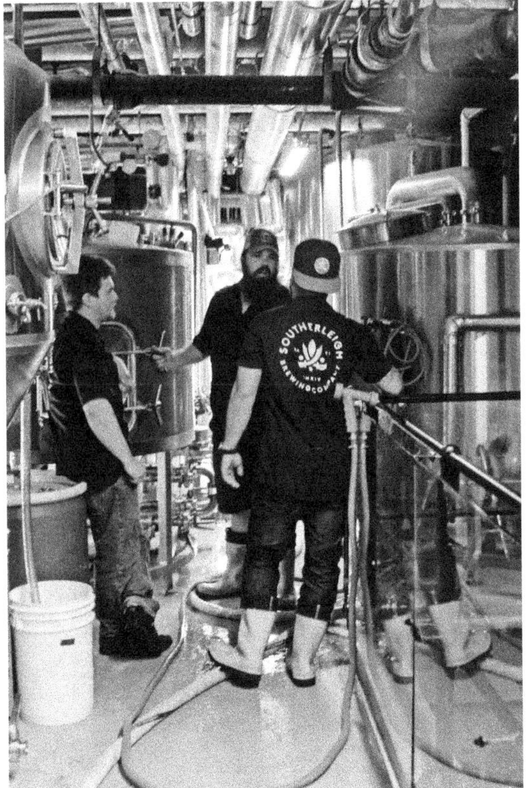

Above: Southerleigh Fine Food and Brewing restaurant manager Philippe Place watches over the brewpub, which now occupies the Pearl Brewhouse. *Jeremy Banas.*

Left: Assistant brewer J.C. Norris and Southerleigh Brewing employees cleaning up after a long day of brewing. *Jeremy Banas.*

many others. Balfour enjoys dazzling patrons with his creativity and passion for traditional foods that often take on a modern flair.

This creativity and innovation does not just stay on the food side of the house. Balfour advised that he and Locke have an open collaboration with the food and beer menus. "We will be constantly working to create beers that have our dishes in mind and vice versa," said Balfour.

This philosophy is shared by Les Locke, who sees a symbiotic relationship with Balfour and the food side of the business. Locke has been known to use unusual ingredients in his beers that can easily pair with almost any dish. "I was excited for the building and equipment to be completed so that Jeff and I could begin working together," said Locke. "He has the same philosophy as I do when it comes to food, and with the unlimited versatility of beer, the pairings are endless."

Southerleigh has ten to twelve house beers and several guest taps. Regular offerings include a California common (steam beer), a German-style Helles and what Locke refers to as Darwinian IPA, an India pale ale that is always evolving. A barrel program that includes sour ales is also in the works, with the Helles being used as the base beer for the sour program. Southerleigh already bottles a few of its regular offerings, and a canning line is on the horizon as well. With all this production, Locke is putting his

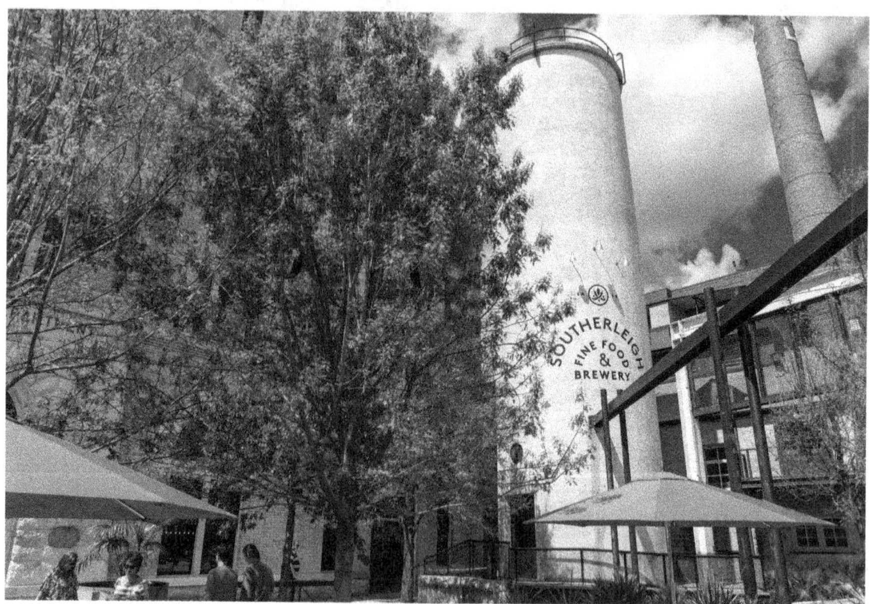

View of Southerleigh. *Jeremy Banas.*

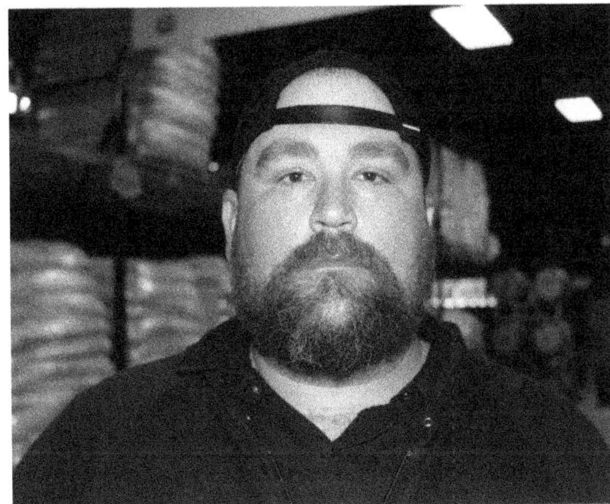

Left: Les Lock, head brewer of Southerleigh Brewing, looks stoic in his role as the latest brewer inside the historic Pearl Brewhouse. *Jeremy Banas.*

Below: Signage directs visitors to the Pearl to Southerleigh. *Jeremy Banas.*

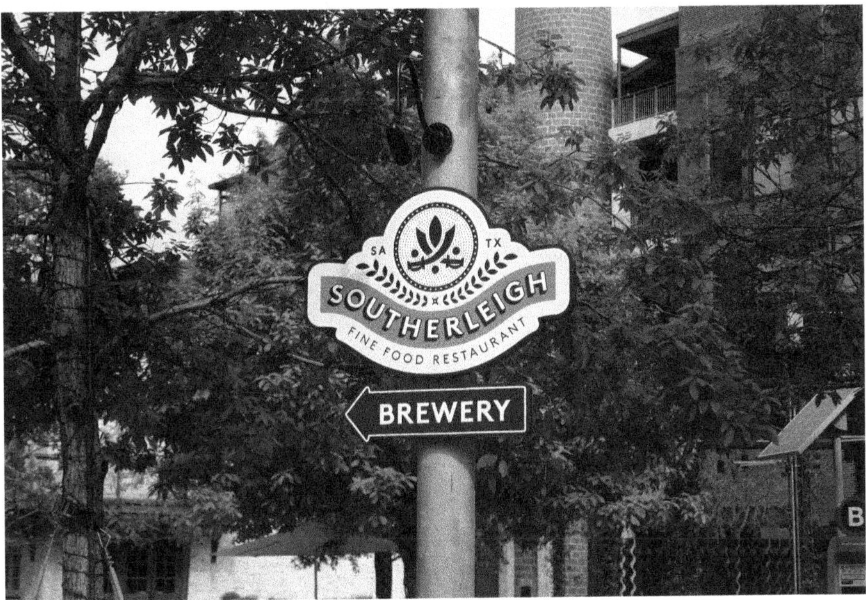

brewing system through its paces, often adding a second brewing shift. To help ease this pace, a production brewery is also in the works.

Southerleigh boasts a fifteen-barrel system from Portland Kettle Works out of Portland, Oregon. "It's important to us that all aspects of the restaurant and brewery reflect an American feel—specifically southern," said Balfour. "We want our customers to feel that they can relate to us when they are here," added Locke. "We want all aspects of the restaurant to be approachable so that regardless of your income level, you'll feel at home here." Don't take this laidback approach for granted, though, as all employees need to meet Balfour's high standards for culinary knowledge, as well as share his philosophy on food, and servers are no different when it comes to the beer side.

Silver Ventures was not finished with the brewhouse, however. Plans had been in motion for a hotel as well. The hotel would take the back half of the brewhouse building adjacent to Southerleigh, with a massive new addition, making the overall building much larger than it had been historically. Dubbed the Hotel Emma in honor of Emma Koehler, this is one killer boutique-style affair. Boasting 146 rooms of a unique caliber, the idea behind the Hotel Emma was to create an experience that screamed refined, sophisticated, classy, historical and welcoming all at the same time. For the brewhouse portion of the hotel, design firm Roman and Williams masterfully melded the historic aspects of the building with a modern flair that made sense, an approach that was replicated with the new addition as well.

The brewhouse tower section of the hotel features six incredibly unique suites, each with a different feel and experience. It is like stepping into the past in a way that makes visitors feel as if they are back in the 1890s. Two of the six suites are named for the original Otto Koehler and Emma Koehler and reflect styles akin to the two Pearl superstars themselves, with the remaining four suites encompassing the feel of the original building and that of San Antonio itself. The remaining rooms of the hotel capture this historic feel yet lend a sense of the modern as well.

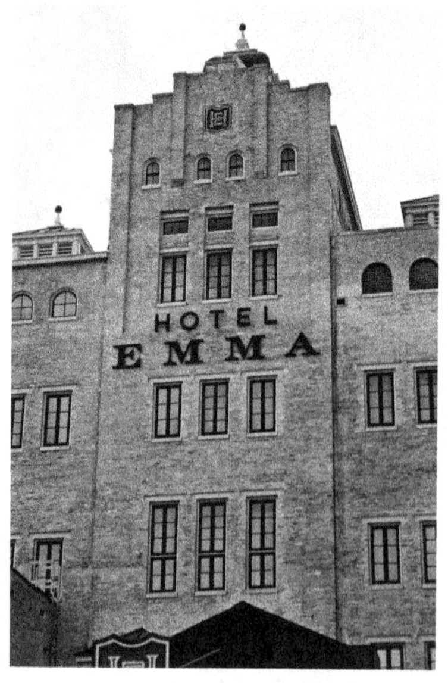

The Hotel Emma. *Jeremy Banas.*

Adding to the overall ambiance of the Hotel Emma is the hotel's focus on a superior food and drink experience. The hotel houses a combination deli and corner grocery store that butchers its own meat. The Larder also carries a wide variety of prepared foods in addition to its mini coffee shop, all with a sophisticated European feel to it. Just down from Larder sits Supper, an elevated approach to a family-style restaurant with both a farm-to-table and bistro approach. Perhaps the crown jewel of the trifecta is Sternwirth, a bar and clubroom that smacks of

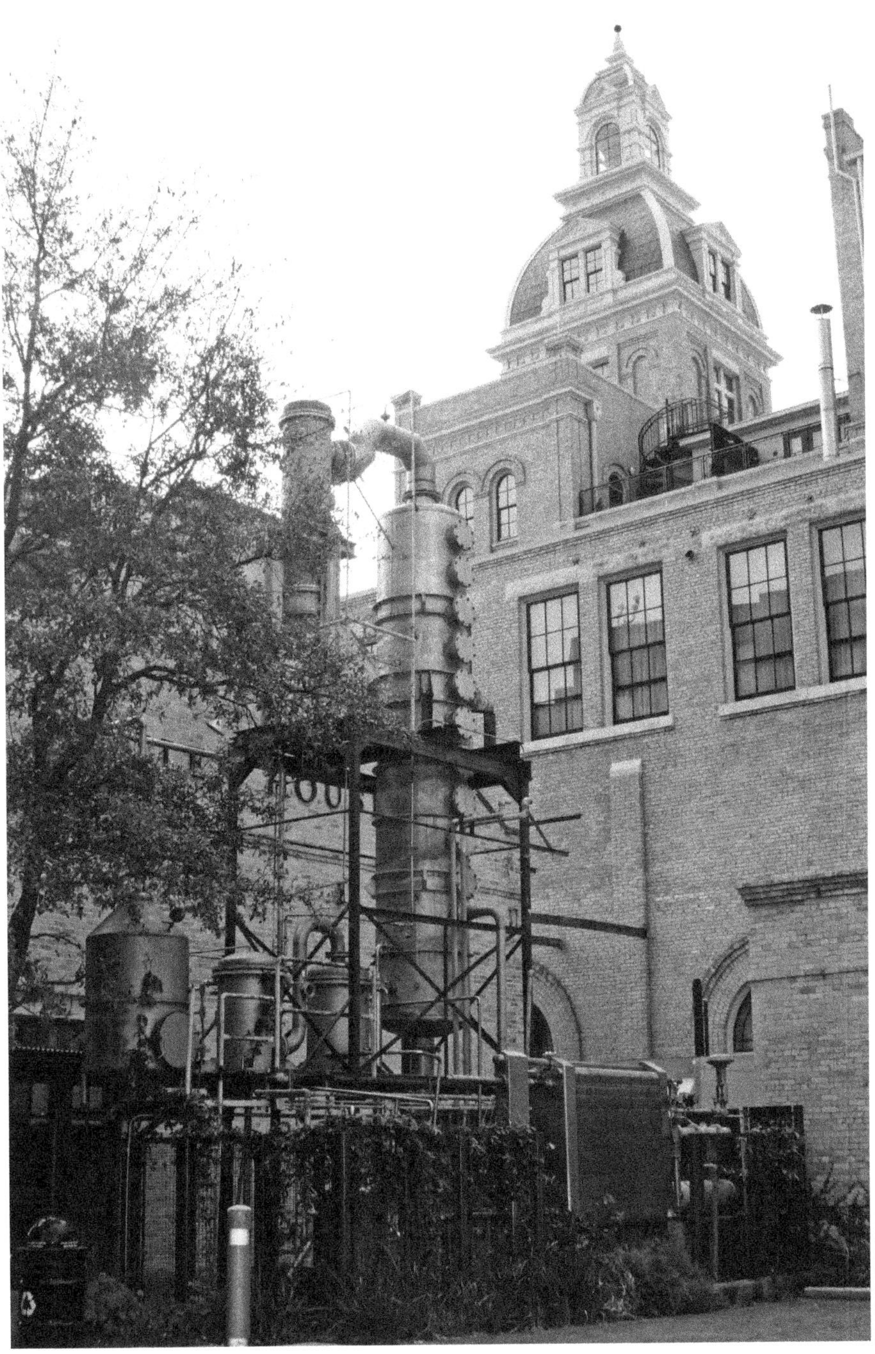

Pearl liquor still no. 2. *Jeremy Banas.*

private English club with classic cocktails, wine and craft beer. Outside of its nineteenth-century English décor, which fits right in with the Pearl's history, Sternwirth features a cocktail aptly named the Three Emmas, which both honors and acknowledges the drama behind its name.

Although Pearl Stables have been many things since they fell out of use with the brewery in the early 1900s due to the advent of motorized transportation—for example, a storage unit and the Jersey Lilly taproom—the stables are now home to a beautiful renovation that houses space for a variety of social events.

Silver Ventures recently re-created another historic building associated with its brewing past. The bottling building, built in 1897, was lost to a fire in November 2003 that was accidentally caused by demo workers who set fire to the cork walls with cutting torches. Goldsbury and Silver Ventures rebuilt the 5,500-square-foot building from the ground up at the original location, using photos to create an exact replica of the bottling building façade. The rebuild was handled by Clayton and Little Architects and included the use of salvaged cornerstones and masonry from the original building. Although the new bottling building will not be packing beer this time, it houses Jazz TX, a throwback jazz nightclub, in its basement and

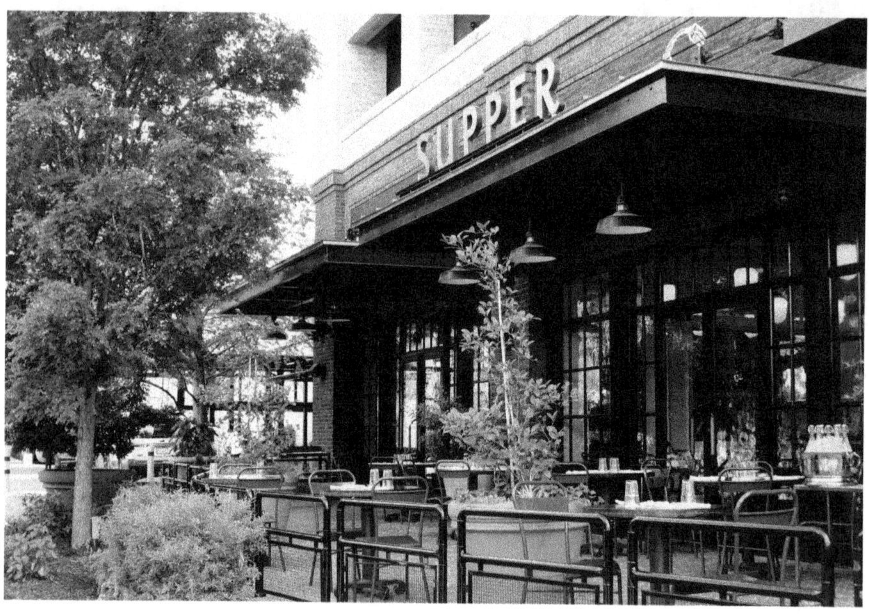

The resident restaurant inside the Hotel Emma. Supper delights both locals and visitors alike. *Jeremy Banas.*

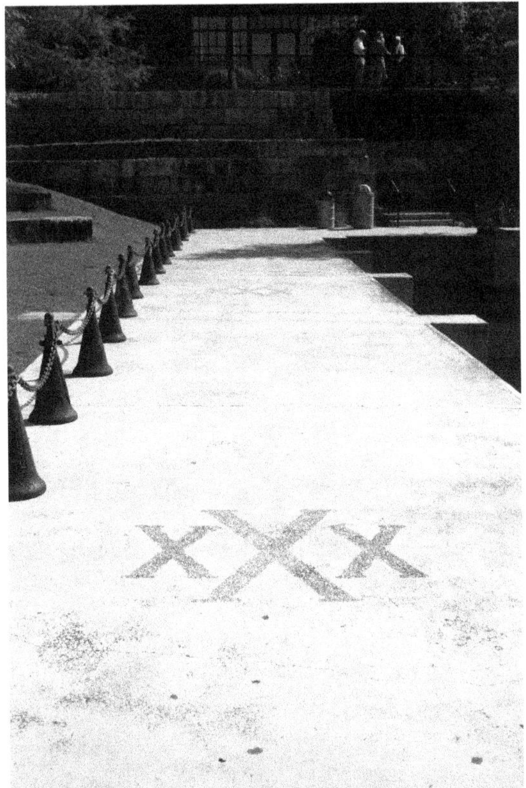

Left: The XXX marker adorns a sidewalk at the Hotel Emma, letting those who enter know that they're about to experience the best. *Jeremy Banas*.

Below: Pearl signage at The Cellars luxury apartments. *Jeremy Banas*.

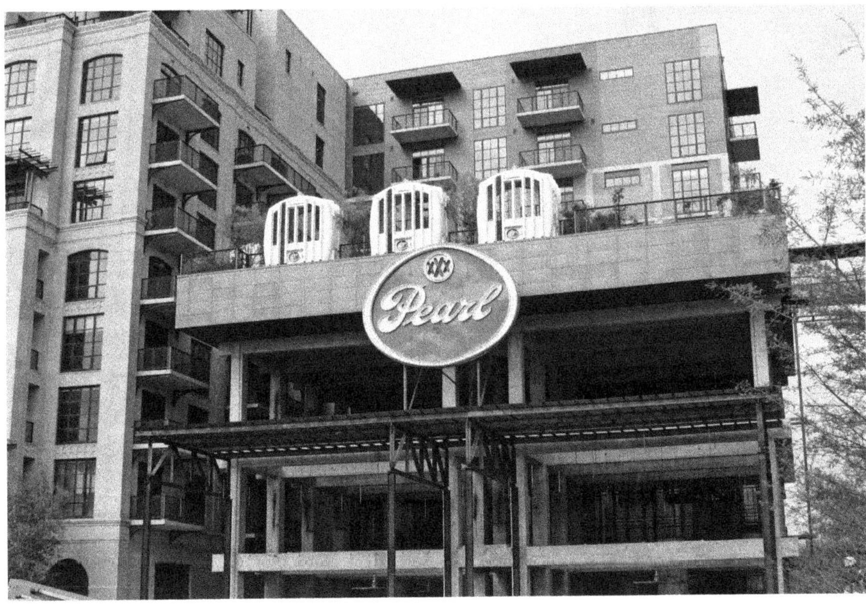

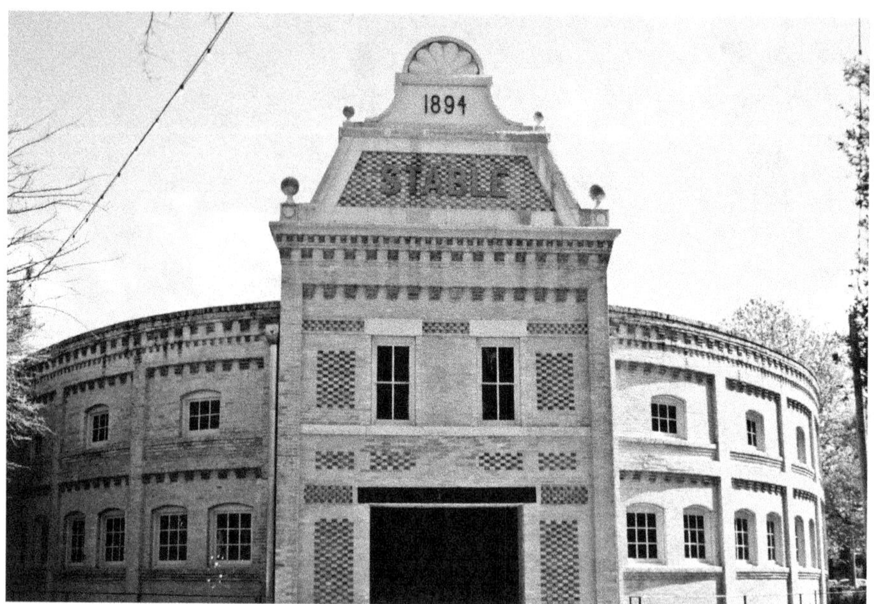

The Pearl Stables today. *Jeremy Banas.*

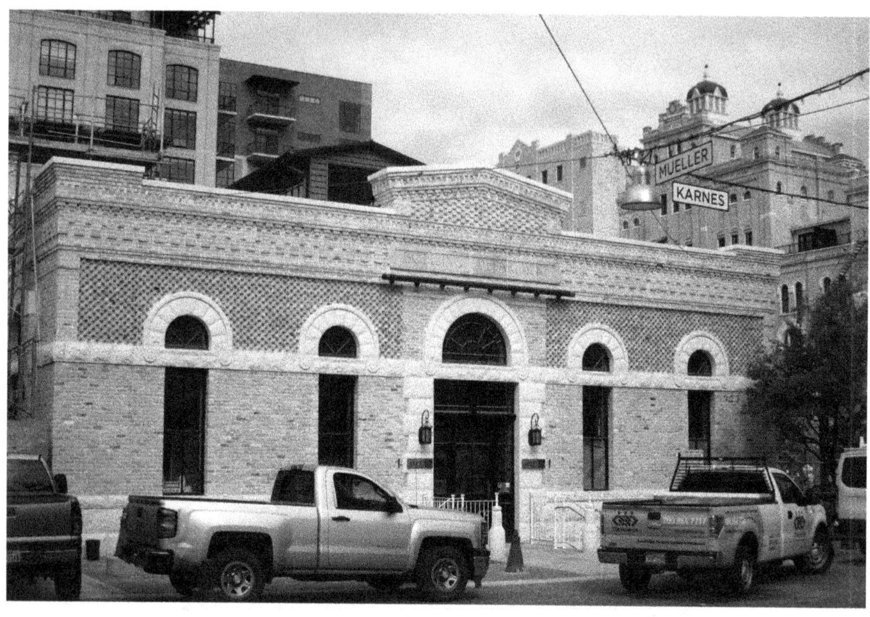

The reconstructed Pearl bottling building, now home to a food hall and jazz club. *Pearl LLC Archives.*

a food hall on the ground floor that houses six food vendors featuring innovative local chefs, as well as a bar. Elizabeth Fauerso, Silver Ventures' chief marketing officer, said that it will feature a communal dining area for visitors in the hope that it acts as a restaurant incubator that will spur culinary creativity.

The Pearl's long and storied history, from its unofficial beginnings in 1883 as the City Brewery to its official beginnings in 1886 and its present period (which began in 2002), has had nothing short of an amazing and irreplaceable influence on San Antonio and Texas in general. It looks to remain so for the unforeseeable future. Perhaps it has another 131 years in it for future generations to enjoy. In all aspects for regional breweries such as the Pearl, it is truly difficult to measure the impact they have. Most of us take for granted the little details. We go about our lives never truly looking at what we have and what it will be like when it is gone.

In the last decades of the Pearl, some would even call into question the actual quality of XXX Pearl Beer and the brewery's other brands. Yes, changes to the ingredients used had an effect on the taste despite the formula remaining the same, but each brewer, each employee on the bottling line and each sales representative put their proverbial blood, sweat and tears into the Pearl, and this cannot be overlooked. Pearl employees were loyal, much as residents of San Antonio are massively loyal to their city. How exactly can you measure that type of overall influence? The simple answer is that none of us can truly put into words exactly the type of impact on history and ourselves that something like the Pearl can have. It ceases to just be a brewery and evolves into a state of mind, a state of being. It embodies what we feel as our community's identity.

We must raise our hats to what came before us, what influences us to do what we do in our own lives. We must respect what came before us, lest we lose any basis for establishing a community or individual identity. We must tip our hats, not only to Otto and Emma Koehler, Otto A. Koehler, Oscar Bergstrom, Otto Wahrmund, J.J. Stevens and B.B. McGimsey but also to every single employee who kept the brewery moving along over its 115-year history, as well as to Kit Goldsbury and Silver Ventures, who are keeping this tradition alive for generations to come. We must never forget to always say, "A bottle of Pearl please."

APPENDIX I

THE KOEHLER HOUSE

The Koehler House has become something of a legend in San Antonio, situated in the Laurel Heights area of San Antonio just north of downtown and a stone's throw away from the Pearl Brewery. Real estate developers began construction of residences in Laurel Heights in the early 1890s, along with other areas such as Alamo Heights and Beacon Hill.

The popular legend as to why Otto Koehler chose this particular location in Laurel Heights was so that he could overlook the skyline of the city; it also gave him a perfect view of his brewery. As family folklore would tell it, Otto Koehler would sit on his porch and watch the brewery to see if they were working or not—allegedly by the color of the smoke coming from the brewery stacks.

The home was designed by local architect Carl Von Seutter and was heralded as the most expensive home in the city. Von Seutter had only worked as a draftsman for another local architect, James Riley Gordon, who also designed the Bexar County Courthouse. Von Seutter finished his professional training as an architect and opened his own firm, Murphy and Von Seutter, with a partner in 1897. In about 1899, Von Seutter left his partnership with Mr. Murphy but remained in the architect's offices, although he would change office locations multiple times over the next thirty years.

Von Seutter enlisted local contractor Jacob Wagoner in the construction of the Koehler residence, going for a flamboyant Victorian style for the façade. Von Seutter combined old styles and new ones more in tune with

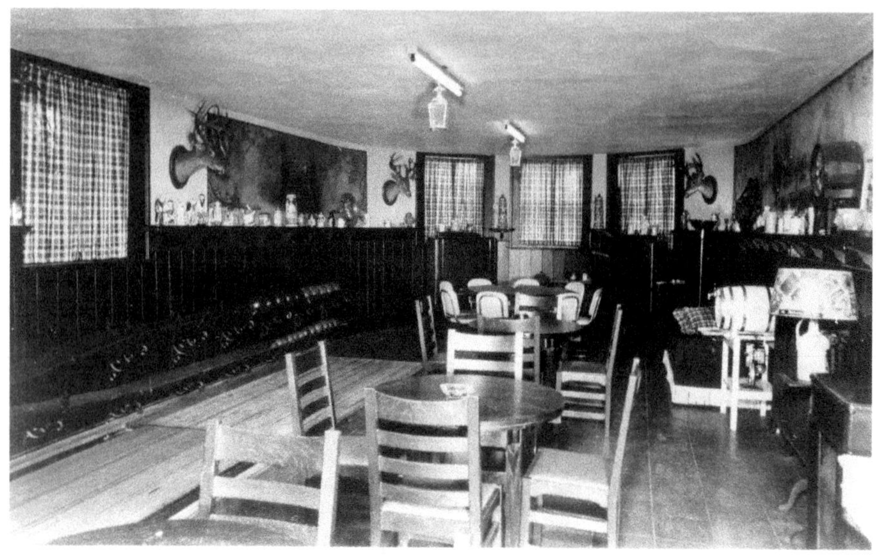

Basement of the Koehler House, 1950s. *San Antonio College and the Alamo Colleges District Foundation.*

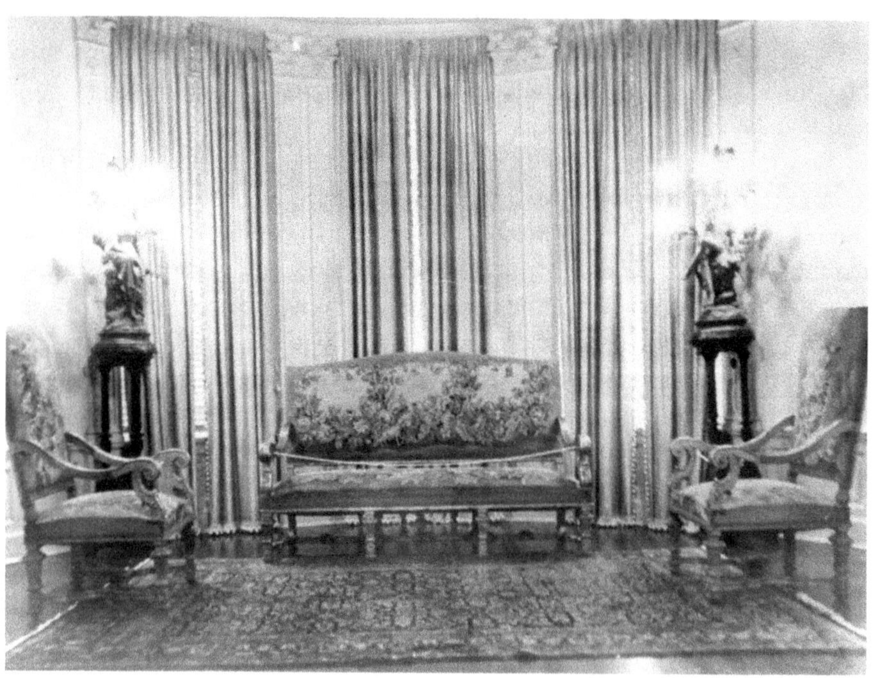

Reading room at the Koehler House. *San Antonio College and the Alamo Colleges District Foundation.*

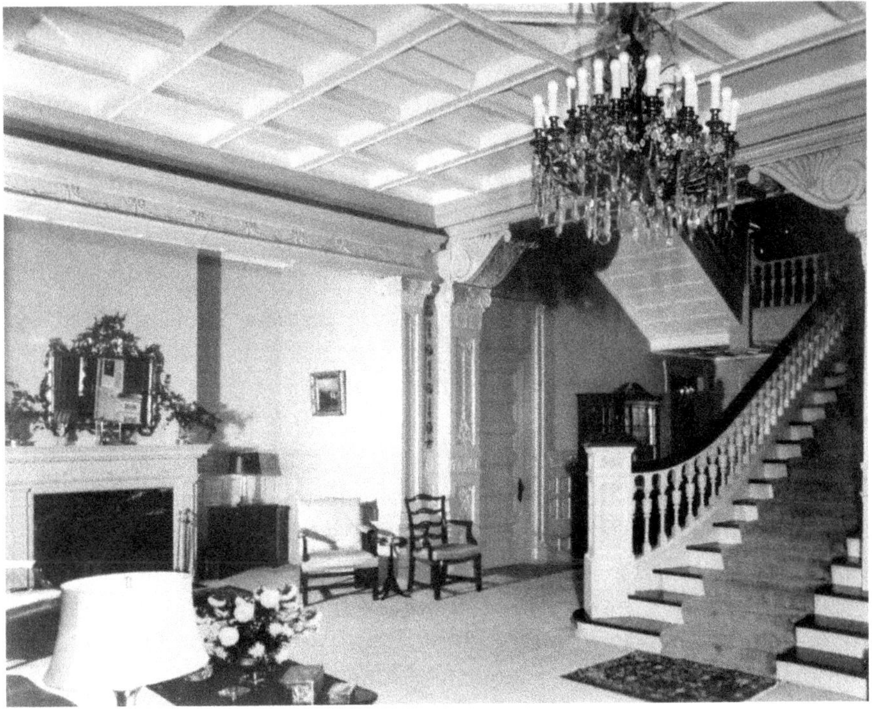

Stairs at the Koehler House. *San Antonio College and the Alamo Colleges District Foundation.*

the times. Many Renaissance elements—such as Italian Palladian windows, balustrades, large columns and sculpture garlands—were incorporated. Near the basement level, massive round arches went in, as well as turrets and a round base with Richardsonian Romanesque tones that he may have learned during his time with James Gordon. The home featured a grand dining room with a rather large solarium on the side that housed hundreds of plants.

The mansion features a sprawling 12,665 square feet, with three main floors plus a basement, and takes up an entire city block. Koehler adorned the mansion with the latest stylings, as well as a few personal luxuries. Koehler had a one-lane pin setting bowling alley installed in the basement designed by Brunswick, and the alley also featured several murals rumored to have been painted by Koehler himself. "I remember running around the house and into the basement," said Dr. Paul Pace, a Koehler descendant. "We used to play a lot on the bowling alley." Dr. Pace also reminisced about holidays at the mansion, running around under the table during Thanksgiving in particular.

Koehler's bedroom was on the second floor, which now houses the grant offices of the San Antonio Community College. The third floor featured a large ballroom that was once used as a speakeasy in the 1940s and a rather large mirror that allegedly has a secret of its own. The ballroom "features a hidden bar that could be brought out during parties and when the lights to the mirror are turned on a hidden semi-nude picture of an unknown woman becomes visible," noted Dr. Pace, whose mother, Margaret Pace Willson, was the great-niece of Otto and Emma Koehler.

Despite the fairly eclectic nature of the mansion, it was, in fact, a home for the Koehlers. Even after Otto's death in 1914, Emma Koehler continued to live in the house until her death in 1943. Emma would host any number of gatherings at her home, including Easter egg hunts and afternoon coffee. "Every Sunday at 4:00 in the afternoon, she received family and friends in the conservatory for afternoons of cake and coffee. She loved to hear all the gossip, and, even as a little girl, I supplied her with all the latest news," wrote Margaret Pace Willson in her memoirs regarding her Aunt Emma. Margaret Pace Willson was the wife of Pace Foods founder Dave Pace and mother to local hand surgeon Dr. Paul Pace and his sister, Linda Pace. Linda would later marry Kit Goldsbury, the current owner of the Pearl.

Pace Willson spent much of her time at the Koehler mansion, enjoying what was essentially a private playground. "I never realized that Aunt Emma's house was grand or large until much later, when my high school friends made comments about how impressive it was. To me it was just an ordinary old house!" said Pace Williams, who also fondly remembered those Easter egg hunts. "My cousins and I delighted in hunting Easter eggs on the grounds. Besides the hard-boiled variety, we also had sugar eggs with lovely scenes inside and chocolate eggs from Germany."

Easter wasn't the only holiday that was done up in high style at the Koehler mansion. Christmas was quite an affair. "Aunt Emma always had a formal dinner on Christmas Eve that included several dozen family members and friends. Everyone set up a small table with their gifts and decorations to distribute to the family in the parlor. It was the job of one of the servants to decorate the large tree so that it would be a surprise for all the guests. At the appointed time everyone entered to see the ceiling-high tree with its glowing light from real candles," noted Pace Willson.

While he was still alive, Otto Koehler was a stickler for formality regarding maintenance of the grounds. He took great pride in the landscaping of the grounds and his home, which included broad terraced

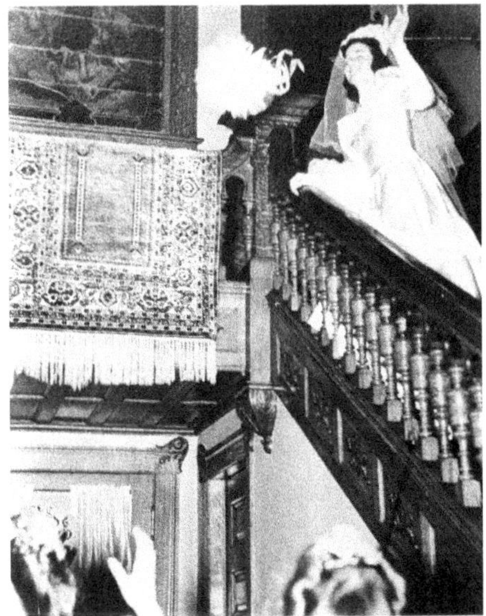

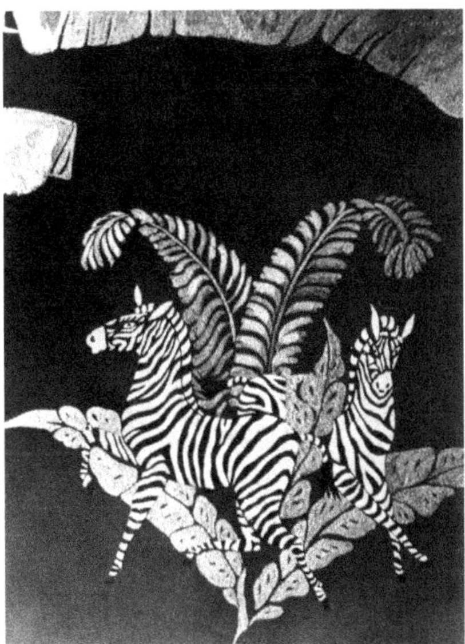

Left: Margaret Bosshardt tossing her bouquet on the main stairway in her Aunt Emma Koehler's home, where her wedding reception was held after marrying David Pace, 1941. Just outside the picture were Otto A. Koehler and Emma Koehler. *San Antonio College and the Alamo Colleges District Foundation.*

Right: Zebra Room print. *San Antonio College and the Alamo Colleges District Foundation.*

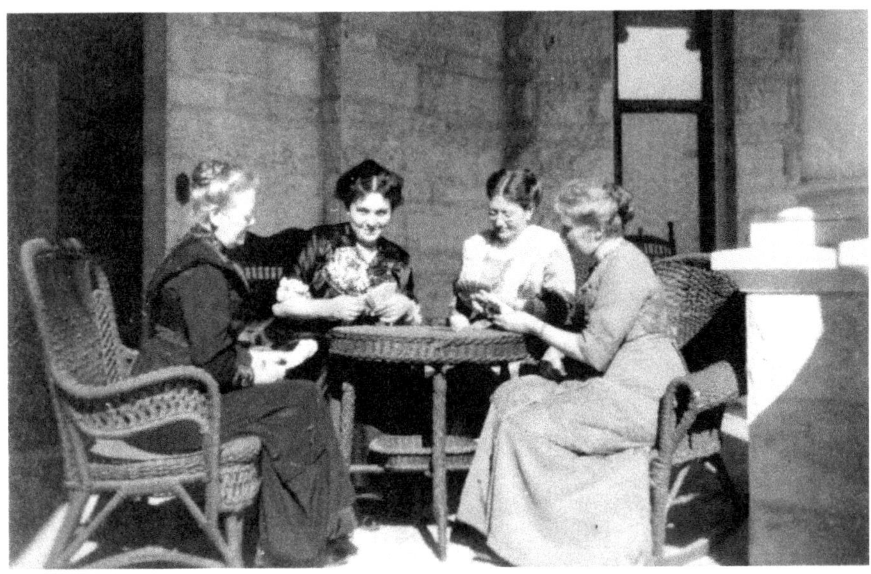

Emma Koehler (*second from right*) playing cards. *San Antonio College and the Alamo Colleges District Foundation.*

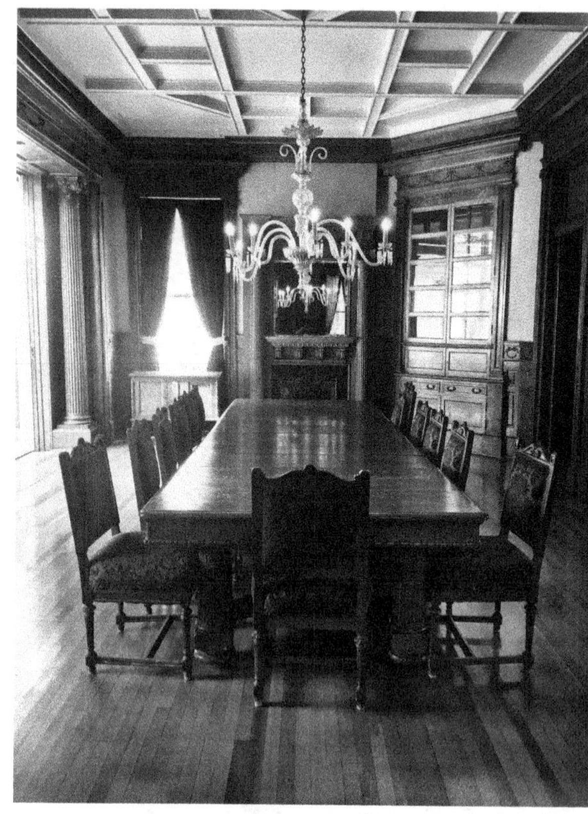

Left: Koehler House dining room, 2017. *Jeremy Banas*.

Below: A work rumored to have been painted by the original Otto Koehler. It sits in the basement of the Koehler House. *Jeremy Banas*.

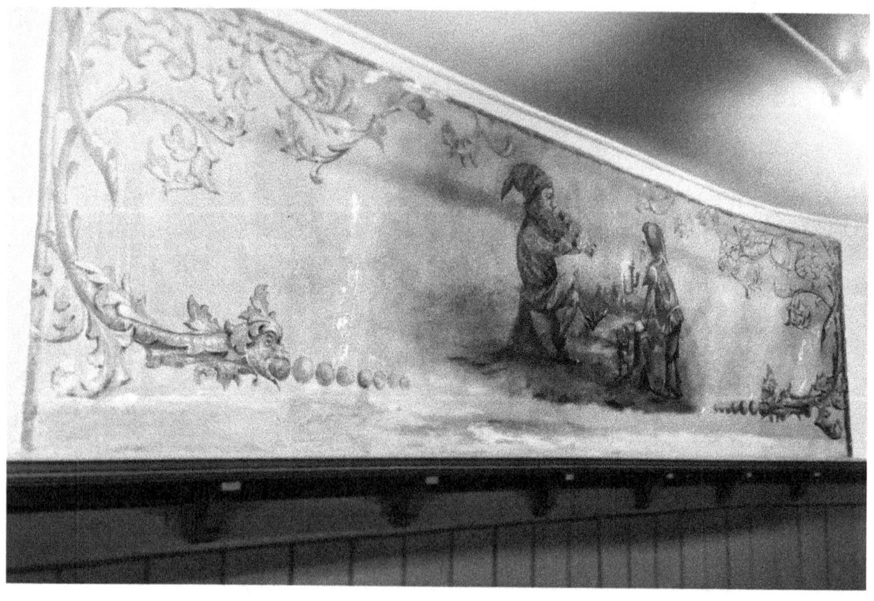

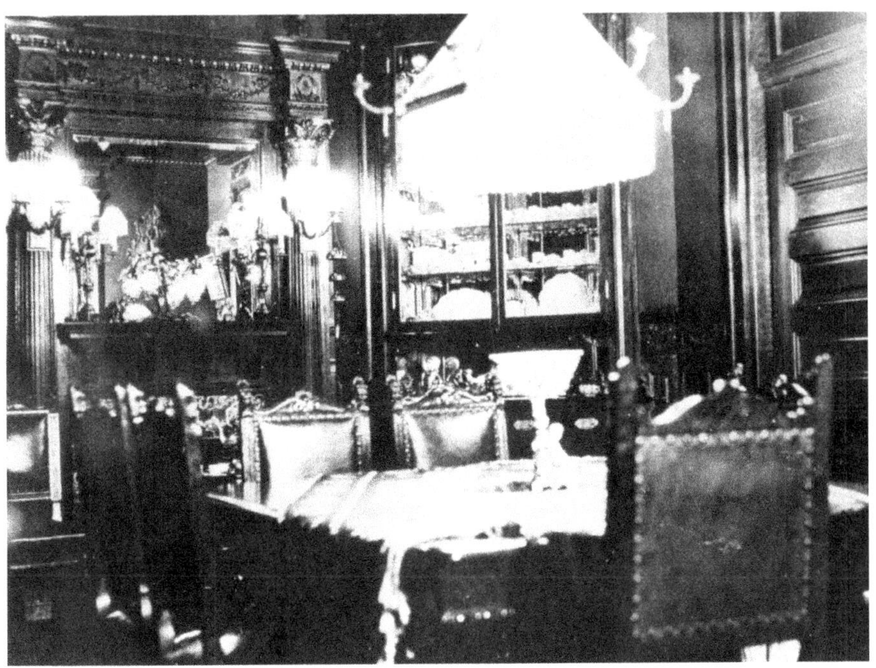

Koehler House dining room. *San Antonio College and the Alamo Colleges District Foundation.*

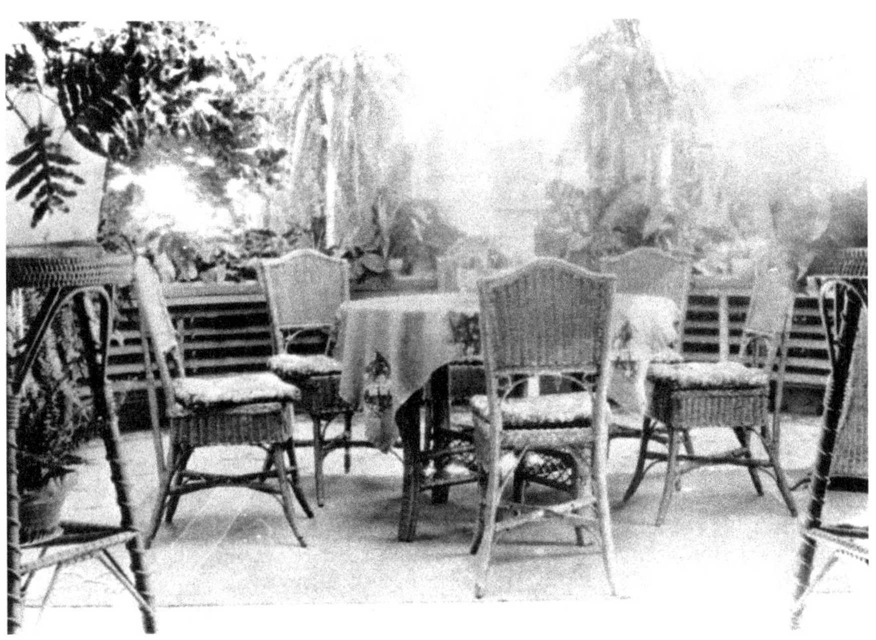

Koehler House patio. *San Antonio College and the Alamo Colleges District Foundation.*

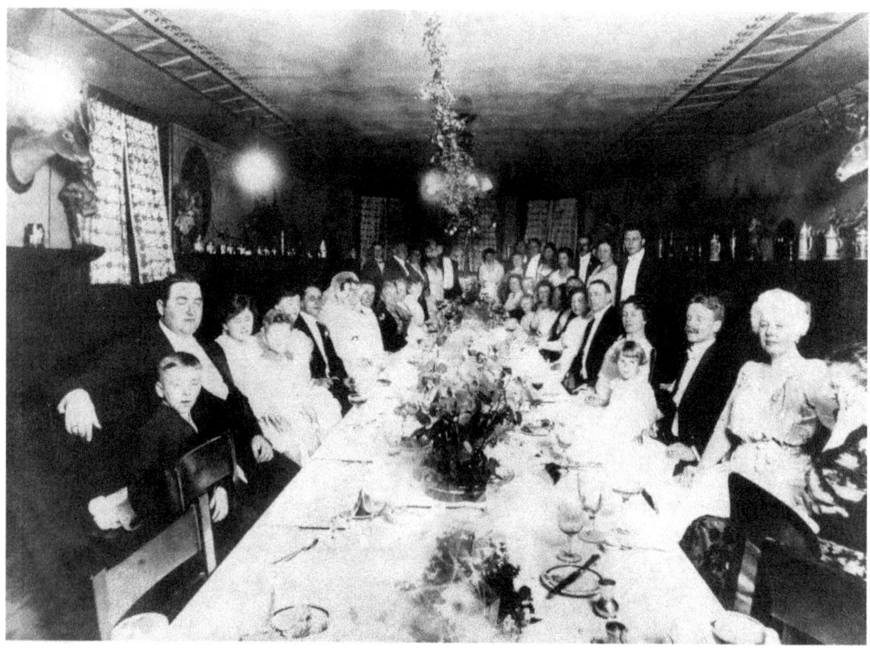

Reception dinner for Margaret Bosshardt at the Koehler House. *San Antonio College and the Alamo Colleges District Foundation.*

lawns. When the home was first built, local landscaper G.A. Schattenburg of Boerne, Texas, was hired for the job. Local lore even indicates that Otto Koehler never left for too long without leaving special instructions to the staff gardener as to the care of his plants, flowers and trees.

When Emma Koehler passed away in 1943, her nephew and namesake of her husband, Otto A. Koehler, moved into the mansion with his wife, Marcia. Otto A. would have been thrilled to be moving back into the home in which he had lived the majority of his childhood. Upon Otto A.'s passing in 1969, the Koehler mansion remained with the family, and in 1971, it was deeded to the San Antonio Union Junior College, now the San Antonio College, by Marcia, under a prior arrangement from Otto A. and Emma Koehler.

Once San Antonio College assumed ownership of the mansion, both the Junior College District and the nearby San Antonio Art League operated it. The mansion was used as an art venue until 1988, at which time it was converted into a mixed-use venue known as the Koehler Cultural Center, which it remains to this day. Now run by the Alamo Community College District, of which San Antonio College is a member, the mansion houses

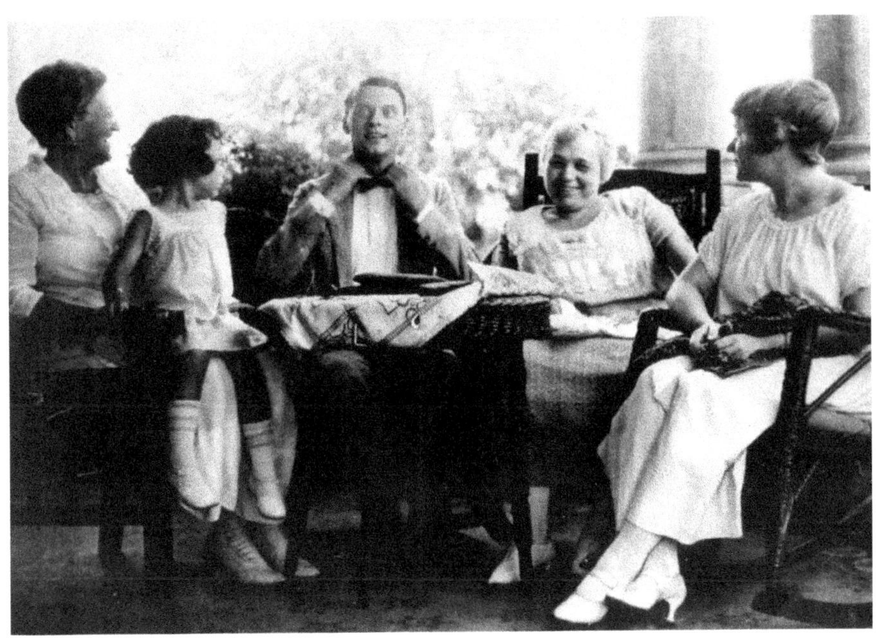

Emma Koehler (*far left*) and family in the solarium. *San Antonio College and the Alamo Colleges District Foundation.*

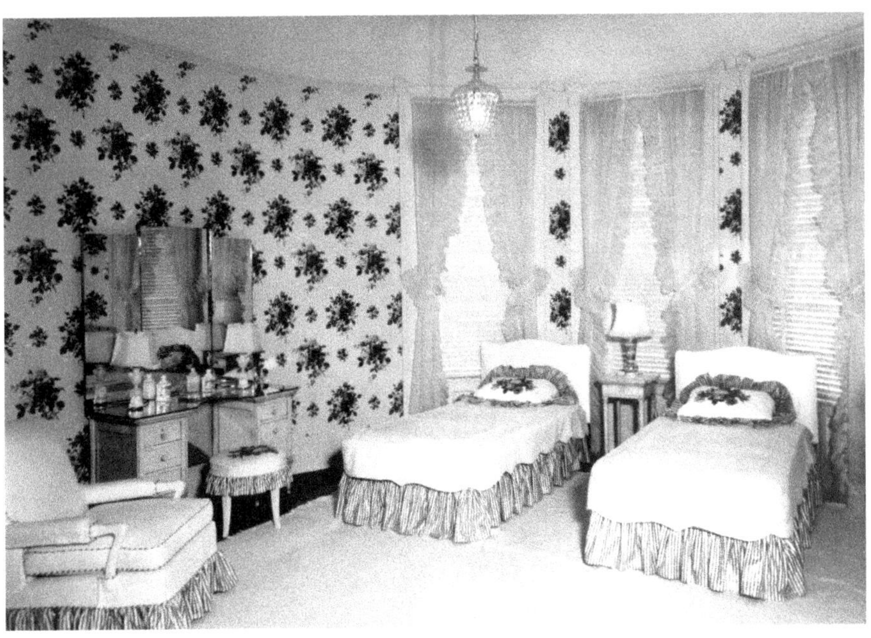

Bedroom at the Koehler House. *San Antonio College and the Alamo Colleges District Foundation.*

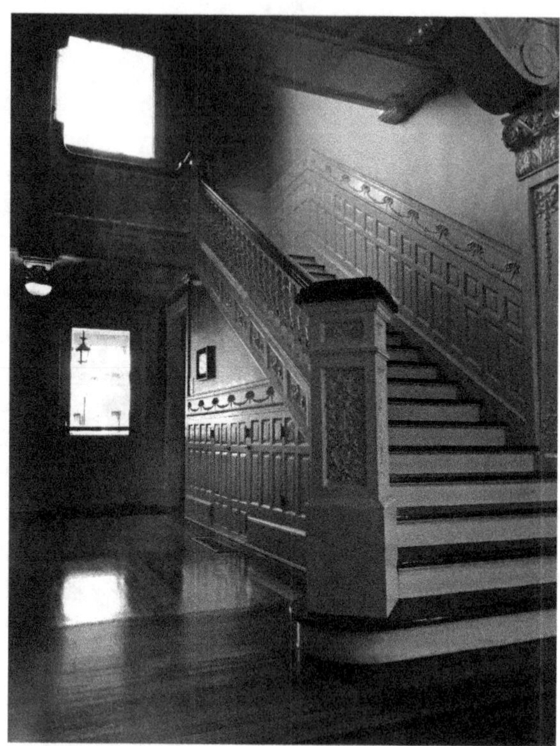

Right: Stairs in the foyer of the Koehler House, 2017. *Jeremy Banas*.

Below: The Koehler House today. *Jeremy Banas*.

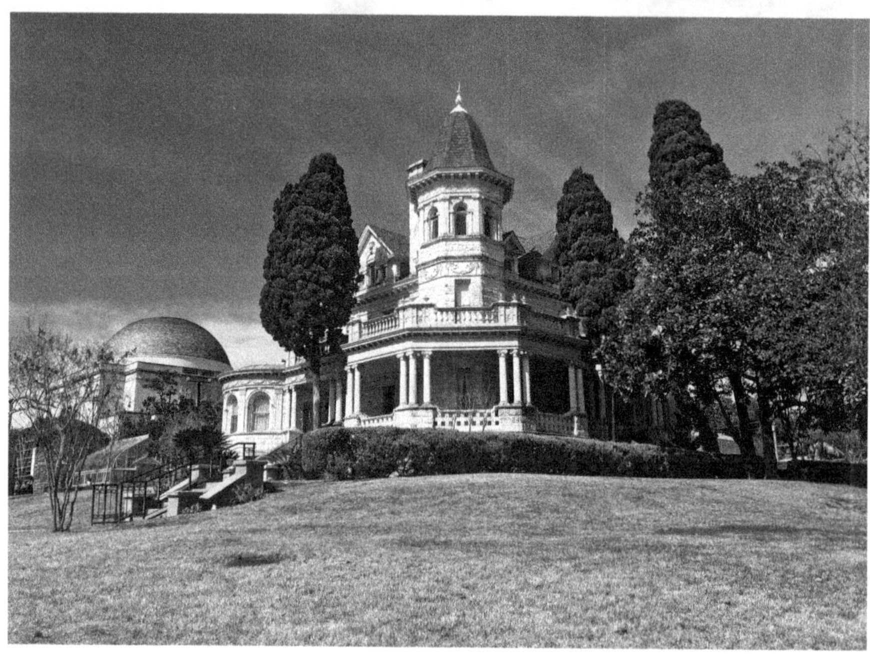

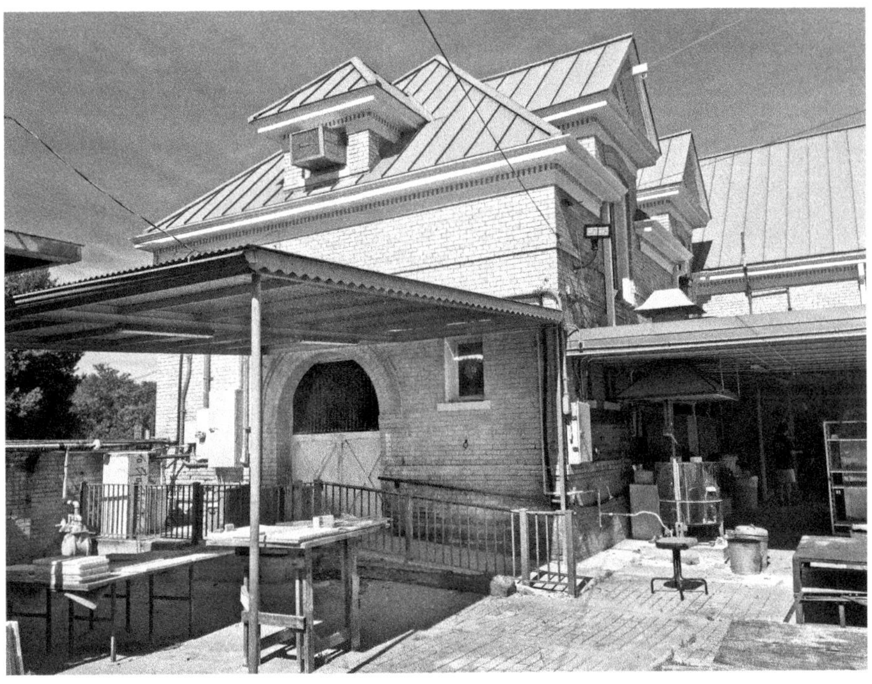

Carriage house at the Koehler House today. *Jeremy Banas.*

some educational offices for the Alamo Colleges, as well as holds events both for the Alamo Colleges and the general public.

The Alamo Community College District has done a great job of preserving the mansion and grounds while also keeping the integrity of the original appearance. As such, it is also preserved as a state historical landmark and looks to continue as a representation of San Antonio's bygone years to be enjoyed by Alamo City residents for decades more.

APPENDIX II

THE TEXAS TRANSPORTATION COMPANY

The Texas Transportation Company was owned and operated by the San Antonio Brewing Association/Pearl Brewery from October 9, 1898, until Pearl closed in 2001. It measured a mere two miles in length, making it the shortest railroad track in the United States and the oldest still operating in 2001. In fact, the track and one of the train cars still exist and can be seen at the Pearl complex today. The first two engines were horse-drawn, with the San Antonio Brewing Association later converting them to run with electricity immediately after purchase.

This short track started by the San Antonio Brewing Association was actually the second to bear this name. From 1866 to 1896, another Texas Transportation Company existed with a line running from Clinton, Texas, all the way to Houston. By 1896, this first iteration had been absorbed into the Southern Pacific Railroad. Ironic, considering the role the Southern Pacific would play with the San Antonio Brewing Association's version. In 1890, the Alamo Electric Street Railway Company arrived and was the city's first electric railway company.

Although trains had been present in San Antonio since the 1880s, the Texas Transportation Company was the first to operate electric freight cars in San Antonio. Although the track itself ran through San Antonio, the railway existed for the pleasure of the brewery. It ran from a station at the San Antonio Brewing Association, proceeding into the city and ending at the rail yards of the Southern Pacific Railroad. To run through the streets of San Antonio, the Texas Transportation Company paid the City of San Antonio $1,000 for each year of its use.

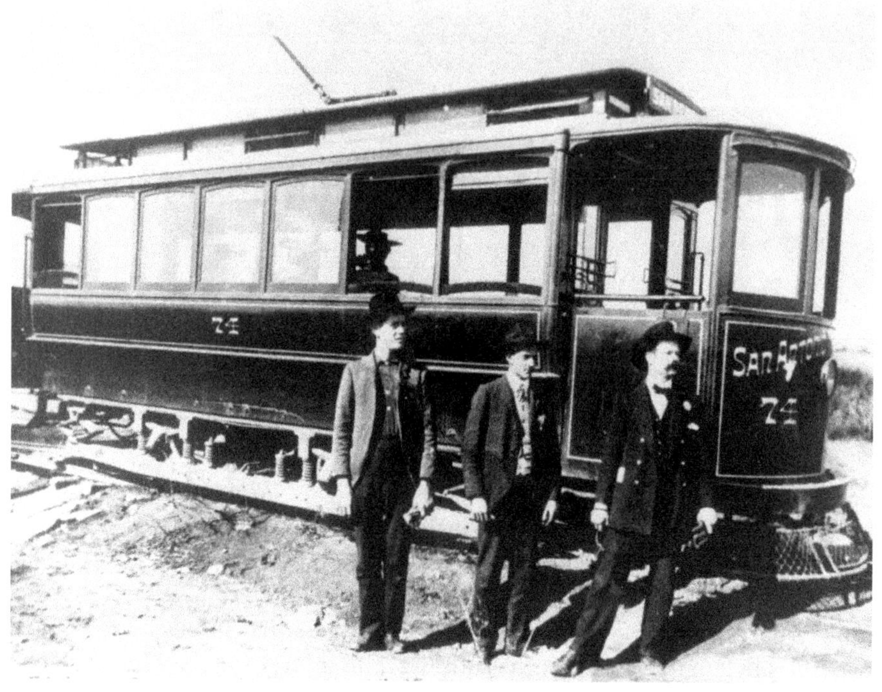

Texas Transportation Company freight car. *Charlie Staats*.

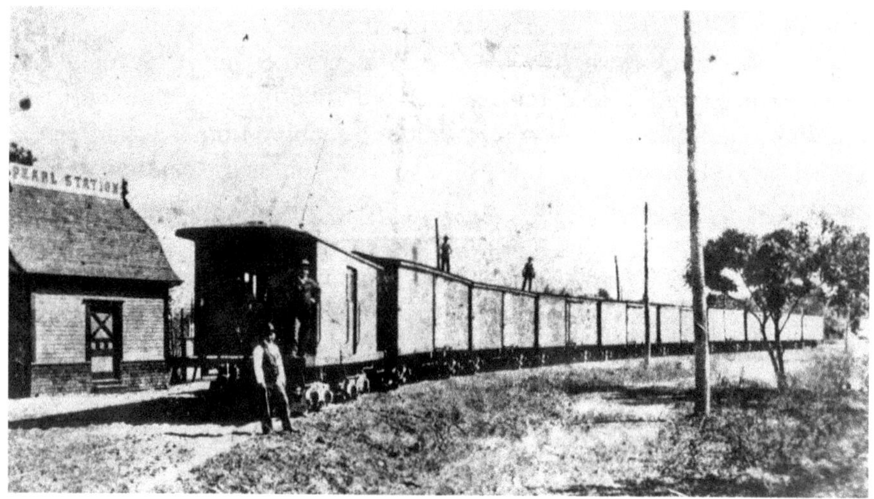

Texas Transportation Company freight car rolling down the tracks with XXX Pearl Beer. *Pearl LLC Archives.*

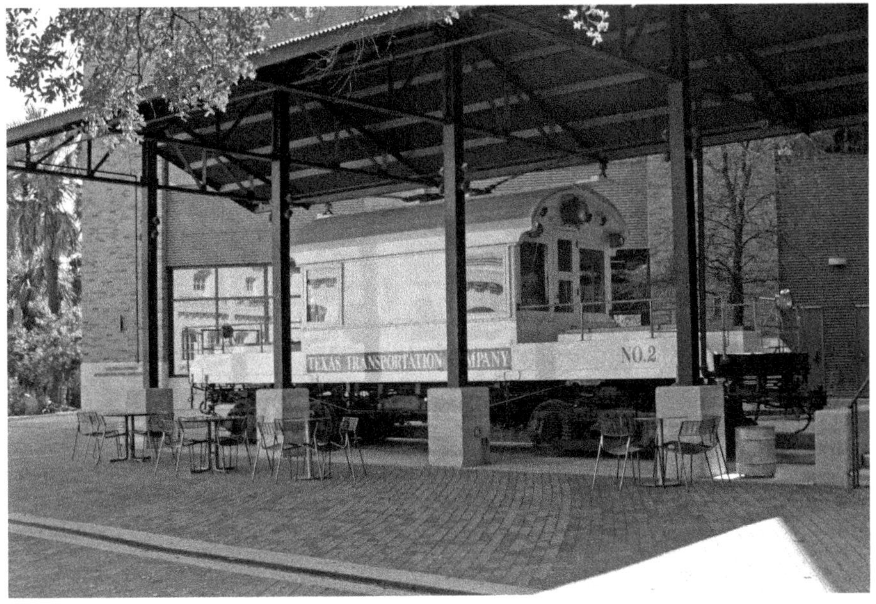

A former train car of the Texas Transportation Company sits on the grounds of the New Pearl complex. *Jeremy Banas.*

The Southern Pacific Railroad oversaw the construction of the new line, with every attempt made to use the best materials available. To this end, extra-heavy copper was used that allowed for very little lag. The train cars were approximately twenty feet long and together would handle the almost 12 million pounds of freight from the San Antonio Brewing Association, which committed to using the Texas Transportation Company exclusively for its freight needs, although the railroad itself was used by other breweries, including the Lone Star Brewing Association.

About 150 poles measuring thirty-five feet each were initially erected for trolleys, or electricity trains, with the trolley wire twenty-five feet off the ground, allowing workers who were on the boxcars to pass without harm. The *Daily Light* reported in September 1898 that the Alamo Street Car Line, headed by Superintendent W.H. Hume, would provide the one-hundred-horsepower electric motors. With part of the track running through the streets of San Antonio, a portion of the streets, including River Avenue, was torn up for the new track line, making it necessary for the Alamo Street Car Line to bring steam rollers into work on that section. Since most streetcar companies in San Antonio used a more narrow-gauge track, Texas Transportation Company needed them widened for commercial freight use. When Otto Koehler bought the Alamo Heights line, these additional track upgrades were initiated for what would become the Texas Transportation Company. In October 1898, the directors of the Texas Transportation Company—J.J. Stevens, Otto Wahrmund and Judge S.G. Newton—would place an order for bigger two-hundred-horsepower engines that provided more power for the train cars, as those provided by the Alamo Street Car Line did not have the needed power for the railroad's train cars.

Once the train began operations, the company was able to rest a bit easier. It had been a long road to get the much-needed rail line operational. To start, the Texas Transportation Company had to get around the illegality of operating a freight train inside an incorporated city. Through a little lobbying, the railroad was able to get the general incorporation law amended so as to allow its railcars to operate. As if that had not been difficult enough, the Texas Transportation Company was the target of an injunction that sought to prevent the rail line from even being built. Once heard in court, the railroad came out the victor, and despite a small delay, construction was able to begin.

Later that first month of October 1898, the Texas Transportation Company filed a request with the State of Texas to set the rates under which it would be allowed to operate. Wahrmund, Stevens and Newton made the trek up from the Alamo City to the capitol in Austin and met with the Texas Railroad Commission.

At some point during Prohibition, the Texas Transportation Company grew weary of that $1,000-per-year fee it was paying to the City of San Antonio. B.B. McGimsey, who was by this time general manager of the brewery in its Alamo Foods Company incarnation, was also manager of the Texas Transportation Company. McGimsey, along with other board members, met with then San Antonio mayor C.M. Chambers to have the previously agreed-on franchise tax removed and refunded.

The basis of their argument lay with the fact that since Prohibition went into effect in 1918, the railroad had lost money and was also serving fourteen other companies. The rumor mill at the time reported that about three-fourths of these fourteen other companies held stock in the Texas Transportation Company. McGimsey and company also stated that an initial reason for the tax back in 1897 was that it was the only corporation in Texas that paid such a franchise tax to a city entity, as it was already paying the same regular taxes to the state that was required of all railroads. When all was said and done, their request for a refund was quickly denied.

Appendix II

PEARL TRANSPORTATION RAILROAD LINE

(Note: Transportation Company's properties hi-lited in yellow & rail line colored red.)

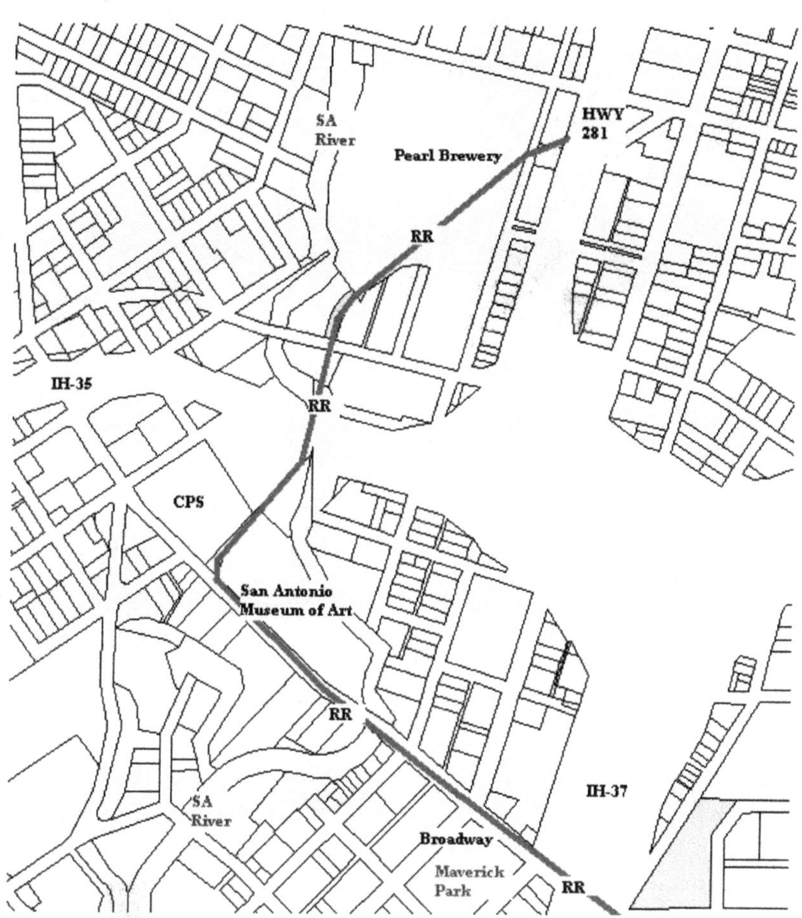

Pearl transportation line map. *Charlie Staats.*

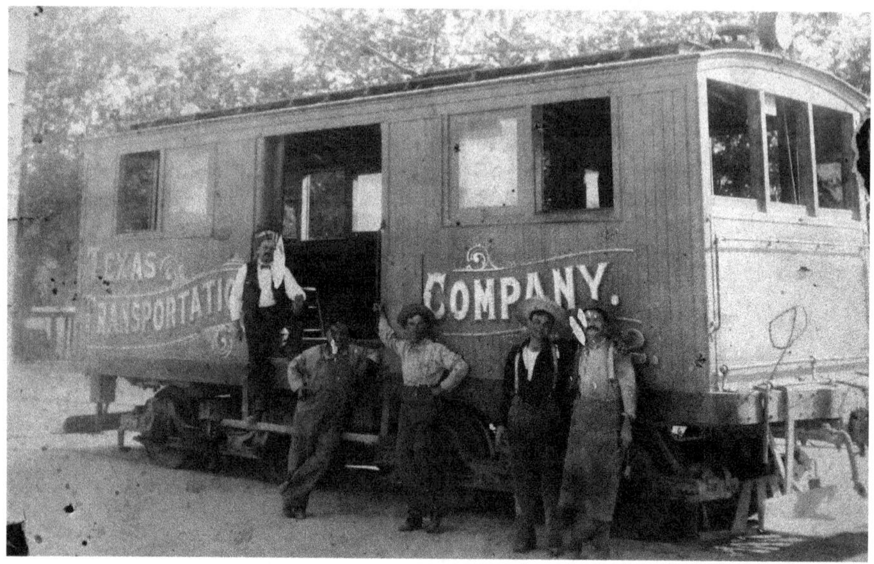

Texas Transportation Company railcar no. 2. *Charlie Staats.*

The decades rolled on, and so did the Texas Transportation Company, continuing to service its parent brewery and other businesses in San Antonio. The Handbook of Texas Online notes, "In the 1990s the railroad had two electric locomotives and remained one of the last freight-hauling electric lines in the United States. The train consisted of an average of twenty-five to thirty cars per day that operated over a six-day week." The railroad continued through to 2000, when the Pearl Brewing Company, owned by Pabst Brewing, ceased its operations. By 2002, one year after Pabst closed the historic Pearl Brewery, the Texas Transportation Company was officially dissolved, ending the last vestige of the Pearl. Even the railroad's overhead wires and tracks were decommissioned, although one plan was to use the tracks for a historic trolley service—to this end, the transit authorities of Bexar County and San Antonio had even conducted a study to see if this was feasible.

BIBLIOGRAPHY

The Anti-Saloon League. *The Brewers and Texas Politics*. N.d.

Atlanta Constitution. February 1915.

Bexar Archives. "Diego de Santos' Certification on Taxes on Aguardiente and Wine Transported from Laredo to Bexar," dated June 11, 1774. Dolph Briscoe Center for American History at the University of Texas–Austin.

Bexar County Census, 1870. Under "Oskar Bergstroem."

Brewer's Journal 28 (April 1, 1904).

Childress Index. April 23, 1974.

Dingus, Anne. "Tapped Out." *Texas Monthly*, May 2001. http://www.texasmonthly.com/articles/tapped-out.

Georges, Mary Hollers. "A Brief History of the Otto Koehler Residence." San Antonio College, 1990.

Gjenvick-Gjønvik Archives. Passenger manifest of the SS *Prinz Frederich Wilhelm*, October 9, 1909. http://www.gjenvick.com/PassengerLists/NorthGermanLloyd/Westbound/1909-10-09-PassengerList-PrinzFriedrichWilhelm.html#axzz4wIXbRx4p.

Greeley Daily Tribune. "Senate Panel Hears 'Horror Story.'" March 30, 1977.

Handbook of Texas Online. "Brewing Industry." https://tshaonline.org/handbook/online/articles/dib01.

Hennech, Michael C., and Tracé Etienne-Gray. "Brewing Industry." Handbook of Texas Online. http://www.tshaonline.org/handbook/online/articles/dib01.

Hix, Martha Rand. "They Made It a Pearl: Pearl Brewing Company's Managers during Its First Three Eras." Privately prepared for the owners of the former Pearl Brewery Complex, June 2004.

Hollern, Madeline. "The Girl with the Pearl Beering." *San Antonio Magazine*, May 2011. http://www.sanantoniomag.com/SAM/January-2011/The-Girl-with-the-Pearl-Beering.

Holt, Jeff. Historic and Modern Breweries of Texas. www.texasbreweries.com.

The Hotel Emma. http://www.thehotelemma.com.

Johnson, Frank. *A History of Texas and Texans*. Vol. 2. Chicago: American Historical Society, 1914.

Kerr, K. Austin. "Prohibition." Handbook of Texas Online. http://www.tshaonline.org/handbook/online/articles/vap01.

Lucio, Valentino. "Development at the Pearl Heating Up." *San Antonio Express-News*, February 6, 2013. http://www.mysanantonio.com/news/local_news/article/Development-at-the-Pearl-heating-up-4254393.php#photo-1063940.

Monroe News-Star. "Pearl, Southdown Planning Merger." July 15, 1969.

Nelson, James L. "Business History of the San Antonio Brewing Association (Pearl Brewing Company), 1886–1933." Master's thesis, Trinity University, 1976.

New York Census, 1910. Borough of Manhattan.

Nikas, Katie. "San Antonio's Hottest District Ushers in Trendy Food Hall." San Antonio Culture Map, January 16, 2017. http://sanantonio.culturemap.com/news/restaurants-bars/01-16-17-pearl-brewery-food-hall/#slide=1.

San Antonio Express. "Four Founders Were Colorful Personalities." October 13, 1953.

———. November 14, 1914.

———. Otto Koehler obituary, November 14, 1914.

San Antonio Express and News. "Pearl Merger." July 12, 1969.

San Antonio Light. January 19, 1918.

———. July 2, 1964.

———. July 5, 1887.

———. November 16, 1914.

———. "Pearl Exec Now on Panel." November 23, 1969.

San Antonio Monthly. "Underdog Pearl Beer Fights Beer Mega Giants." December 1991.

SCAD. "Cured at Pearl Brand Identity." http://portfolios.scad.edu/gallery/32097443/CURED-at-Pearl-Brewery-Brand-Identity.

Silva, Tricia Lynn. "Aveda Institute Has Decided to Vacate." *San Antonio Business Journal*, April, 2 2013. http://www.bizjournals.com/sanantonio/blog/2013/04/aveda-institute-has-decided-to-vacate.html.

St. Louis Post Dispatch. June 9, 1974.

Tedesco, John. "Judson Gave Field Trips at His Candy Factory." *San Antonio Express-News*, December 10, 2010. https://www.google.com/amp/www.mysanantonio.com/obituaries/amp/Judson-gave-field-trips-at-his-candy-factory-923187.php.

Thirty-Seventh District of Bexar County, Texas. *Bergstrom v. Alamo Industries*, April 1921.

Tovey's Brewer's Directory of the United States and Canada. Chicago, 1891.

Waco Tribune-Herald. "Attorney Tries to Free Millionare from Hospital." May 3, 1974.

Werner, George C. "Texas Transportation Company." Handbook of Texas Online. http://www.tshaonline.org/handbook/online/articles/eqt17.

Wichita Falls Daily Times. August 5, 1918.

———. December 23, 1914.

INDEX

A

African safaris 79
Alamo Colleges 137
Alamo Electric Street Railway Company. *See* Texas Transportation Company
Alamo Foods Company 57, 58, 59, 62, 63, 65, 142
Alamo Industries 25, 50, 54, 55, 57, 58, 62, 66
Alamo Street Car Line. *See* Texas Transportation Company
Anheuser-Busch 28, 33, 34, 67, 92, 99
Anti-Saloon League 38, 39, 61

B

Balfour, Jeff 114
Bean, Judge Roy 67, 94
Belohradsky, J.B.
  arrest 18, 23, 29, 54
Bentzen, Emma 65
Bergstrom, Oscar 18, 23, 24, 25, 27, 29, 31, 34, 45, 55, 62, 66, 125
Biting, Bill 98
Blue Bell Creamery 59
Boehler's 67, 71
bottle cap salvaging machine 75
bottling building 34, 122
Boys Club of San Antonio 71
Boysville 78
Branch, Oscar 38
Brewettes (team) 72
Brooks, Matron 48
Brunswick. *See* Koehler House
Burgermeister, Emma 40, 41, 42, 46, 47, 48, 49
Busch, Adolphus 18, 22, 28, 31, 32, 62

C

Chambers, C.M. *See* Texas Transportation Company

Citrus in the Valencia Hotel. *See* Balfour, Jeff
City Brewery 18, 22, 23, 24, 29, 34, 54, 99, 125
Cordt, Henry 47

D

Degen, Charles 18, 21, 43, 53
dry camp 38, 51, 60, 61
Dumpke, Emma 40, 41, 46, 47

E

Eickenrot, H.J. 84
Emory John Brady Hospital 88
Etter, Gustav 35, 57

F

Fox Motel 109
Frank, A.B. 28

G

Galveston Brewing Association 38
Goetz Brewery 81
Goldsbury, Christopher "Kit" 20, 100, 101, 103, 125, 130
Gordon, James Riley. *See* Von Seutter, Carl
Granary 'Cue and Brew, the 34, 110, 112, 113, 114
Gregg and Company 62, 66
Gregg brothers 62
Griesedieck, Anton 28, 30

H

Haeglin, Harry 76
Hartz, Frederick 18, 24, 29
Hobby, William 54, 55
"Hook Jacket" 81
Hotel Emma, the 100, 120, 122
Hot Wells 32, 40
Houston Colt .45s (Houston Astros) 84
Hrovat, Ignatz 34, 110
Hunstock cottage 40, 42, 49

I

Isaacs, William "Billy" 50, 51
Issleib, Lutz 66, 95

J

James Street 81
Jazz TX 122
Jersey Lilly 94, 122
Jersig, Harry 85
Jones, Bill 98
Judson Candy Company 84, 85, 92

K

Kaiser-Beck Brewery 30
Kalmanovitz, Paul 20, 94
Kelly Field National Bank 83
Kline, Aubrey N. 66
Koehler Cultural Center. *See* Koehler House
Koehler, Emma 18, 39, 40, 41, 42, 46, 49, 54, 55, 56, 57, 59, 60, 62, 63, 65, 66, 75, 95, 103, 120, 125, 130, 134

Koehler House 35, 40, 42, 45, 103, 127, 129, 130, 134, 137
Koehler, Karl 27, 60, 75
Koehler mansion. *See* Koehler House
Koehler mining interests 31, 60, 63, 90, 99, 109
Koehler, Otto 18, 19, 20, 24, 27, 28, 29, 32, 34, 35, 36, 38, 39, 40, 41, 42, 43, 45, 46, 47, 48, 49, 50, 51, 55, 56, 57, 59, 60, 61, 62, 65, 66, 75, 88, 96, 120, 127, 130, 142
Koehler, Otto A., Jr. 88, 89, 90
Koehler, Otto Andrew 60, 61, 62, 75
Ku-Winda 80

L

Liberty Bar 71
Linden, W.C. 46, 47
Local 1110 98, 99
Locke, William Les 114, 115, 118, 119
Lone Star Brewing Association 18, 22, 23, 28, 30, 32, 38, 53, 66, 141
Lone Star Brewing Company 36, 85, 96

M

Mahaffey, David 99
Maritzen, August 34
Marmor, Al 76
Marsden, Crosby 48
McAskill, Duncan 47
McGimsey, Benjamin Brooks "B.B." 56, 62, 63, 64, 65, 66, 78, 83, 88, 125, 142
McHugh, Steve 110, 113
Menger, William 18, 21
Miss Pearl Brewery 75
Mueller, Ernest Charles 34, 110
Muenchener 35

N

Neo-Rite system 72
Nimitz, Charles 29

O

O'Brien, Hiram B. "Pat" 66, 67
Onion, James F. 47

P

Pabst 20, 51, 83, 94, 96, 98, 99, 102, 144
Pace, David 102, 130
Pace Foods 102, 130
Pace, Linda 102, 130
Pace, Paul 103, 129, 130
Pace Willson, Margaret 40, 103, 130
Passport to Danger 80
Pearl 17, 18, 19, 20, 28, 29, 30, 32, 33, 34, 35, 38, 46, 51, 53, 58, 59, 61, 64, 66, 67, 71, 72, 75, 76, 77, 78, 80, 81, 83, 84, 85, 86, 88, 90, 92, 94, 95, 96, 98, 99, 100, 101, 102, 103, 109, 110, 113, 114, 115, 120, 122, 125, 127, 139
Pearl Brewing Company 17, 20, 51, 78, 81, 86, 88, 90, 92, 98, 144
Pearl Corral Hospitality 77
Pearl Cream Ale 95

Pearl Gunslingers 84
Pearl Malt Syrup 59
Pearl-O-Lure 81
Pearl Parkway 81
Pearl Stables 18, 34, 122
Prides (team) 72
Priest, Corwin 55, 57, 62
Prince Carl of Solms-Braunfels 56
Prohibition 18, 19, 27, 28, 36, 50, 51, 53, 54, 55, 56, 58, 60, 61, 62, 63, 65, 66, 67, 75, 96, 142
Pure Food Law of 1906 36

R

Range, A.J. 84, 88, 90
Rattray, Alex 110, 112
Rattray, Tim 110
RC Cola 86, 88
Roman and Williams. *See* Hotel Emma, the
Roosevelt, Franklin Delano 61

S

saloons 33, 47, 60
San Antonio Brewing Association 17, 18, 19, 24, 25, 27, 29, 30, 31, 32, 33, 34, 35, 38, 39, 40, 43, 45, 47, 49, 50, 51, 53, 54, 55, 57, 59, 60, 61, 62, 63, 64, 65, 66, 67, 72, 75, 76, 77, 78, 86, 110, 139, 141
San Antonio Community College 35, 130
SCAD 113
Schattenburg, G.A. *See* Koehler House
Schreiber, Oscar Oswald 35
Siebel Institute 50, 96, 112
Silver Ventures 100, 102, 103, 106, 109, 110, 113, 114, 120, 122, 125
Society of Melbourne 56
Southdown Corporation 20, 88, 90
Southerleigh Fine Food and Brewery 100, 114, 115, 118, 119, 120
Southern Pacific Railroad 139, 141. *See also* Texas Transportation Company
Spinosa, Frank 95
Stevens, J.J. 28, 29, 34, 45, 125, 142

T

Texas Brewing Company 36
Texas Consolidated Brewing Association 36, 38, 51
Texas Dry Corporation 66
Texas Pride 35, 38, 72, 80, 94, 95
Texas Society of Professional Engineers 50
Texas state legislature 54, 61
Texas Transportation Company 31, 32, 139, 141, 142, 144
Three Emmas, the. *See* Hotel Emma, the
Twenty-First Amendment 61

U

United States Brewmasters Association 35

V

Von Seutter, Carl 127

W

Wagoner, Jacob. *See* Koehler House
Wahrmund, Otto 18, 29, 32, 34, 43, 45, 50, 54, 55, 56, 57, 62, 125, 142
Wahrmund, William 56
Western Brewery, the 18, 21
Wilson, Woodrow 53
Wood, Grant 96
World's Fair 86

X

XXX Pearl Beer 29, 30, 33, 53, 58, 76, 78, 80, 94, 125

ABOUT THE AUTHOR

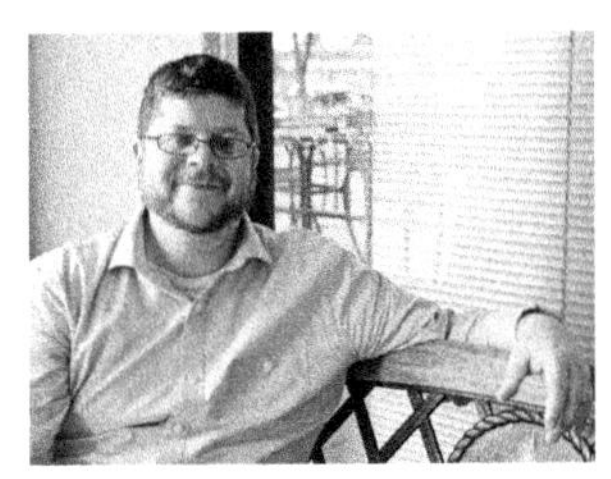

Jeremy Banas is a freelance beer writer who writes for such publications and websites as the *San Antonio Current*, *Antonio Magazine*, TheFullPint.Com and the Brewers Association's craftbeer.com, as well as his own website, RuinationPress.com. He is also the author of a previous book, *San Antonio Beer: Alamo City History by the Pint* (co-authored with Travis Polling). He has judged numerous beer competitions, serves as a founding member (and committee member) of San Antonio Beer Week and hosts beer dinners and lectures.

Jeremy also comes from a proud brewing tradition. His cousins, Carl and Joseph Occhiatio, were the last owners of the historic Tivoli Brewing Company in Denver, Colorado, from 1965 to 1969, where his grandfather also worked. Jeremy has achieved the designation of Certified Beer Server in the Cicerone Certification Program and is working toward his Cicerone Certification. He resides in San Antonio, Texas, with his three boys: Quinn, Jack and Maxwell.

www.ingramcontent.com/pod-product-compliance
Lightning Source LLC
LaVergne TN
LVHW010933100826
845153LV00001B/19
9781540227942